MIKHAIL IVANOVICH GLINKA

*Memoirs*

# MIKHAIL IVANOVICH GLINKA

*Memoirs*

Translated from the Russian by
RICHARD B. MUDGE

University of Oklahoma Press : Norman

Library of Congress Catalog Card Number: 63–8993

Copyright 1963 by the University of Oklahoma Press, Publishing Division of the University. Composed and printed at Norman, Oklahoma, U.S.A., by the University of Oklahoma Press. First edition.

*Translator's Preface*

MIKHAIL IVANOVICH GLINKA was born on the family estate of Novospasskoe in 1804 and died in Berlin in 1857, probably chiefly of syphilis, although Soviet writers like to say "of causes still unexplained." In his fifty-three years he wrote two great operas, many light, lyrical songs, and a dozen or so notable instrumental works; he traveled in Switzerland, Germany, Poland, France, and, especially, Italy and Spain, for Glinka loved the lands where the oranges grew but (as he once too frankly told the Empress) he even preferred the climate of Warsaw to that of Petersburg; he consulted countless doctors all over Europe about his real and imaginary pains; he made love (he says) to countless women of all qualities; and he consumed countless bottles of his favorite red "church wine." It seems to have been a life of wine, women, song, and doctors.

Glinka was not a stuffy type genius. He could compose a charming love song riding toward Warsaw in a coach with a pretty companion, and he could sit in his parlor, a flock of his pet birds flying around his head and three or four friends talking and carousing at his elbow, and happily write down his *Kamarinskaya*. He was a lively human being—except for times of illness and, in in his last eight years, times of disillusion and maybe boredom— who, sometimes almost incidentally, took the trouble to create some fine music. He apparently had no mean opinion of himself, and then, too, in talking freely of all his ills throughout his life he must not always have been too appealing, although in his case and among his good friends there might have been, finally, something almost comical about it.

As everyone knows, Glinka was the founder of art music in Russia and of Russian "national" music—"the Prophet-Patriarch," as Liszt called him—and the guide and inspiration for the famous "Five" (Balakirev, Cui, Borodin, Moussorgsky, and Rimsky-Korsakov), each of whom avowed his indebtedness to him. Truly, he revolutionized Russian music; his *Ruslan and Ludmila* "created almost at one stroke the essential style of modern Russian music."

Quite a lot of Glinka's music is available in the United States on records—the very familiar overture to *Ruslan*, the *Kamarinskaya*, *A Night in Madrid*, the *Waltz Fantasie*, the *Jota Aragonesa*, for example. There should be some of these on hand, of course, to accompany the reading of this book. I have enjoyed playing *A Life for the Tsar*, by the Bolshoi Theater Choir and Orchestra (Artia Records MKR 216), which I obtained from my good friends at Dike Blair's Vermont Book Shop, Middlebury, Vermont.

Mikhail Ivanovich wrote better music than memoirs. Oh, the latter are interesting, all right, and frank and revealing the way Russians (pre-Soviet, at least) seem to be when they write about themselves. But after all, Glinka was not a writer, and besides, he only set down what he called "Notes" two years before his death because his sister Ludmila made him. It should be remembered, too, that he was really not writing a book for publication (no part of it appeared in print until nearly fifteen years after his death, and then only in a newspaper): he was simply putting down thoughts on his life, and on events and people of the recent past, for an audience of that more or less intimate company which comprised aristocratic and intellectual Russia. His readers, then, knew without needing all the details spelled out who Ivanov was and of the mystery of his failure to return to Russia from Italy, and they knew, for example, all the gossip about Glinka's troubles with the jealous and bureaucratic Kapellmeister Lvov. This is why there is a certain lack of coherence now and then and sometimes a vagueness in transition, or a question, perhaps, of just who is being mentioned. I would much prefer to have such things ascribed to Mikhail Ivanovich Glinka than to me.

I should like to thank the following persons for their help: Alan Carter, director of the Vermont State Symphony Orchestra and head of the music department at Middlebury College; Nina Ragsdale Mudge, my wife; Mrs. E. J. W. Ragsdale of Palo Alto, California, my mother-in-law; Vladimir Seduro, professor of Russian at Rensselaer Polytechnic Institute; Helen D. Willard, curator of the theater collection, Harvard College Library; George Freedley, curator of the theater collection, New York Public Library; and Professor Walter M. Pintner of the department of history, Cornell University.

Richard B. Mudge

WALTHAM, VERMONT

MARCH, 1963

# Contents

Translator's Preface                                                    v

## *May 20, 1804,* TO *April 25, 1830*

1   Birth. Life with Grandmother                                   3
2   First Feeling for Music                                        6
3   Early Education                                                9
4   Graduation from Blagorodny School                             11
5   First Trip Abroad                                             22

## *April 25, 1830,* TO *December, 1836*

6   Travel Abroad. Return to Russia                               55
7   Novospasskoe, Moscow, and St. Petersburg. Marriage.
    First Performance of *A Life for the Tsar*          91

## *December, 1836,* TO *June, 1844*

8   Kapellmeister of the Imperial Chapel Choir. Little
    Russia. *Ruslan and Ludmila*. Retirement from
    Official Service. Dissolution of Marriage          113
9   First Performance of *Ruslan and Ludmila*                    149
10   Trip to Paris                                               175

| | | |
|---|---|---|
| 11 | Sojourn in Paris | 187 |
| 12 | Spain. Return to Russia | 195 |
| 13 | Novospasskoe, Smolensk, Warsaw, and St. Petersburg | 209 |
| 14 | Second Stay in Warsaw. St. Petersburg | 219 |
| 15 | Third Trip Abroad and Return to Russia | 230 |

## *Appendices*

| | | |
|---|---|---|
| 1 | Chronology | 245 |
| 2 | Glinka's Family and Relatives Mentioned in His Memoirs | 248 |
| 3 | *A Life for the Tsar* | 250 |
| 4 | *Ruslan and Ludmila* | 251 |
| | Index | 253 |

# Illustrations

Mikhail Ivanovich Glinka as a Young Man     *facing page* 68

The Finale of *A Life for the Tsar*     69

Glinka, K. P. Brullov, and N. A. Kukolnik     84

The Grand Imperial Theater in 1839     85

The Title Page from an Edition of *Ruslan and Ludmila*     164

Glinka at the Piano     165

A Set Designed by A. A. Roller for *Ruslan and Ludmila*     180

Mikhail Ivanovich Glinka in His Later Years     181

*May 20, 1804, to April 25, 1830*

# I

---

## *Birth. Life with Grandmother*

Tsarskoe Selo, June 3, 1854

I was born at daybreak on May 20, 1804, in the village of Novospasskoe,[1] which belonged to my father, Ivan Nikolaevich Glinka, a retired captain. This property was about fourteen miles from the town of Elnya in the government of Smolensk; it lay along the Desna River (near its source) surrounded by impenetrable woods merging with the great forest of Bryansk. Soon after I was born my mother, Evgeniya Andreevna (nee Glinka), was forced to leave my early upbringing to my grandmother, Fekla Aleksandrovna (my father's mother), who, in taking charge of me, moved me into her own room. I passed three or four years with her as my foster mother and governess, only rarely seeing my parents.[2] I had a weak constitution, a scrofulous condition, and an extremely nervous disposition; my grandmother, a woman in her

[1] This was the patrimonial estate of the Glinka family. After the composer's death Novospasskoe passed to his sister Olga and then to her husband, N. A. Izmailov. The latter eventually sold it to a Kolomna merchant named Rybakov. The house and all outbuildings were completely destroyed in World War II.

[2] Glinka's father, Ivan Nikolaevich Glinka, was born May 7, 1777, and died March 4, 1834. His mother, Evgeniya Andreevna, nee Glinka (second cousin of Ivan Nikolaevich), was born December 24, 1784, and died May 31, 1851. Left an orphan, she was brought up by her older brother, Afanasy Andreevich Glinka (1772–1828), proprietor of the estate Shmakovo. A. A. Glinka, a passionate lover of music and the theater, had his own serf acting troupe and orchestra. These were inherited by his younger brother, Ivan Andreevich Glinka (1777–1852), also a lover of music, a good pianist, and a generally well-educated man who

declining years, was nearly always sick and therefore kept her room (where I lived) at a temperature of at least 77° F. Despite this, I always wore my fur coat. At night and often in the daytime I was given tea with cream and a lot of sugar, plus cracknels and several kinds of crackers; I was seldom allowed out in the fresh air, and then only in warm weather. There is no doubt that this early upbringing had a great effect on the development of my physique and that it also explains my irresistible longing for warm climates. Even now, at fifty years, I must say that I really prefer to live in the south and that I suffer there less than I do in the north.

My grandmother spoiled me unbelievably, denying me nothing; nonetheless, I was a gentle, good-tempered child and it was only when someone disturbed me while I was busy that I became *touchy* (like a mimosa plant), and indeed I am inclined to be like that to this day. One of my favorite pastimes was to lie on the floor and draw trees and churches with a piece of chalk. I was very devout and church services, especially those held on solemn-festival days, filled my heart with the liveliest poetic rapture. I learned to read very early and would often astonish my grandmother and her sisters by reading sacred books to them. My musical aptitude was first indicated at this time by a *passion* for the ringing of bells (chimes); I would listen hungrily to the sharp, shrill sounds and could skillfully imitate the bell ringers on two copper bowls. When I was sick, little bells would be brought to my room for my amusement. I had poor nerves from babyhood; for example, for several days before my grandmother died she was being treated with a foul-smelling plaster. No force whatever

---

had a part in stirring Glinka's interest in music. Ivan Nikolaevich and Evgeniya Andreevna had ten children. Of his brothers and sisters, Glinka was closest to Ludmila Ivanovna Shestakova (1816–1906). After his death she tirelessly devoted the rest of her life to the preservation of his memory; she arranged for publication of his operatic scores and symphonic works, actively promoted the erection of monuments in Smolensk (1885) and St. Petersburg (1906), organized a Glinka museum in St. Petersburg, and wrote her reminiscences of her famous brother.

could compel me to go to her, and I was not present at her death, despite my love for her.[3]

I could mention several amusing anecdotes here, although my recollections of this period are not entirely clear in my mind— but such stories are probably beside the point, since they have no direct bearing on my artistic life, and besides, I have no wish to copy the Sage of Geneva.

[3] Fekla Aleksandrovna Glinka, nee Sokolovskaya, died in 1810. According to Glinka's sister Ludmila, she was the one really in command of the family, virtually taking Mikhail Ivanovich away from his parents.

# 2

---

*First Feeling for Music*

W HEN my grandmother died, my way of life changed somewhat. My mother spoiled me less and even tried to accustom me to fresh air, but these efforts were for the most part not successful. As for the women in the household, well, besides my sister, a year younger than I, and my nurse, another nurse, Irina Fedorovna Meshkova, the widow of a surveyor, was soon engaged. She had a daughter a little older than I. This nurse was a simple and unusually goodhearted woman. Mother did not spoil us, but she loved us and everything was fine at home. Later on, Irina Fedorovna was joined by a Frenchwoman, Rosa Ivanovna. Meanwhile, an architect hired by my father had put a pencil in my hand instead of chalk and began to give me drawing lessons, explaining how to handle eyes, nose, ears, and so on, unreasonably demanding of me a purely mechanical imitation; nevertheless, I managed to make rapid progress. Furthermore, a distant relative, a hearty old man eager for knowledge and of an agreeable nature, often visited us at this time. He loved to tell tales of far-off lands, of wild tribes, of different climates, and of the products of tropical countries. Noting my keen interest, he brought me a book one day entitled *Travels and Wanderings*,[1] published in the reign of Catherine II.

I eagerly set about reading this book, which, if I remember cor-

[1] Complete title of this twenty-two-volume edition: *The History of Travels*

rectly, contained an account of the voyages of the celebrated Vasco da Gama. Later on, this same relative gave me other volumes in this collection of travel stories and when I read descriptions of the islands of Ceylon, Sumatra, Java, and other islands of the Indian Archipelago, my imagination was so inflamed that I began to pore over accounts of these delightful places and even started to make a précis of the books, which later served as the foundation for my great love of geography and travel.

My feeling for music was still in a latent state. Even in my eighth year, when we escaped the French attack on Orel, I was listening with my earlier eagerness to the ringing of the bells, distinguishing the chimes of each church, and then painstakingly imitating them on my two copper bowls.

Always surrounded by women, and playing with no one but my sister and the nurse's daughter, I was not really much like other boys of my age. A passion for reading, for maps, and for drawing, in the last of which I had begun to make visible progress, also often drew me away from children's games; and, as always, I was of a quiet and gentle disposition.

Sometimes guests and relatives would gather at my father's house, especially on his name day or when there was someone whom he wished to entertain in style. On such an occasion my uncle (my mother's brother), who lived about five miles away, was usually called upon to send us some of his musicians. These people generally stayed for several days, and when the dances for the departing guests were over, they would play various pieces for us. Once (I believe it was in 1814 or 1815, in other words, when I was ten or eleven years old), they played Crusell's quartet with clarinet; this music made an inconceivable, fresh and delightful impression on me—after hearing it I remained for the rest of the day in a sort of feverish condition, deep in an undefinable, bittersweet mood, and the following day I was confused and for-

*in General to All Parts of the Earth, the Work of M. Prévost, Abridged in the Latest Manner by M. La Harpe* (Moscow, 1782–87).

7

getful at my drawing lesson. My state of mind was still more disturbed the day after, and my drawing teacher, seeing that I was working in much too slipshod a fashion, reproved me repeatedly and finally, suspecting what was the matter, remarked that I seemed unable to think of anything except music. "And what is the point of that?" he asked, to which I replied: "Music is my life."

And, actually, from that time on I did love music passionately. My uncle's orchestra was for me the source of the keenest delight. When it played dances, such as *écossaises*, *matradurs*, quadrilles, and waltzes, I would take a violin or a small flute (piccolo) and follow along with the orchestra, by the tonics and dominants, of course. My father frequently became annoyed with me for not dancing and for not mixing with the guests, but at the first opportunity I would always come back to the orchestra.

At supper, Russian songs scored for two flutes, two clarinets, two horns, and two bassoons were usually played. I fully understood the sadly tender sounds, and they pleased me immensely (I could scarcely endure penetrating sounds, even those of horns on low notes when they were played loudly). It may be that these songs which I heard in my youth were the basic reason why I dwelt primarily on Russian folk music later on.

# 3

## *Early Education*

IT was about this time that my parents sent for a governess from Petersburg, Varvara Fedorovna Klammer. She was a girl of about twenty, tall, severe, and exacting. If I am not mistaken, she had been educated at the Smolny Monastery. She undertook to teach us Russian, French, German, geography, and music, as well as to get us started on grammar, conversation (dialogues), brief descriptions of lands and cities, and other things. All this had to be learned by rote; that is, when she asked a question, we had to reply without hesitation, neither changing nor leaving out a single word of the fixed response. Although she also taught us music—piano and the reading of music—in the same mechanical fashion, I made rapid progress in this department. Varvara Fedorovna was clever. As soon as my sister and I began to learn the notes and to hit the right keys, she had a board fitted over the piano so that although we could play, we could not see our hands or the keys. So it was that from the very first I became accustomed to playing without looking at my fingers.

Soon after this one of my uncle's first violinists began to teach me the violin. Unhappily, he himself did not play as well as he might have, using the bow very awkwardly (*raide*), a bad habit that he passed on to me.

Although I loved music almost without thought, I remember

well that I preferred pieces which were more within the limits of my musical understanding of that period. Generally speaking, I loved the orchestra most of all, and of the orchestral numbers, after Russian songs, I preferred the overtures: Boieldieu's *My Aunt Aurora*, Kreutzer's *Lodoiska*, and Méhul's *The Two Blind Men of Toledo* (*Les deux aveugles*). I readily played these last two on the piano, as well as some Steibelt sonatas, especially the rondo *The Storm*, which I did quite well. I did not like the Czech Gyrowetz at all, partly because I found his sonatas too long and involved, and even more because they had been very badly printed, and on dark and cloudy days I had a hard time making out the music, so that quite often my teacher would whack my fingers with her pencil.

# 4

---

*Graduation from Blagorodny School*

$\mathbb{A}$T the beginning of winter, 1817, my mother, her brother (the uncle who had the orchestra), Varvara Fedorovna, I, and my sister set out for St. Petersburg. The purpose of the trip was to enroll me in the newly opened Blagorodny Boarding School at the Main Pedagogical Institute. Although even now I can clearly remember certain details of this trip, I shall pass over them, since they are irrelevant to the business at hand.[1]

As we entered our northern capital the appearance of the massive, well-proportioned houses and wide streets had a magical effect on me, and for a long time I retained that impression of rapture and astonishment. My ideas of architectural worth were then just as vague and disordered as my ideas on music; I thought the Russian-style cathedrals with five cupolas a triumph of art, and did not care for the Kazan cathedral at all.

My father arrived soon afterward, and, making the acquaintance of the inspector of the school, Lindquist, at once, and finding out about everything, got down to business.[2] Our school was

[1] Family tradition has it that on this trip Glinka kept telling his little sister that he was going to discover a new land, new countries: "Columbus discovered America, you know—well, I shall discover some land or other, they will write about me in books, and in the new land I shall arrange various concerts, have orchestras, music, and there will be lots of good musicians."

[2] Glinka entered the school, a part of the Main Pedagogical Institute, on February 2, 1818.

located in the Otto House at the Kalinkin Bridge, close to the hospital. My father did not waste money on me, and I was therefore lodged with three other students of the same age and a private tutor (W. K. Kuchelbecher)[3] on the entresol of the school building; here there was even room for a piano, soon replaced by a Tischner grand piano. At that time Tischner was the best artisan in Petersburg, and the mechanism of his grand pianos was such that they could be played with the highest degree of precision.

I shall not list all the subjects they taught us; I shall say only that I, especially at first, applied myself very diligently in all my classes. Later on, my favorite subjects were languages: Latin, French, German, English, and then Persian. Of the sciences I liked geography and zoology. I made such rapid progress in arithmetic and algebra that I could tutor others in the latter. After getting through geometry I gave up mathematics altogether, very likely because in the higher grades the number of subjects to be taken increased substantially.

The professors in the more advanced classes were persons of knowledge and were well educated; most of them had attended German universities. In a word, the higher grades were taught by the professors of the Pedagogical Institute. These included the eminent Raupach, professor of German literature; Arseniev, professor of geography and statistics; Kunitsyn, law and other subjects.

Some of the teachers in the lower grades were quite eccentric fellows, and among the tutors also we found comical characters such that I and all my schoolmates still remember them. Let me mention a few.

*Gospodin, Monsieur, Mister Bitton* (as the *dyadki*[4] called him) was a rough, rather unmannerly Englishman (probably of the

[3] Wilhelm Karolovich Kuchelbecher (1797–1846), poet, Decembrist, and friend of Pushkin and Griboedov. He taught Russian literature at the Blagorodny School. He was dismissed in 1820 when he gave a public reading of poems dedicated to the then banished Pushkin.

[4] With us, the people who waited on table at dinner and supper were called

seafaring sort). He had an extreme liking for rice pudding, and on days when it was served he would select several victims from the younger students, who would then unfailingly either not know the meaning of the English words he threw at them or would pronounce them improperly, at which Mister Bitton would cry out in a loud voice, "On your knees!" tripping up the unfortunate student so forcefully after the third command that he would fall to the floor. After supper, the waiter Saveli would carry all the portions of rice pudding confiscated from the boys who had been punished to Gospodin, Monsieur, Mister Bitton's quarters, who would that night greedily devour his plunder.

Gospodin Höck, a German who wore a red wig, had a different system. Quite often, toward the end of a meal we would hear his affected voice meting out punishment to the guilty in the following manner: "Messieurs tel et tel privés du jardin et du dernier plat."[5]

The lively French master, Trippe, would play *lapta* with us, but we did not like him much because of the coarse way he treated us. According to rumor, he had formerly been in retail trade.

In this same category I must also include Ellena, the malicious Piedmontese, who tormented us with marching and drilling, of which he himself knew nothing at all. The Pole, Yakukevich, of extremely sloppy appearance and with no knowledge of anything except billiards, and the Finn, Lumberg, always a little bit drunk, completed our collection of characters. But Ivan Ekimovich, our good Assistant Inspector Ivan Ekimovich Kolmakov, was both a relief from the others and a pleasure in himself. His presence would always hearten us, and his diverting behavior, accompanied by blinking and odd grimaces, made him known by word of mouth to many who did not know him personally.

---

*dyadki* [literally, of course, "little uncles," a word of many colloquial uses in Russian].—Glinka.

[5] "Messieurs so and so are not to walk in the garden, nor to have their dessert."

We would sing this "historical chant," as we called it, at dinner and supper. The two rooms that formed our dining hall (for more than one hundred students) were rather narrow but long; the tables were arranged lengthwise so that the distance from one end to the other was considerable. As soon as we were seated, Ivan Ekimovich, being assistant inspector, would come into the room, wearing tasseled boots, gray trousers, a light-brown dress coat, and with a bald spot on the top of his head. He would walk importantly up and down, blinking his eyes and fidgeting with his vest. Sobolevsky (who was later to write such brilliant epigrams) once took it into his head to celebrate Ivan Ekimovich in song. I matched his verses to the then popular song by Cavos, *Oh, My Darling!* It was not hard to learn it, since we all knew the melody, and we liked the words. Although we were all fond of Ivan Ekimovich, we could not resist having some fun at his expense, all the more so in that I. E. *was pleased to get angry* (his own words) in a most entertaining fashion. At such times his flat, pockmarked face, with a nose like a button, would redden; his convulsive movements, as he blinked and adjusted his vest, which was pushing up, grew more violent and his voice rose to the sharpest and shrillest notes of a *soprano*.

Well, once at mealtime Ivan Ekimovich was pacing up and

down with his usual air of importance, and then something in the way of a serenade, in a subdued tone, started up in one corner of the room. I. E. stopped, listened—grew suspicious—and then finally heard his very own name being mentioned. Guessing by now what was up, he strode resolutely in the direction of the sounds. No use! We all went on chewing innocently, but very earnestly, on the unappetizing dish that comprised our poor fare that night, while the singing, without ever stopping, broke out on the opposite side of the room. Ivan Ekimovich ran over there, only to find the same concentration with the food, while then, as before, the singing centered on the other side. He halted, reddened, quivered in frustration, and exclaimed in his squeaky soprano voice: "You ill-bred, ignorant clowns and knuckleheads!"

All this did not prevent us from amusing ourselves by singing our song on various occasions, and, if I remember correctly, I. E. would invariably become angry but never punish anyone. He was, on the whole, a good and honest man; he would say of himself, when in a happy mood, "Vanka Kolmakov's a good fellow and an honest Christian," or "an honest fellow and a good Christian."

I. E. loved the society of his friends—and did not disdain the gifts of Bacchus. After about the eighth glass of punch he would remark that his tongue was getting badly twisted, but would add: "I'm swaying. I don't want to fall down. It's enough!"

The sciences were for I. E. a genuine delight—his ruling passion. He knew everything, remembered everything, and was always happy to take the place of any absent professor. He would discuss any difficult point with any student on the very least excuse. Even in another's classes he would try to prompt any boy who had not learned the lesson thoroughly, despite frequent reprimands from the inspector, Yakov Vasilevich Tolmachev, who was wont to call him a fool.

Love of the sciences stirred I. E. to an extraordinary degree. As his enthusiasm mounted and took possession of him, his language would become inventive and resourceful. Unexpected turns of phrase, ingenuity, jokes, unusual transpositions of words, and succinctness of speech (*laconisme*) were distinctive features of his way of talking. Once, for example, in telling us of one of his youthful adventures, he concluded with the words: "We knew, but there were no suspicions; it was known, but we did not suspect!"

By the end of the year I. E. had become a favorite and always entertaining friend of ours. At school, he helped me to read excerpts from Ovid's *Metamorphoses*, and it is to him I owe my initial acquaintance with Latin literature.

When I first arrived in Petersburg I studied piano with the eminent Field,[6] but, unfortunately, I had taken only three lessons when he left for Moscow. Although I did not hear him very often, even now I well remember his vigorous yet sensitive and precise playing. It seemed to me that he did not actually strike the keys, but that his fingers simply fell, as if they were raindrops, scattering like pearls on velvet. Neither I nor any other sincere lover of the art of music can agree with Liszt, who once said in my presence that Field played languidly (*endormi*); no, Field's playing was often bold, erratic, and varied, but he did not disfigure art like a charlatan, nor did he "make mincemeat,"[7] as do most of the latest fashionable pianists.

In the three lessons I took, I learned his *Second Divertissement* (E Major) and received flattering approval from him.

After Field left, a pupil of his, Oman, became my teacher. He started me with Field's *First Concerto* (E Flat Major). After him, Zeuner[8] further improved the mechanics of my playing and even

---

[6] John Field (1782–1837), who has been called "that Chopinist before Chopin," was a British pianist and composer. In his *Pioneers in Music*, David Ewen writes of Field: "His name became something of a household word, and to become his pupil was the highest aspiration of every young music student in highest society."

[7] Literally, "chopping hamburgers (cutlets)" as the Russians do, with the edges of their hands; in other words, jerkily and a little bit clumsily.

[8] Karl Zeuner (1775–1841), pianist and composer.

did something for my style. However, my instruction in theory, that is, of intervals with their inversions, did not go so well. Zeuner made me study his lessons by rote, and this bored me, so later on I took for my teacher Charles Mayer, who in time became my friend. More than the others, he helped to develop my musical talent. On the day of my graduation in 1822, I played Hummel's A minor *Concerto* in a public recital as Mayer accompanied me on a second piano. I was not so successful on the violin. Although my teacher, the concertmeister Böhm,[9] played truly and precisely, he did not have the gift of passing his knowledge on to others, and when I played poorly he would say: "Messieur Klinka fous ne chouerez chamais du fiolon."[10]

Despite the fact that I had not really accomplished much, I was able to play in my uncle's orchestra. In 1819, 1820, and 1821, I visited my family during vacations. Uncle's orchestra had been improved and enlarged with several boys my father had sent away to study so that he himself might have his own dance music. Moreover, a governess had been hired for my younger sisters. Her husband, Karl Fedorovich Hempel, son of the Weimar organist, was a good musician and in his free time went with me to my uncle's— Afanasy Andreevich. We were both delighted by the music, but I now realize how ignorant I was then; I was to some extent acquainted with the overtures of Cherubini and Méhul, and I listened with great satisfaction to Rossini's overtures. Of these, *Cenerentola* so pleased me that Hempel and I transcribed it for four hands and frequently amused ourselves by playing it. About this time, or earlier, there also lived with us the Italian Todi,[11] who taught voice and was just as bad a musician as all the other "canaries" like him.

While I was away at school, and even just after my arrival in

---

[9] Franz Böhm (1789–1846), violin virtuoso and concertmeister for the St. Petersburg Theaters.

[10] "Mesoo Klinka, yoo vill nott effa blay ze fiolon."

[11] Todi taught voice to Glinka's sisters.

Petersburg, my parents, other relatives, and their friends would take me to the theater; opera and ballet threw me into indescribable rapture.

It should be noted here that the Russian theater of that day was not in the sad state it is in now as a result of the constant inroads of the Italians.[12] Ignorant, but inflated by their fancied worth, the Italian songsters were not then inundating the capitals of Europe like corsairs. I was glad there were none of them in Petersburg and that the operatic repertoire was therefore a varied one. I saw Cherubini's *The Water Carrier*, Méhul's *Joseph*, Nicolo Isouard's *Joconda*, and Boieldieu's *The Little Red Cap*. The tenors Klimovsky and Samoilov and the bass Zlov were most notable singers; so was our well-known singer Sandunova, although she no longer appeared on the stage. She did take part in important concerts, though, and I heard her in oratorios. At that time I did not have a good understanding of serious singing; rather, I found my major delight in instrumental soloists and orchestras. On one of my father's visits to Petersburg he took me to Lvov's, and the sweetly delicate sounds of Aleksei Fedorovich's entrancing violin became deeply engraved on my memory.

In the winter of 1821–22, the last year of school for me, Uncle Afanasy Andreevich came to Petersburg and I used the poor state of my health as a reason for visiting him for a while. We lived in General Vasily Vasilevich Engelhardt's house (he was a nephew of Field Marshal Prince Potemkin-Tavrichesky).[13] He was well disposed toward me, and I continued afterward on friendly terms with his sons and their families. Vasily Vasilevich's grandson, Vasily Pavlovich, educated at the School of Law, had a strong love of music in his early years. He now has all my manuscripts

[12] Written in 1854. The Italian opera was founded in St. Petersburg in 1843. Its popularity forced the Russian operatic group from the Bolshoi Theater (sometimes called the "Grand Theater") to the Aleksandrinsky. In 1846, the Russian opera moved to Moscow.

[13] Vasily Vasilevich Engelhardt (1758–1828), general, senator, and nephew of Potemkin. Glinka's Uncle Ivan Andreevich managed the Engelhardt properties for thirty years, and it was this circumstance that brought the two families together.

that we could find and copies of those that were lost. I owe a large part of my musical pleasure in recent years to his active and devoted friendship.[14]

I was always very happy indeed whenever the Engelhardts got a short leave for me from my boarding school. The old general was very indulgent with me. I soon became friends with my cousin Sofiya Ivanovna, a girl of my own age with an excellent education, kind, pretty, and a lover of music and books. Her father, Ivan Andreevich (brother of Afanasy Andreevich), was a good musician. He had a large collection of various pieces, mostly piano overtures for four hands by Cherubini, Méhul, Mozart, Righini, Spontini, Paër, and Rossini. We played all of these well enough to entertain our friends and acquaintances. I never missed a chance to attend a concert—anywhere—and whenever possible I would be taken to P. I. Yushkov's, where they played and sang every week.[15] The orchestra, although not full, was a good one. One time Uncle Afanasy Andreevich took me to see the famous Hummel, who was then performing in Petersburg. He listened politely as I played the first solo from his A minor *Concerto.* Afterward, he improvised for us: he played smoothly, as if he himself had composed the piece and learned it by heart.

In the early spring of 1822, I was introduced to a family at whose home I met an attractive young lady; she played the harp well and, above all, had a delightful soprano voice. Her singing resembled no instrument at all; it was a pure, resonant, silvery soprano, and she sang naturally and with great charm. Her excellent qualities and cordial attitude toward me (she called me her "little nephew," and I called her my "dear aunt") inflamed my heart and stirred my fancy. She loved music, and often, for hours on end as she sat by the piano while my uncle and I were playing,

14 Vasily Pavlovich Engelhardt (1828-1915), astronomer, musician, man of affairs, friend and admirer of Glinka, collected the composer's manuscripts and later gave them to a public library. He was the grandson of V. V. Engelhardt.
15 Peter Ivanovich Yushkov (1771-1847), owner of a serf orchestra in St. Petersburg.

she would sing her favorite passages along with us in her resonant, silvery voice. Wishing to do something for her, I thought of composing variations on a theme she liked (C Major) from Weigl's opera *The Swiss Family*. I then wrote variations for harp and piano on a Mozart theme (E Flat Major) and finally a waltz of my own devising for piano (F Major). More than this I do not recall; I know only that these were my first attempts at composition—although I still did not know thorough bass—and that at this time I first got to know the harp, a delightful instrument if used appropriately.

This ideal manner of passing the time distracted me from more serious matters, and in my last year at school I always found means, by feigning illness, to visit my uncle; up to that time I had been a model student, I had behaved myself, and I was as well liked by my fellow students as I was noted favorably by my professors. In 1819, 1820, and 1821, I made the honor roll and was awarded an engraving and other prizes. I may say apropos of this engraving that I would undoubtedly have attained a certain degree of proficiency at drawing, but the academicians Bessonov and Sukhanov wearied me by making me draw enormous heads for them and, by demanding a slavish imitation, line by line, brought me to the point where I simply refused to study under them. I had taken a dislike to mathematics when we got to analytics; criminal and Roman law pleased me not at all. I was no good at dancing, nor at fencing. In the latter subject our instructors were Severbrik and Havemann. The first often said to me, "Ei, Glinka, I'll stick you," and, in point of fact, he did stick me.

I had my greatest success in languages. To the amazement of my professor, I learned German in half a year. Latin with I. E. and English and Persian with Professor Dzhiafar went along fine. I knew geography well and history adequately, and I loved the natural sciences, especially zoology. Even before going away to school I had begun to note the marvelous diversity of nature's works. Uncle Afanasy Andreevich had a great number of birds

in cages and in a part of the parlor separated by netting, where
they could fly about. I enjoyed watching them and listening to
them sing. Another uncle (my father's brother) left us a lot of
birds when he died. The very year I left for Petersburg I had
birds flying all about my room, and when we lived at the Kalinkin
Bridge above the entresol, where, as I said, my father had put me,
we had several kinds of pigeons and rabbits thriving in the garret.
What did most to develop my passion for zoology was a visit to
the "Cabinet of Curiosities,"[16] where Professor Zembnitsky, our
guide, explained the objects to us.

Some time before graduation I took up the sciences, counting
on my memory to see me through, but I couldn't catch up with
my fellow students. I had long ago abandoned mathematics, of
course. As for criminal law, I well remember that, having learned
only one case, I had to answer the professor's question on an entirely different tack, but so adroitly that the examiner, Professor
Zyablovsky, was quite satisfied despite the poorly concealed rage
of my regular law professor. In a word, partly because of previous
hard work and partly because of dextrous maneuvers, in the early
summer of 1822, I was graduated first[17] in my class and given a
tenth-class civil service ranking.

[16] Or *Kunstkammer*. A museum founded by Peter I. Yakim Grigorevich
Zembnitsky was professor of natural sciences at the Blagorodny School.
[17] Glinka graduated *second*.

# 5

## First Trip Abroad

I did not enter government service immediately. I believe I visited my parents and, after returning to Petersburg, settled down not far from our former school inspector, Lindquist, with whom I arranged to breakfast and dine for a fixed fee. My father wanted me to serve in the Foreign Office, which was regarded at that time as the most select service. A. A. Lindquist was an editor of the *Journal de St. Petersbourg* and could have been very useful in familiarizing me with French diplomatic language. But this project failed—the language did not seem at all poetic to me; somehow, I could not grasp the feel of it or get it into my head. On the other hand, I got along well with Mayer from the first, and even with Böhm. I don't remember, though, whether I composed anything at this time or whether I was studying theory. I do know that I took some lessons from Fuchs, but I can't say just when.

In the first part of March, 1823, my father sent word that he approved of my profiting from a certain favorable opportunity for a trip to the Caucasus, where I could perhaps be helped by the mineral waters.[1] I wasted no time in making ready for the journey, all the more so since the departure of Uncle Ivan An-

[1] On a vacation visit to my parents a married cousin who was being treated (and later cured) with mesmerism said, when in a state of clairvoyance at a séance, that the Caucasian mineral waters would be good for my scrofulous condition.—Glinka.

dreevich and his two daughters, Sofiya and Evgeniya Ivanovna, offered a very convenient and agreeable means of traveling to our village of Novospasskoe. We set out in March, that is, when the roads were at their worst, so we made abominable progress in our old four-passenger covered droshky[2] with screens to protect our legs. The journey was a pleasant one nonetheless. I had met Sofiya Ivanovna previously and was on friendly terms with her; Evgeniya Ivanovna, just graduated from the Ekaterinsky Institute, was a very pretty and very amusing young girl. The simplest things would give her pleasure. As an example, once, while stopping for the night at a posthouse, we met a group of cadets; one of them seemed to think himself a prankster and would hide his comrades' shoes each night. After we had gone about 250 miles, our droshky got stuck so deep in the slushy snow that our post horses could not pull it out and we had to send for help. Happily, this happened not far from the estate of a wealthy landowner, Zherebtsov, who sent some fine carriages for us and then had us spend several days with him, during which time he entertained us with unsurpassed hospitality. He himself was a cheerful, talkative person who loved the gay life. He had a private theater where he put on amusing shows, but the rehearsals were even more amusing. At the one for Kauer's *Rusalka* the actors—house servants—appeared in the most diverse and fantastic costumes, each suited to the wearer's duties or employment.

I returned home and stayed there until the last of April. My father supplied me with a light carriage, a valet (my former attendant, Ilya), and a cook, Afanasiya. We left Novospasskoe in wet, very cool weather, but several days later, near Orel, we could feel the warm breath of spring; after crossing the Oka, I knew I was in a different region, the southern zone, quite new to me. Oak groves replaced our birch trees, and in the ravines, instead

---

[2] Glinka uses the word *lineika,* a long droshky, usually open but evidently covered in this case, in which the passengers sit back to back on benches running lengthwise.

of bare branches, apple, cherry, and pear trees were blossoming. The look of the fields and the villages, with their white, mud-walled huts instead of the dark, timbered ones of the north, arranged in irregular but picturesque fashion, drew my attention by day, while at night the clear sky, strewn with brightly shining stars, enraptured me. I reached Kharkov on May 10. My father wanted me to go on to the Caucasus because an acquaintance of his was going there—an educated and responsible person, the former director of the Smolensk District Office, Petrovsky-Muravsky. Moreover, a Smolensk physician, Lazar Petrovich Bykovsky, was traveling to the same destination with his family. I was to meet the first of these people in Kharkov. In order not to lose time, on the advice of a Petersburg acquaintance, I introduced myself to a General Vitkovsky,[3] who in those days had a very good music store in Kharkov. My playing of the first solo from Hummel's A minor *Concerto* made such a good impression that I was immediately introduced to the proprietor's talented family, and they entertained me with music until my friend arrived.

When my traveling companion finally did appear, with his brother, we set out on our way. Endless steppes soon replaced the picturesque Ukraine. We crossed the Don at Oksaya and found ourselves in Asia, which inexpressibly gratified my imagination. I must say, however, that until we reached the sulphur waters (now Pyatigorsk) we saw nothing to delight the eye; on the contrary, there was nothing but the limitless steppes, overgrown with thick, tall, sweet-smelling grass. Pyatigorsk was at that time completely wild, but somehow grand nonetheless; there were few houses and no churches or gardens at all. But then, as now, the snow-covered ridges of the Caucasus Mountains stretched away majestically and in the valley, like a ribbon, wound the Podkumok, while multitudes of eagles circled above us in the clear sky.

[3] Ivan Matveevich Vitkovsky, violin virtuoso, composer, conductor, and teacher.

My companions and I moved into a modest little house. Life was pleasant: my friend had brought a supply of books and the kitchen was in good order. Excellent mutton, chicken, game, and superb fruit enabled our cooks to feed us well, while bottles of Santurino wine (which I still like to drink) replaced the expensive bottles we had brought with us. Generally speaking, I was quite well satisfied, especially in Pyatigorsk. Among other things, I saw a Circassian dance, the games and races of the Circassians, and, of course, the peaceful Caucasian villages, or *aulas*. I also had some pet wild goats.

Soon after our arrival we started the cure, that is, we took hot sulphur baths and drank water from the so-called sulphuric acid spring. Later on, I bathed, or, rather, I was boiled, in a sort of bathtub cut out of the rocks by the Circassians where a stream of sulphurous water flowed at a temperature of 115° or 117° F. The waters helped my companion a great deal—indeed, put him on his feet again (he had been getting around with difficulty). It is likely that I, too, would have received considerable benefit from them if only my jangled nerves had been taken into account and if I had been made to drink less and allowed to bathe in water that had been diluted with cool water, as is done at Aachen.

After taking a few "sulphuric acid" baths, we went on to the iron waters, located in a forest halfway up a mountain. Their site was wild but extremely picturesque. At that time there was only one wooden house where visitors could stay. Anyone not finding refuge there would pitch a felt tent; at night, when fires were gleaming all around, the place looked like the camp of wild nomad warriors. The rest of the mountain was covered by thick woods up to the very top. A wild vineyard had entwined great numbers of bushes and small trees, and, as always, the eagles flew about just above our heads. Once I watched as a cloud moved toward us and soon cloaked everything in a dense fog.

After several baths of iron water at 104° F., I began to feel bad, and presently, severe headaches forced me, and my friend, too, to leave these springs. We went to Kislovodsk, accompanied by a convoy and a cannon. The reason for this became clear the following year, 1824, when the Circassians launched a big attack and cut several near-by villages to pieces.

Kislovodsk was more attractively situated than Pyatigorsk, but in my time it still had few houses and no trees at all. On the flat summits of the hills, lying in tiers very much like the *páramos* around Valladolid, a thick, aromatic grass (this in July and August, when in the ravines everything had already been burned up by the heat) rose as high as a horseman's cap.

I had to drink and bathe in carbonic mineral water[4] (50° F.) — and matters went just as badly for me here as they had at the iron waters. I soon felt a loss of sleep and appetite, and Dr. Bykovsky himself was convinced that the carbonic treatment was doing me harm. To repair my upset stomach, he prescribed (not without success) bitter herbs steeped in wine. My insomnia was not relieved immediately, partly because it is not easy to calm nerves once distraught and also because of the fleas, which made it impossible for me to close my eyes at night.

On the return trip, after leaving my companion in Kharkov, I had attacks of fever as I approached Orel, and while staying over with a merchant acquaintance there, I fell desperately ill with fever and abscesses where I had had herpes from birth. After a few days, however, my illness went away of its own accord, and with it the herpes. Everyone assumed that I had been fundamentally cured, but this was quite untrue, as later developments were to reveal.

In the first part of September I returned to Novospasskoe and, after a rest, took up my music with renewed energy. During my four months of travel I had had a piano only at Kharkov—and, of course, I played the violin very badly. Moreover, the irritating effect of the mineral waters and the multitude of new impressions

[4] Called *narzan* water, from the name of the great spring at Kislovodsk. The water has a high content of free carbonic acid.

had overexcited my imagination, and so I set to work in the following fashion: in order to obtain greater precision, whenever musicians arrived (this happened about twice a month, and they would stay for several days, sometimes about a week), before a full rehearsal I would go over each individual's part with him—except for a few of the better ones—until there was not a single false note or even a doubtful one in his playing. I thus found a method of orchestrating most of the best composers (Gluck, Handel, and Bach I knew only from what I had heard about them). I would next listen to the over-all effect of the piece, or, in our first rehearsal together, I would conduct the orchestra myself, playing the violin, and if the piece went all right, I would go off a certain distance and in that way follow the effect of the instrumentation that had already been mastered. For the most part, the repertoire consisted of overtures, symphonies, and sometimes even concertos. Among the overtures were:

| Cherubini: | *Medea* |
| | *Hôtellerie portugaise* |
| | *Faniska* |
| | *Lodoiska* |
| | *Les deux journées* |

The first two were my favorites.

| Méhul: | *Joseph* |
| | *Le trésor supposé* |
| | *L'irato* |
| Mozart: | *Don Juan* |
| | *Zauberflöte* |
| | *Clemenza di Tito* |
| | *Nozze di Figaro* |
| Beethoven: | *Fidelio* (E Major) |

Bernhard Romberg (E Flat Major) and Maurer (E Flat Major), for which the alto part was missing. However, I spread the other parts out on chairs and after comparing them wrote the alto—entirely without mistakes, I believe.

There were three symphonies:

27

Haydn, B Major
Mozart, G minor
Beethoven, *Second*, D Major

I particularly liked the last one.

Rossini's overtures were no longer being played. Toward the end of my stay in Petersburg, Mayer had substantially advanced my musical taste. He did not confine himself to merely demanding from me a precise and unconstrained performance. He resolutely opposed affected or elegant expressions in playing, and, as far as possible in view of the state of my musical knowledge at the time, he also explained to me, naturally and without pedantry, the worth of various pieces, distinguishing the classical from the good and the latter from the bad. As for compositions generally, thorough bass, counterpoint, and other conditions basic to a good method of composing, my ideas were so indefinite that I took up my pen without even knowing how to begin.

I started to write first a septet and then an adagio and rondo for orchestra. If these pieces have survived among those of my manuscripts[5] in the keeping of V. P. Engelhardt, they will serve only as an indication of my musical ignorance at that time.

In March or April of 1824, I returned to Petersburg and found a room at Kolomna. I made no haste, though, about deciding to enter the civil service. With me at the time, besides Ilya, were two musicians: Yakov (later well known from N. Stepanov's caricatures) played the cello a little, while his brother, Aleksei, was already quite a good violinist.[6] They later studied under the first violinist of P. I. Yushkov's orchestra; as for me, I worked at the

---

[5] The manuscript of the unfinished septet for oboe, flute, horn, two violins, cello, and bass, as well as the manuscripts of two unfinished orchestral pieces—*Adagio* and *Andante cantabile*—are in the Archives Division of the M. E. Saltykov-Shchedrin State Public Library.

[6] The brothers Yakov Netoev and Aleksei Ulyanovich were two serfs who were with Glinka for many years. Yakov was his personal attendant, or valet, on the trip to the Ukraine in 1838. Aleksei took violin lessons with Glinka from Franz Böhm. Excerpts from Aleksei's reminiscences of the composer were published in 1888.

piano and violin with new vigor. Charles Mayer no longer gave me lessons; he had once said: "Vous avez trop de talent pour que je vous donne des leçons, venez en ami tous les jours et nous ferons de la musique ensemble."[7] I recall with sincere gratitude these expressions of friendship, which were not merely empty words. Nearly every week, I visited Mayer, who lived with his mother and sisters; I often played four hands with the elder, Henriette (later Mme. Garegnani). Mayer himself, as before, assigned me various pieces, sometimes his own but more often Hummel's. Examining my experiments with composition most tolerantly, he would explain to me, insofar as he was able, the rules of the art,[8] but he never used himself or his own style as models. On the contrary, in such instances Mozart, Cherubini, Beethoven, and other classicists were pointed out as representing the peak of accomplishment. At that time the celebrated contrapuntalist Miller[9] was in Petersburg, but somehow I did not meet him. Who knows? Perhaps it was for the best. Severe German counterpoint does not always mix well with sprightly fantasy.

In the spring of this same year, 1824, I met another distant relative, who, at his brother-in-law's house, presented me to the office director for the Transport Council. He had a well-paying position open for an undersecretary. At this time my father was having difficulty meeting the expense of my music and language lessons; in any case, I had been thinking of entering the civil service somewhere or other—it was all the same to me—and I believed I might then even transfer into the Foreign Office, although, truth to tell, I was not particularly drawn toward the diplomatic service. Thus

---

[7] "You've got too much talent for me to be giving you lessons; just come around every day and we'll play some music together."

[8] Among the works composed at this time there are also some piano variations on an original theme with the dedication: "To whom—I shan't say."

[9] Johann-Heinrich Miller (1780–1827), student of musical theory, composer, pianist, and violinist. In 1803, he settled in St. Petersburg, where among his pupils in the theory of composition were A. A. Alyabiev, A. N. Verstovsky, A. S. Griboedov, Mikhail Yu. Vielegorsky, and V. F. Odoevsky.

it was that on May 7, 1824, I went to work as undersecretary at
the chancery of the Transport Council, an event which was to
have an important bearing on my life. On the one hand, I had to
be at the office only from five to six hours a day, no work was ever
taken home, and there were no responsibilities and no required
attendance, so that as a consequence I could devote the rest of my
time to my favorite occupations, especially music. On the other
hand, my position in the civil service quickly secured me an
acquaintanceship that was most useful in a musical way.

Papers came to our office from the Ministry, and we had to
prepare reports from them for the Transport Council, which consisted of four generals. The senior member was Count Sivers, a
learned man with an inquiring mind and a great lover of good
classical music. Countess Sivers sang first soprano. She had a pleasing voice, true and resonant. Mme. Kryukovskaya sang second
soprano. Kryudner, the Countess' brother, and Hippius, both fine
musicians, sang the bass parts. The first tenor was Hippius' brother, and I would sing second tenor when necessary. We sang only
classical pieces, among others the finale to the first act of *The
Water Carrier*, in which even I played a part as Antonio. Mayer
usually accompanied us on the piano. Sometimes we did other
things besides singing; I remember that on one of our musical evenings there were two quintets—one Mozart, the other Beethoven
(both E Flat Major)—for wind instruments.

In addition to visiting at Count Sivers' home, where I was most
cordially received, I had many other acquaintances whom I met
through our office director, Aleksander Nikolaevich Bakhturin.

During the summer of that year (1824), I moved into Faleev's
house (also in Kolomna). I was soon joined by a relative, Aleksander Ivanovich Kiprianov (husband of my cousin who was being treated with mesmerism), an extremely intelligent, educated,
and agreeable person. Noting the fierce intensity with which I
gave myself to composition, he tried to divert me from this occu-
pation, which was in his opinion a pernicious tendency, asserting

that a talent for playing the piano and violin, aside from the personal satisfaction it might give, could in fact provide me with agreeable and useful acquaintances, while from composition, as he said, there was nothing to hope for but envy, vexation, and embitterment. I later found there was some truth in what he said.

Aleksander Ivanovich and I witnessed the flood of November 7, 1824. When the water first appeared in the streets, people were coming from Mass and the women had to draw their skirts up to their knees, which we found diverting. But when the water began to rise considerably, I turned to the upstairs tenants (our room was on the lower floor) for permission to move my grand piano in with them for the time being. The German housekeeper, in the absence of her mistress, wrung her hands and wept bitterly, accompanying her sighs and groans with expressions of compassion, in broken German and Russian, for a cow that had been drowned. We moved the piano, but, as it turned out, when the water had reached our threshold, it began to subside.

At that time I did not care for the company of men, preferring that of women and young girls whom my musical talent pleased. I was soon convinced that I should learn to dance, and began taking lessons from Holtz. I spent about two years with him and got as far as *entrechats doubles, ailes de pigeons*, and other steps with which a clever dancer of that day could cut quite a figure.

During this same period or a little later, I'm not quite sure, I met the Italian singer Belloli and began to study voice (Italian) with him. I had a powerful, somewhat nasal voice—and an indeterminate one, that is, neither tenor nor baritone. I must say that although I did have an excellent ear, I did not sing truly during the first few months, since I was not accustomed to hearing myself. Belloli taught well and still had a voice good enough to sing everything he was teaching me. I could soon do *musica buffa* quite well.

Despite frequent sessions with Mayer, his explanations of things, and the constant, intensive effort with which I worked, I was still getting nowhere in composition. I remember that at this time I wrote a quartet for two violins, viola, and cello (D Major), but this attempt fared no better than had previous ones.

In 1825, I met the family of Princess Khovanskaya, whose eldest son, Yuri Sergeevich, had been educated at the Tsarskoe Selo lyceum; we became friends, and before long I was being treated as one of the family. Besides the daughters and other relatives, a young Viennese girl named Liglya was living with them. She taught music to the Princess' daughters, played excellently at sight, and could accompany. I played four hands with her quite often, mostly Haydn quartets, Haydn symphonies, Mozart, and even some Beethoven. At that time they were living in Tsarskoe Selo. Occasionally I would visit them for several days, and my appearance always made everyone happy, for they knew that where I was, there could be no tedium. Actually, at that time (happy days!) I knew how to entertain my friends in various ways, especially by doing scenes from *opera buffa*.

I also became acquainted with D. P. Demidov, whose daughter, Elena Dmitrievna, was regarded as one of the finest amateur singers in the capital. She had a very strong contralto voice, but she could also sing soprano parts. Liglya usually accompanied us on the piano, although Belloli and she quite often sang duets by various composers. In all truth, I owe a lot to these musical activities at the Demidovs'.

It was about this time that I wrote the first allegro of a D minor sonata for piano and viola; this composition was more tightly constructed than the others, and I performed it with Böhm and Liglya, in the latter instance playing the viola myself. I wrote the adagio later, but did not get around to the rondo (I recently used its Russian-style motif in a children's polka).

My first unsuccessful attempt at composition with a text was made about this same time. It was a romance to words by Konstantin Aleksandrovich Bakhturin, son of our office director.[10] I

[10] Glinka's first song was *My Harp* (words by K. A. Bakhturin). It is very likely that, as E. Kann-Novikov suggests, this romance was originally intended

can't remember when I composed my first successful romance, *Tempt Me Not Without Need!* (words by Baratynsky), but on reflection, I imagine it was sometime in this same year, 1825.

At the end of summer I moved to Nechaev's house on Zagorodny Prospekt to room with Alcksander Yakovlevich Rimsky-Korsak, a former schoolmate from my own government. Our very comfortable room was on the second floor (*au premier*) of a small wing opening onto the courtyard. It had a garden, which we were entitled to use, and here there was an arbor with the edifying inscription: "Why look any further? It's good here."

I presented my friend at Bakhturin's house; soon . . . .[11]

Toward the end of this year I would sometimes come across former companions, one of whom reproached me for having given up serious matters in order to waste valuable time in, as he put it, frivolous amusements. I believe I answered him to the effect that I would be a success later on but that now I thought it well to pay heed to my own inclinations and my age. This very same fellow indeed became the victim of his *own* imprudence—in 1826 he was sentenced to loss of rank and nobility and sent to Siberia.

Early in the morning of December 14, the elder son of Lindquist (our former inspector at school) paid us a visit. We went into the square just as the Tsar was coming out of the palace. I still clearly retain in my heart the memory of the majestic and inspiring presence of our emperor. It was the first time I had seen him. He was pale and somehow looked sad; with his arms folded across his chest, he walked, slowly and calmly, directly into the center of the crowd and addressed them: "Children, children, disperse!" We stayed in the square for several hours, until I, com-

to be part of an opera, which Glinka was then considering, based on Sir Walter Scott's poem *Rokeby.* The words were an abridged translation of Edmond's romance from this poem.

[11] This sentence was not finished in the original. From the words "I presented my friend" to "who listened amiably and dismissed me" in Glinka's manuscript, the entire text and the notes referring to it were x'd out from top to bottom in black ink.

pelled by hunger (for I had not had breakfast), went back to Bakhturin's. It may be that this apparently trivial circumstance saved me from death or injury, since soon afterward we heard cannon firing at the rioters.

Several days later there was a noise at our gate in the middle of the night. The door to our room was opened, and Colonel Varentsov, staff officer on duty in our area, entered and imperiously ordered me to appear at once before His Highness. Imagine me, scarcely awake, knowing nothing of what was going on, and add to that the fact that I had had many acquaintances among the rioters! In a word, I felt (although only for a short while) that feeling which we call *terror*. My heart froze, and I was, as they say, frightened out of my wits. Recovering myself in a moment, I dressed, and en route to the office of Chief Director of Transport Count Wurtemberg, brother of the Empress Dowager Maria Fedorovna, I asked the Colonel to tell me of what I was accused. One word sufficed to reassure me. This is what the whole matter was all about.

Kuchelbecker,[12] a participant in the riot, had two nephews (the sons of his sister Ustina Karlovna), Dmitri and Boris Grigorich. He had run off after the events in the square, and it was thought that he might be hiding in the capital with one of these nephews. It was an easy matter for me to clear myself of suspicion in a few words, all the more so since Dmitri and Boris were the children of Grigori Andreevich Glinka, former chevalier in attendance on the sovereign Nikolai Pavlovich when he was still a grand duke. They had been reared at the expense of the crown and were distinguished by their particularly fine behavior.

All this I quietly and in quite good French (in which I had improved myself with the help of the former tutor[13] of Princess

[12] Kuchelbecker first stayed with us on the entresol as a special tutor for me and my friends, but later he taught Russian composition and syntax [Glinka lived with Kuchelbecker from 1818 to 1820].—Glinka.

[13] His name was Romulus Godefroy and, as they said, he had been born dur-

Khovanskaya's children) explained to the Count, who listened amiably and dismissed me.

At the end of December, Korsak and I went to the village, I because of the betrothal of my sister Pelageya Ivanovna to our neighbor Yakov Mikhailovich Sobolevsky, a charming and cultivated man.

Soon after my arrival I went to Smolensk with some relatives. We stayed at the apartment of another relative, one Aleksei Andreevich Ushakov, a cheerful and jolly person, who, however, had the fashion of gradually exaggerating any story he might be telling into the most inept lie, sometimes calling in his servants as witnesses in an attempt to convince his listeners. His pretty eighteen-year-old daughter played the piano well. It goes without saying that there was much music played during my stay with them. To oblige my charming niece, I composed piano variations on the then popular Italian song *Benedetta sià la madre* (E Major).[14] These were corrected here and there by Mayer and subsequently published (exactly when, I don't remember). This was therefore my first composition to appear in print.

Among the families then living in Smolensk was that of the retired General Apukhtin. He liked to keep open house, and since dances were not permitted because of the universal mourning, he conceived the idea of putting on a performance which was in accord with the prevailing circumstances, that is, a "Prologue" on the occasion of the death of Tsar Aleksander and the accession to the throne of Nikolai Pavlovich. The tutor wrote the words, in French, at the General's house. I composed the music, which consisted of a chorus (C minor), an aria (B Major), which was to be the conclusion of the "Prologue," and a triumphal chorus, also in B Major. All this music was accompanied by piano and bass. K. F. Hempel played the piano and sang high tenor in the C minor

ing the Terror (*on naquit du temps de la terreur*). He was living with us.—Glinka.

14 Literally, *Blessed Be Mother.*

chorus. I sang the B Major aria dressed as a spirit (I don't remember whether we had torches and wings). In spite of some awkward moments (*gaucheries*) and the incongruity of the C minor and B Major tonalities, I believe this cantata was the first successful experiment in vocal music on a large scale. I had written with straightforward sincerity, and I recall that this piece interpreted the words quite faithfully.

After my sister's marriage I returned to Smolensk to enjoy Shrovetide. Home again, I acquired sixteen birds of various kinds, including a blue-throated warbler, a hedge sparrow, a black-headed warbler, and others of the warbler family (*genre fauvette*).

In the evenings and at dusk I loved to sit and dream away at the piano. Zhukovsky's sentimental poetry pleased me extraordinarily and on occasion moved me to tears. (Generally speaking, in my youth, I had a romantic disposition and loved to weep sweet, sentimental tears.) I think that two of my melancholy romances, *Moonbeams on the Graveyard* and *The Beggar Singer* were written at this time (spring of 1826).

In May of the same year I set off again for Petersburg. Before doing so, however, I sent a certification of my illness to the proper authorities and requested an extension of leave. The summer of 1826 was dry and hot—there were many forest fires—and I suffered from insomnia (because of the sulphur waters in the Caucasus). No doubt I was occupied with music even through this year, but I really don't know what I accomplished.

At the end of that winter (1826) my father came to the capital on business and stayed with us for a while, since he was anxious to see me.[15] He was then forty-nine years old; his face radiated good

---

[15] Sometime in the fall of 1836, Glinka went to Moscow to visit a schoolmate, N. A. Melgunov (although he does not mention this in the *Memoirs*). Pushkin was also in Moscow that fall, and among other occupations, at various houses he visited he was reading *Boris Godunov*, *Songs of Stenka Razin*, and the just recently finished prologue to *Ruslan and Ludmila*. It is not known whether Pushkin and Glinka were in Moscow at precisely the same time, but in any case they had

health and strength, although he already had quite a few gray hairs. He loved me and his other children very much, but with me in particular he acted like a comrade, confiding in me his plans and his secrets, his joys and his sorrows.

Since our apartment at Nechaev's house on the Zagorodny Prospekt was too small, we moved into Piskarev's house on Torgovy Street, Theater Square, in the early part of 1827.

In early spring my father had to return to the village for a month or two, but we stayed on with Korsak. One time a young girl (Katenka) called with a lady friend of Korsak's—and made a great impression on me. In our first meetings I believed myself supremely happy, but soon I felt the opposite. Her heart belonged to another, and all my scheming and conniving calculated to arouse a reciprocal feeling in her, proved fruitless. I expressed the grief of this state in a piece of music for which Korsak supplied the words:

> "I love," you said,
> And I believed.
> But you loved another
> While you passionately said,
> "I love, I love!" *etc.*

Prince S. Golitsyn later wrote some French verses for my music, and this romance is known as *Le baiser*. Physical suffering was soon added to my lovesickness.

On a visit from the village one time my father met at some social affair a certain Dr. Brailov, who, when he learned that I had a history of scrofula, offered his services. To be cured in a radical manner, he said, I would have to drink about thirty or more bottles of a decoction of some kind or other. My God! What

many friends in common and Glinka would most likely have known about the readings in one way or another. In a letter to N. F. Findeizen dated May 26, 1893, V. V. Stasov wrote: "Who knows? Perhaps it was here, during those glorious days and nights passed with ardent Muscovites of the world of art, that Glinka, subtly inspired by *Boris Godunov*, got his first subconscious idea of *A Life for the Tsar!*"

a decoction that was! Astringent, spicy, thick, and of a repulsive, swampy-green color. It certainly did work, though: I was purged most outrageously, and suffered tormenting aches and pains, but not only was I neither refreshed nor cooled—the blood was driven to my head to such a degree that for a long time I simply could not get a wink of sleep. I did not by any means immediately regain my health after I had, with exemplary fortitude, finished off all the bottles.

Despite all this, I went on with my composing; besides the romance *Woe Is Me!* written in 1827 with words by Korsak, I composed several separate theatrical scenes to be sung with an orchestra, namely: duet, with recitative for bass and tenor (A Major); chorus on the death of a hero (C minor); aria for baritone (A Flat Major)—I later used the adagio of this piece for the canon in the first-act finale of my opera *Ruslan and Ludmila*—and finally *Prayer*, for three voices, F Major.

My activities were interrupted by a scrofulous inflammation of the left eye, very likely the result of the continued flow of blood to my head. They seated me in a dark room and sent for the eminent oculist Lehren—but I did not get off without purgatives this time, either. This terribly violent use of internal medicines evidently damaged my health and prepared the way for further tribulations.

When my eye trouble had disappeared, I went to work with renewed vigor. Two circumstances in particular were in my favor: our apartment had a large foyer and an acquaintance of mine, Count Dever, played the violin most expertly. More important than that, perhaps, he was regimental adjutant in the Horse Guards Regiment, and now and then I was able to gather, on far from burdensome terms, the number of wind instruments I needed for my compositions. The string instruments I lacked were obtained through similar, most economical arrangements. In the vocal line I was assisted by Varlamov, who himself gladly sang the bass parts and with singular efficiency produced (from the stables, if I am not mistaken) the number of singers required for the choruses. In this way I was able to hear the effect of what I had written. About this time, too (as it seems), I became acquainted with the violinist Rémi. In a few lessons he set me straight on how to use my right hand; unfortunately, it was too late—my passion for composition utterly distracted me from musical exercises. As for the Persian language, I had given that up soon after I left boarding school.

At this time my circle of acquaintances expanded a bit, and I remember quite well that the Tolstois often came to see us in the evening. There were four of them. The younger Tolstoi, Feofil Matveevich (Rostislav),[16] had a very pleasing tenor voice (*voix sympathique*). They belonged to high society but were nevertheless kind, gay people who did not disdain boiled potatoes and onions, which we prepared to perfection at our place.

In the spring of 1827, when my father was in Petersburg, something happened that was to have an important effect on my later well-being. In Torgovy Street opposite our apartment there lived in a private dwelling the councilor of state, Pogodin, now senator and court lieutenant in the active army. When he heard that my father wished to undertake an important large-scale operation, he, knowing the reputation my parent had earned as a well-informed and upright man, approached him himself and, after he had been vouched for, proposed taking a half-interest, entrusting to my father a capital sum of 500,000 paper rubles against pledges. The profit made in this venture proved to be enough to free our property completely from its burdensome debts.

During that winter my health gradually worsened. Despite the sometimes severe pain, I was often able to pass the time pleasantly and happily. Since moving in with Korsak I often saw our school-

16 Feofil Matveevich Tolstoi (1809-1881), dilettante composer and singer, critic (pseudonym: Rostislav). After writing several unsuccessful operas he devoted himself to musical criticism, notably opposing "The Five." He wrote articles on Glinka and A. N. Serov, as well as reminiscences of them. Glinka had a poor opinion of Tolstoi's capacities.

mate Lukyanovich (now office director for the Disabled Veterans Committee). He was gay, amusing, and kind; he loved literature and had written a number of articles with Korsak. As for myself, feeling guilty, and stirred by their good example,[17] I set to work again. Before long, Ivan Ekimovich also began dropping in, frequently bringing a friend, Aleksei Grigorevich Oginsky—the translator of Goldsmith, Gillies, and other English historians—a scholarly and hard-working person.[18] In physical appearance he stood in striking contrast to Ivan Ekimovich. Aleksei Grigorevich was tall, quite bald, and his face looked somewhat like a baboon's. He spoke gravely, nonetheless, slowly, and somewhat nasally in a deep bass voice, all the while moving his right hand with deliberation to further impress his audience.

Our friendly talks about literature, aided by some punch, nearly always wound up in philosophical discussions. By the third or fourth round, I. E. would be thrown into an ecstasy of enthusiasm which led him to cry out from time to time: "I'm going to argue, I'm going to argue—and that's all there is to it!"

In the winter of 1827–28, Korsak's brother-in-law, Ravinsky, came to visit us; in his youth he had been a gay, witty man who loved to say the most outrageous things with a completely deadpan expression. Korsak and I decided to divert him with some of our eccentric characters. I was ill at the time, but despite that, even now I cannot recall without laughing the little conversation we arranged for Ravinsky. The punch had been spiked; soon I. E. began to yell:

"Aleksei Grigorevich, I quote from the Word! Vanka Kolmakov's drunk; I shall lead! I am the Way, the Truth, and the Life!"
Oginsky (laughing): "You'd never make it."
Kolmakov: "I shall lead, I tell you!"
Oginsky (laughing harder): "You won't."

[17] Glinka's poem *Ansald*, written at about this time, was obviously influenced by Pushkin's southern poems.
[18] Aleksei Grigorevich Oginsky (1770–1848), professor of classical languages at the Blagorodny School.

Kolmakov: "Listen: the fact Vanka Kolmakov is drunk, is proved."

Oginsky: "*Demonstratur.*"

Kolmakov: "Very pretty!"

Oginsky: "*Ruber* est."

Kolmakov: "He's staggering."

Oginsky: "*Vacillat.*" etc."

After this exchange our orators entered into such amusing and ingenious talk that Ravinsky had to rush headlong out of the room lest he choke to death with laughter.

In March, 1828, I went to visit my parents, where I saw for the last time my oldest sister, with whom I had spent the first years of childhood. She died in 1828. At the end of April, I set out for Moscow in an open post carriage. Near the city of Gzhatsk the wind blew so constantly into my left eye that it became inflamed and I had to travel all the next stage covered by a mat. At Gzhatsk, I looked for a doctor but was told the doctor there was no good; the barber, on the other hand, was said to be a very clever fellow. He gave me rosemary and some sort of vegetable oil, which drove away the pain in a few hours and reduced the inflammation so much that I reached Moscow in pretty good condition.

The purpose of this trip was to meet my schoolmate and friend Nikolai Aleksandrovich Melgunov.[19] Because of poor health, he had not remained in school very long. I had often visited him after he left and enjoyed talking with his charming parents. My father, in Petersburg at the time, also became acquainted with them and very nearly permitted me to go abroad with Nikolai Aleksandrovich and his father. But *my* father was a sober-minded man; he concluded that a Russian should not become a Frenchman and, moreover, did not consider a tenth-class civil service rank, on completion of school, to be without value.

I stayed with Melgunov only until May 9 (his name day), but in those few days I wrote the adagio (B Major) for the D minor

[19] Nikolai Aleksandrovich Melgunov (1804–1867), writer, musician, literary and music critic.

*Sonata* and I recall that I had some fairly clever counterpoint in this number. By taking the post carriage in the morning, I reached Petersburg on the evening of May 9, before my leave was up, but in any event, I did not remain long in the service. I resigned for the following reason.

Ivan Savvich Gorgol (one of the generals in the Transport Council) had a wife and three daughters. One of these, Polixena, had studied singing with Belloli, and I often accompanied her and sang with her, too. My circle of acquaintances had widened about that time and I went less frequently to the home of General Gorgol. To tell the truth, the General's wife and his little daughters were such that I did not really want to be with them very often. They had lived for a long time in Kiev and to their unnerving provincial usages they had added a mania for talking very loudly, all four at the same time, so that neither their guests nor the General himself could get a word in edgewise, even when addressed directly.

I was just an undersecretary, but they made me read aloud to them reports from all three bureaus. As my visits to the General's came to be farther and farther apart, it was not hard to detect a marked change in his attitude toward me. But the matter was not confined to this. In examining some papers one day, the General found that the commas were not in their proper places and that correct grammar had not been observed throughout. Although, in all justice, I could not be held responsible for all three desks in our chancery, I, with all due respect, said not a word to my chief, but I thought to myself, "Aha! I see here the hand of that little darling, Polixena," and determined then and there to cease my visits altogether. The General, of course, became even more exacting, so much so, in fact, that without wasting time I requested retirement and thus left the service—all on account of a comma.

On arriving in Petersburg, I settled down at Barbasan's house (no, Zhukov's, if I am not mistaken), on the corner of Nevsky Prospekt and Vladimirsky Street, in the apartment of my schoolmate Chirkov. My health soon became noticeably worse: the scrofula began as herpes in two fingers of my right hand and these soon became so inflamed that I could neither write nor play the piano. Lehrer cured me, but the scrofula continued to bother me; no doubt I might have found some simple remedy, if not to eradicate, then at least to alleviate the disease, but this was not to be.

A distant relative, Aleksei Stepanovich Stuneev,[20] who loved me devotedly, was more than once the innocent cause of misfortunes in my life. For example, he introduced me to a Dr. Gasovsky of the Military Academy. This doctor was a good man, but that made things no easier for his patients (two of my brothers and my father became victims of his curative methods). Later on he became a homeopath and said himself that when he had worked allopathically he had indeed been an enemy of mankind. He actually prescribed great doses of strong, heroic remedies without any reason whatsoever; his favorites were mercury, sulphur, quinine, and opium. For one whole month he subjected me to external and internal applications of the first of these favorite remedies—without any particular reason and without having examined or questioned me in any great detail. I spent the month in a stuffy room, despite the heat of summer and then, when released from confinement, was ordered to take a series of sulphur baths.

As a result of this unintelligent treatment, which, moreover, did not suit my strained nerves, I felt at that time only a slight irritation in the *plexus solaris* and a false appetite.

I diligently applied myself that year. Tolstoi and I began to study Italian with Maroketti and with someone else whose name I have altogether forgotten.[21]

I also took lessons in composition from the son of the well-known Italian *buffo* Zamboni, who was in Petersburg at that time.

[20] Stuneev was an army major serving at the Military Academy.

[21] F. M. Tolstoi wrote in his *Recollections of M. I. Glinka* (1871): "We were studying the Italian language at that time, preferably with Zamboni's daughter, who had so charmingly sung the contralto role in Rossini's *La Gazza Ladra.*"

He assigned me an Italian text and made me write arias, recitatives, and so forth, as well as two-part fugues without words. I cannot boast about the latter experiments, although I was indeed already acquainted with Seb. Bach's *Clavecin bien tempéré*.

In addition, I wrote:

(*a*) A serenade for which Tolstoi had given me Italian words: *O mia dolce, mia carina*. At the time, this serenade was well received.

(*b*) An F Major quartet for soprano, alto, tenor, and bass accompanied by two violins, viola, and cello (*Come di gloria al nome*).

(*c*) A quartet for the same voices and instruments in G minor (*Sogna chi crede esser felice*). These last two pieces were performed at Demidov's, and the F Major quartet again, later on, at Lvov's.

(*d*) I also wrote these romances: Batyushkov's *Heart's Remembrance*, for A. S. Stuneev, and to words by Prince Sergei Golitsyn, *Pour un moment* and *Tell Me Why*.

I cannot list in chronological order the most important events of this period, but it doesn't really matter.

My acquaintance with Prince Sergei Grigorevich Golitsyn[22] greatly influenced the development of my musical talents. He was a kind and cheerful, sometimes witty young man who had a good knowledge of music and sang very agreeably in an excellent deep bass voice. I was then extremely shy; he knew how to give me self-confidence and brought me into the company of young people of good society. Thanks to his friendly intervention, I acquired a host of pleasant and useful acquaintances. He himself could cleverly excite me to action; he wrote verses for me and willingly played my compositions. Before I set out for Moscow, he gave me a letter to Nikolai Nikolaevich Norov[23] (now deputy minister of finance) containing only this laconic statement: "The bearer of this note is Glinka." Norov received me kindly and we

[22] Sergei Grigorevich Golitsyn (1806–1868), amateur poet, composer, and singer.

[23] Nikolai Nikolaevich Norov (1802–1860), composer and senator. He became Deputy Minister of Finance in 1845.

soon became good friends. He was a person of rare spirit and talent, and I am grateful for having known him.

At this time the *Kammerjunker* Evgeni Petrovich Shterich[24] was circulating among the young people of high society. Although he was an *élégant* in the full sense of that word and loved to shine in salons, he was also distinguished by some worth-while qualities of a somewhat higher order. Among other things, he was a good musician, had studied with Mayer and played the piano with precision. I soon became friends with him and quite often, along with Sergei Golitsyn (whom we called "Firs"), I visited him at Pavlovsk, where he spent the summer months. There I was presented to our famous poet Vasily Andreevich Zhukovsky. I had known Count Vielegorsky[25] earlier, but at Pavlovsk I became better acquainted with him and I believe we each wrote a canon, thus trying our skill at composition. Before Mikhail Yurevich Vielegorsky took up his pen, I managed to devise a canon (which has apparently survived) for these words by Prince Golitsyn:

> In this sacred holy place
> We spend the days in prayer;
> We know not the worldly race,
> Here we find contentment rare.

Prince Sergei Golitsyn and I journeyed to the Black River to visit Prince Vasily Petrovich Golitsyn,[26] who had a good tenor voice. At the end of August, Tolstoi and I got together with some other young people to entertain the public with a serenade. The rehearsals were most interesting, and in the evening crowds of men and women would gather beneath the windows of Prince Golitsyn's house to listen to us. On the day set for the serenade,

---

24 Evgeni Petrovich Shterich (1809–1833) was an amateur composer and friend of Glinka.

25 Mikhail Yurevich Vielegorsky (1788–1856), high government official and patron of the arts.

26 Vasily Petrovich Golitsyn (1800–1863) was District Marshal of the Nobility in Kharkov from 1841 to 1852. He had a notable art collection, was a lover of music and a singer (tenor).

two barges adorned with lanterns appeared on the Black River; we occupied one, and the trumpeters of the Horse Guards Regiment occupied the other.

A small piano had been set up on the stern, where I played the accompaniment and directed the chorus. I can't remember all the pieces we played. The agreeable voice of Feof. Mat. Tolstoi had a charming effect when heard on the water as he sang the Venetian barcarole *Da brava Catina*. The chorus from Boieldieu's *Dame Blanche, Sonnez, sonnez, cors et musettes*, was done quite well. After each number the powerful, harmonious, triumphal notes of the trumpets resounded. Instruments with valves were not then in use, so that ears sensitive to music did not suffer from the false, distressing sounds by which we are unmercifully besieged today. Count Mikhail Yurevich's mazurka, composed expressly for trumpets, made a strong impression on me. Even the march and finale in my opera *A Life for the Tsar* were written especially for simple trumpets without valves, and if it were possible now to find a chorus of trumpets similar to that which took part in our serenade, there is no doubt that the finale of the opera would be more effective.

The serenade was favorably reviewed in the *Northern Bee*, and this first success spurred us on to further enterprises of a similar nature. A group of about sixteen of us performed for Count Kochubei (then chairman of the Imperial Council); in addition to Prince Golitsyn and me, there were Bashutsky,[27] Count Protasov (he is now Procurator of the Holy Synod), and others, plus a full orchestra. Charles Mayer played the piano. I, in a white muslin dress and red wig, took the role of Donna Anna in the introduction to Mozart's *Don Juan* and also improvised on the piano. We presented a program at Tsarskoe Selo, where we performed my serenade and couplets with chorus: *Lila in the Black Mantilla* (words by Prince S. Golitsyn). Ivanov sang the couplets and the court singers sang the chorus. There was a small part for

[27] Aleksander Nikolaevich Bashutsky (1800–1876), man of letters.

Prince S. Golitsyn, too. Finally, we traveled about one hundred miles to Count Stroganov's village of Marino in Novgorod Government. Here I played Figaro in several scenes from Rossini's *Il Barbiere di Siviglia*. For our efforts, we were entertained there for several days.

In the summer of this same year, 1828, Mikhail Lukyanovich Yakovlev, the composer of some well-known Russian romances and a good baritone, introduced me to Baron Delvig, one of our eminent poets. I visited him quite often; that winter, the young girl Liglya was there and we played four hands on the piano. Baron Delvig rewrote the song *Oh, Night! Oh, Gentle Night!* for my music; I also composed the music to his words *Grandfather, Once Maidens Told Me*, a song that M. L. Yakovlev sang beautifully.

Along about this time I often saw our famous poet Aleksander Sergeevich Pushkin, whom I had known before when he used to visit his brother at my school. I enjoyed his acquaintance right up to his death.

I spent nearly one whole day with Griboedov (author of the comedy *Woe from Wit*). He was a very good musician and gave me the theme of a Georgian song for which A. S. Pushkin shortly thereafter wrote the romance *Sorceress, Sing Not for Me!*[28]

I first heard Ivanov about this time, too, and could not fail to be impressed by his sweet and resonant voice. At first he was so shy that he sang only up to high F and G; I persuaded him to visit me and in a short while, by having him sing gradually higher and higher pieces, he unconsciously reached up to high A and B Flat. Subsequently, he often took part in our musical evenings at home.

It was also at this time (as far as I can remember) that I met the well-known pianist Shimanovsky. He had two daughters, Tselina

---

[28] The manuscript of this song, now reposing in the Glinka Archives, bears a notation by Kukolnik: "This Georgian national melody was given to M. I. Glinka by A. S. Griboedov; the public had long known the words, written by A. S. Pushkin to a melody he had heard by chance."

and Elena, who sang fairly well. I was the *maestro* at Shimanovsky's musical mornings, when we sometimes played my compositions. It was on one of these occasions, if I am not mistaken, that I met the poet Mickiewicz, who was then courting Tselina, whom he later married.

In 1828, Prince S. Golitsyn and I undertook to publish the *Lyrical Album*, but it was quite a while before the affair went at all well. Nikolai Ivanovich Pavlishchev[29] then busied himself with the publication, and the album did indeed finally appear in 1829.

In the latter part of 1828 my health began to deteriorate again —I started to have pains, especially when it was cold and wet. Gasovsky prescribed Dr. Nemich's May balsam, which produced a rash over my entire body and I felt worse and worse. Around March of 1829, Salomon (later well known as a surgeon) undertook to cure me. For two whole months he kept me in a hot room and made me take *sublimatum* pills, in steadily increasing doses, so that I unquestionably ate from eighty to one hundred of the things on a very strict diet. Such treatment so weakened me that when Prince S. Golitsyn, on his way to join the active army (he served in the war[30] and was adjutant to Count Ridiger), came to say good-by, he found me in a terribly sick state. Nevertheless, at this time I wrote the romance *Will I Forget You?* (words by Prince Golitsyn). His romance *Where Art Thou, O Youth's First Longing?* must relate (I think) to 1828.

In May, after several sulphur baths, I felt better for a while. I often visited Baron Delvig; besides his very dear and charming wife, there was also the lovely Madame Kern.[31] In June, the Baron and his wife, together with Madame Kern and Orestes Somov (a

[29] Nikolai Ivanovich Pavlishchev (1802–1879), man of letters and amateur composer. He married Pushkin's sister, Olga Sergeevna.

[30] This, of course, was the war against Turkey, 1827–29, brought about by the Greek situation.

[31] Anna Petrovna Kern (1800–1879), known for her biography of Pushkin, who had dedicated to her the poem *I Recall That Wondrous Moment*. Glinka had a serious affair with her daughter, Ekaterina Ermolaevna (1818–1904).

writer, and a very intelligent and amiable man),[32] traveled to Imatru[33] in a four-passenger droshky; Korsak and I followed them in a peasant cart. Stopping off in Vyborg, we all walked together through Baron Nikolai's beautiful garden. We then did some sightseeing in Imatru and returned to Petersburg. One of the Finnish coachmen sang a song that pleased me very much; I made him repeat it several times so I could learn it by heart, and I later used it for the principal theme of Finn's ballad in *Ruslan and Ludmila*. This trip would have been still more enjoyable for me if I had not been ill. Before the trip, despite the fine weather, a severe case of neuralgia had begun to develop, and by the time we reached Petersburg it had increased to such a degree that it bothered me every day and came to be accompanied by burning fits of fever and delirium. The paroxysm would end in severe and abnormal sweating. It is no doubt because of these miseries that I can't remember this period too well.

In the summer of 1829, I wrote the romance *O Gentle Autumn Night* (words by Korsak). Toward the end of summer, I frequently visited the Delvigs and listened to Naryshkin's horn-music on the Neva.[34] Shimanovsky's *Viliya*, consisting entirely of arpeggios, enchanted me in particular. Why did they disband this marvelous orchestra and introduce those horrible *trompettes à clefs*?

I remember that soon after coming back from Imatru, we successfully entertained the Delvigs, Madame Kern, and Somov by presenting them to Kolmakov and Oginsky.

Delvig wrote a romance for me: *Not the Heavy Autumn Shower*. I later took the music to these words for Antonida's song

[32] Orestes Mikailovich Somov (1793–1833), man of letters, assistant to Baron Delvig in publishing *Flowers of the North* and the *Literary Gazette*.

[33] In Finland, noted for its waterfall.

[34] Dmitri Lvovich Naryshkin (1765–1838), a court chamberlain; he had a topnotch serf horn orchestra. The so-called horn-music was a singular type of music that developed in Russia in the second half of the eighteenth century. The orchestra was a collection of copper horns of various sizes, each of which sounded a single note only.

*'Tis Not for That I Grieve, My Darling* in my opera *A Life for the Tsar*.

In the autumn of this same year, one time at Shterich's I heard a Persian song sung by the secretary of Minister of Foreign Affairs Khozrevamirz. I used this motif for the chorus *The Deep of Night Falls o'er the Field* in *Ruslan and Ludmila*.

During that same autumn, I used to visit the Lvovs, where I wrote my quartet in F Major: *Come di gloria al nome*.

About this time, too, I suffered from pain, especially in the cervical glands, that eventually reached such a high degree of intensity that I would roll on the floor and bite myself out of unbearable torment. Soon (probably from a cold) a persistent, spasmatic ache developed in the back of my neck, and although it could be relieved by very hot baths, I informed my parents of my condition. In October, my mother and sister Natalya Ivanovna came and took me back to the village.

Before we left I had been advised to see an Italian doctor, whose name I can't recall. He prescribed pills of opium and mercury to soothe my aches and pains. I saw him many times during the winter and spring, and his treatment did, in fact, give me some relief, but the general state of my health became increasingly poor.

In the periods between illnesses (nearly always accompanied by burning fits of fever and delirium) I went on with my music. I learned Hummel's *Septet* and played it several times with accompaniment. I improved my piano playing by constant work on the *études* of Cramer and Moscheles, and sometimes I even tackled Bach. I composed several light pieces which may be found in the green notebook at V. P. Engelhardt's. I wrote the romance *Voice from the Other World*, words by V. A. Zhukovsky. Finally, in the early spring of 1830, I wrote an F Major quartet for stringed instruments. Thanks to V. P. Engelhardt, I was able to hear the performance of this rather amateurish work several times, and it seems to me that it must reflect the poor state of my health at that period. In addition, I wrote six contralto *études* for my sister Natalya Ivanovna. I also taught geography to my sister Ludmila Ivanovna (later Shestakova). She testifies that she studied gladly under my direction and that she still has several pages of my notes. For my younger sisters and brother I built a wooden mountain inside the house, down which they could slide in copper pans.

Even before going back to the village the idea of traveling abroad had occurred to me. This desire, born of the hope of ending the miseries of my poor health and of perfecting my music, was intensified by my reading of travel books. I recall that just before setting out for the village I read a book about travel in Spain, and from that moment on I dreamt of that fascinating country.

I returned to the village with the hope of getting my father's permission to go abroad. He refused me decisively, his great love for me notwithstanding. I was mortified to tears, but did not dare even to think of acting contrary to his wishes, despite our generally friendly relationship. My mother, with her usual kindness and concern, tried to calm me down. Meanwhile, my illness worsened despite the efforts of our fine old local doctor, Wilhelm Danilovich Hindenberg. I again had recourse to the Italian doctor's pills and without a doubt in the world swallowed hundreds of them in six months, to the great detriment of my health.

Happily for me, toward the end of the winter of 1829 the regimental physician Shpindler visited us. My father had known him at Bryansk (Orel Government) and held him in high esteem. After inquiring in detail about my troubles, he looked me over and explained to my father that I had a whole troop of illnesses and that to be rid of them I should have to spend *not less than three years* abroad in a warm climate.

Thus it was that my trip to Italy and Germany was ultimately decided upon.

I wanted to go with my father to Petersburg to arrange a concert there for Ivanov so he could accompany me. Seeing that the wretched state of my health would not enable me to make this journey in the winter, my father took it upon himself to make all these arrangements for me. In fact, with the good-natured insistence natural to him, on the one hand he *prevailed upon* (*c'est le mot*)[35] Ivanov, who had not committed himself and was vacillating, and on the other he begged the director of the Imperial Chapel Choir, Fyodor Petrovich Lvov, to grant Ivanov permission to go with me. Ivanov was given a two-year leave and some financial assistance, while my father signed a note so that Ivanov would not lack means of subsistence. Ivanov thus owed his future lot more to my father than to me.

In the spring my health got progressively worse, and when Ivanov arrived near the end of April, I was in very bad shape and was groaning and moaning a lot. Everything had been readied for our departure, however, and it was determined that we would set out on April 25, 1830.

[35] "That's the word for it."

*April 25, 1830,* TO *December, 1836*

# 6

## *Travel Abroad. Return to Russia*

AND so, on Friday, April 25, 1830, Ivanov and I left the village of Novospasskoe. My mother went along with us to Smolensk, and from Smolensk to Brest-Litovsk we had the company of my brother-in-law Yakov Mikhailovich Sobolevsky and a fellow named Aleksei (a violinist). It was now the first part of May and the weather was cold and snowy. I felt tired at each post stop and the first few days I often had to lie down and rest a bit at the various stations. Before long, however, I was feeling better, and when we got to Brest, I was already walking about quite easily. Here we said good-by to my brother-in-law and Aleksei, after which Ivanov and I continued on to Warsaw in a big four-wheeled cart.[1] From there we rode to Dresden in an open carriage along with three candymakers from Graubünden.

In Dresden I consulted Dr. Kreisig (that was the fashionable thing to do, even then); he prescribed for me, first the waters at Ems, then those at Aachen. From Dresden we went via Leipzig to Frankfurt am Main in a rented carriage. We had as traveling companion a student (Jewish, I think) who sang bass. Whenever we stopped for dinner or for the night—if we could find a piano—we tried singing together. Ivanov was first tenor, I second tenor,

[1] A Jewish peasant cart—used by peddlers traveling from village to village.

and the student bass in well-known operatic selections: the chorus and trio from the first act of *Der Freischütz* went particularly well, and the villagers would gather around to listen to us.

From Frankfurt we went to Mainz and from there by steamboat down the Rhine; before reaching Koblenz we went ashore and walked on to Ems. Three weeks of taking the waters there greatly weakened me. We went on to Aachen, where in a very short while I felt I had been helped considerably; but here, too, the same thing happened as in the Caucasus; they made me drink too much and bathe too often, although they did not cook me (as they had in the Caucasus) in unbearably hot water.

At that time a fine group of touring German singers from Paris were playing at the Aachen theater. The soprano, Madame Fischer, sang quite nicely. Geitsinger and Eichberger were at that time quite properly thought to be the best tenors in Germany. I heard the first as Florestan in *Fidelio* and the second as Max in *Der Freischütz*. They were splendid. The first time we heard *Fidelio*, Ivanov and I did not understand it, but the second performance brought tears to our eyes. Of other operas, I remember hearing Spohr's *Faust*.

Toward the end of my treatment the consumption of sulphur waters had ended by irritating my cervical glands and giving me a very severe toothache. At that point we heard from Shterich, who, also traveling for his health, had arrived at Ems, where he wanted us to come for a visit. We had been friendly in Petersburg, so it is not necessary to describe my pleasure at seeing him. Dr. Bers (his brother served with the management of the St. Petersburg imperial theaters) eased my pain temporarily with baths consisting of a mixture of water and chaff. After a short stay in Ems we went to Schlangenbad and then to Frankfurt, along with Shterich, his mother, and some traveling companions of theirs. This was in August, but nevertheless we had to have fires in the fireplaces at night. We saw the celebrated statue of Ariadne and went to Cherubini's opera *Medea*. I confess I understood only the overture, which was excellently done; for the rest, it was all beyond me and I can remember none of it.

We traveled by coach from Frankfurt to Basel, arriving there the same time as the Shteriches. On one occasion we made a trip in a hired carriage through Solothurn, Bern, and Lausanne to Geneva. I still recall how we were all delighted by the marvelous Swiss countryside, which we saw in perfect weather, as we traveled from Solothurn to Geneva. Once we journeyed to Milan, the Shteriches in their carriage and we in the coach. During this trip a young Englishman, on his way to Corfu, sat with me in the rear compartment of the coach. When we had nearly reached the top of the Simplon, the driver let us out and allowed us to walk the steepest part of the way. When we were at the very top, though, and were supposed to get back inside, the Englishman was nowhere in sight. We started looking for him, and calling to him, and finally caught sight of him sitting quietly on a rock separated by a deep fissure from the principal rock formation and hanging out over a fearsome abyss.

"Que faites-vous donc, Monsieur?" cried the driver.

"J'essaie le sentiment du danger," replied the Islander.

"Mais ne voyez-vous donc pas, que vous risquez de rouler dans le précipice?" said the driver.

"C'est parce que je risque, que j'éprouve effectivement le sentiment du danger," replied the Englishman, and then resumed his proper seat in the coach.[2]

After leaving the Simplon, where it was dark, damp and cold from the fog and drizzle, we found ourselves before long entering the delightful Domodossola Valley. That evening, in perfect weather (this was the beginning of September), we came to Laveno, facing the Borromean Islands on the shore of Lake Mag-

---

[2] "What the devil are you doing there, Monsieur?" cried the driver.
"Why, I'm getting the feel of danger," replied the Islander.
"But don't you know you might fall off?" said the driver.
"It's because of the risk that I am actually getting the feel of danger," replied the Englishman, and then resumed his proper seat in the coach.

giore. In the afternoon of the next day we reached Milan, at the same time as the Shteriches, and stopped for a while at the Albergo del Pozzo, not far from the Duomo di Milano.

The sight of this great, white, marble cathedral and of the city itself, the transparency of the sky, the dark-eyed girls of Milan with their mantillas—surviving from the days of Spanish rule—all this pleased and delighted me beyond measure. Shterich stayed with us for only a short time, since he had to hurry on to Turin where he had been assigned to our embassy at the court of Sardinia. We occupied ourselves in looking for lodgings and soon moved to No. 626 Corso di porta Renza (*orientale*), opposite the column Leone della porta Renza and the San Babila Church. Our landlady was a widow of about forty or more, and not too beautiful in external appearance. She was swarthy and sort of yellowish, but as a matter of fact she was a very kind woman and, since she herself suffered from periodic attacks of nerves, she could sympathize with the troubles of others—a quality I put to the test almost immediately.

Our apartment consisted of one large room with three windows looking onto the street (the main street of Milan, please note), a small *calorifère*,[3] and two sofas on which we made up our beds in the evening. We went out to taverns for breakfast and dinner. Once, by mistake, instead of going to the second floor of a tavern, we found ourselves on the first floor, where servants customarily ate, and there we fared very poorly indeed. That night Ivanov and I were awakened at about the same time by spells of dizziness and severe stomach pains accompanied by nausea. These turned into the most severe gripes and vomiting; we thought we were dying, when a fellow lodger (an inferior tenor) came into our kitchen and, seeing the sorry state we were in, quickly made us each a large glass of camomile tea. It turned out that the cause of our illness was the spinach sauce, which had been prepared in a dirty pan.

[3] "Stove."

Next morning, Signora Giuseppa Abbondio declared to us that although she never did any cooking for any of the lodgers, she would do so for us, and not only did she faithfully keep her word, but each time she came back from the market she made us inspect all the things she had purchased.

A few days after this we went to Turin to visit Shterich; there, as a consequence of the poisoning, we both fell ill: Ivanov had blisters, and I, well, as for me, my nervous troubles (neuralgia) returned. Shterich's doctor, Battaglia, prescribed mercury and sulphur pills for me again.

In Turin I heard the comic opera *Le Cantatrici Villane*[4] performed magnificently. The prima donna, Unger, sang particularly well and acted in a most unaffected manner. I also heard Dupré there, and although his voice was not strong then, it was fresh; even at that time, though, he sang somewhat in the French fashion, that is, *il relevait chaque note avec affectation*.[5]

On our return to Milan in early November, Ivanov suggested that I study voice with Eliodoro Bianchi. He was an elderly person of self-important mien and with all the earmarks of a deliberate charlatan. He was a *tenor serio*[6] and had even sung in London. Since Italian *maestri* preceding Rossini did not write roulades and embellishments but simply commonplace musical phrases, without color, which the singer himself had to adorn and vary according to his own view, on every possible occasion Bianchi would display his own cleverness at what he called "dressing up the singing." He spoke of Rubini with some contempt, saying that he did not sing with a pure chest voice but often resorted to a head voice and thus could not "tread in buskins" (*vestir il coturno*), that is, play the Roman, as he, Bianchi, could.

---

[4] *The Village Singers*, an opera by the Italian composer Valentino Fioravanti (1770–1837). He wrote about fifty comic operas, but only two, of which this is one, had any notable success. According to Grove, they all "possessed a genuine vein of comedy, a freshness, and an ease in the part-writing which concealed their triviality and want of originality, and made them very popular in their day."

[5] "He brought out each note with exaggerated feeling."

[6] Dramatic tenor.

I was also advised to look up the director of the Milan Conservatory, Basili,[7] as a teacher of composition. He set me to work writing for four voices in the following manner: one voice took the theme in whole notes, the second in half notes, the third in quarters, and the fourth in eighths. This head-splitting exercise, in Basili's opinion, would help to sharpen my musical capacities, "refine your inspirations," as he said; but my lively fantasy could not be subjected to such dry and unpoetical work and I soon gave up my lessons with him.

We had a piano with a pedal that enabled us to produce drumbeats. With this "percussion instrument" we entertained our landlady and our neighbors. Before long we would have around us of an evening a society of neighbors, old and young, male and female, singers of the third rank. The young man who had rescued us from poisoning was a bad tenor, as I have said, but he knew very well how to amuse us at the game of forfeits.

Among our neighbors I must mention one nice-looking young girl. Her name was Adelaida—Didina in Milan. The first thing that brought us together was the sound of our piano, and then simply the matter of seeing each other frequently; she lived in the same house we did. Quattrini (now an orchestra conductor in Warsaw), who had recently come from Spain with his mother, began to teach me Spanish, while she (a dancer) taught Ivanov the art of mimicry.

On December 26, 1830, the inhabitants of Milan, and we also, were impatiently awaiting the opening of the theaters. The impresarios of the two theaters—the large La Scala and the small Carcano—had entered into competition. The impresario of the first, relying on custom to bring him business, since his theater had been the usual gathering place, had acquired only one good singer, Giuditta Grisi, sister of the subsequently world-famous

[7] Domenico Andrea Basili, appointed director of the Milan Conservatory in 1827. He obviously did not understand Glinka's genius and is, of course, known as the man who refused Verdi admission to the Conservatory.

Julietta Grisi. In the little Carcano Theater, on the other hand, Pasta, Rubini, Galli, and others were singing, while the conductors were Bellini and Donizetti. Ivanov had taken an orchestra seat at the Carcano in one of the first rows, while at the same theater I was going to use the front box of our ambassador to the Sardinian court, Count Vorontsov-Dashkov, who, with Shterich, had come to Milan for diversion.

The first performance of Donizetti's *Anne Boleyn* was given for the opening of the theaters. To me, there seemed something somehow magical about it; Rubini, Pasta (who played Anne Boleyn with distinction, especially in the last scene), Galli, Orlandi, *etc.*, all had parts. And since from our front box one could not miss the very softest *sotto voce*, in which, incidentally, Rubini did not at that time indulge to the absurd degree he did later on, I was wallowing in rapture, all the more so since I was not then indifferent to *virtuosité*, as I am now. Of the other operas I recall Rossini's *Semiramide*, Zingarelli's *Romeo e Giulietta*, and Donizetti's *Gianni di Calais*. Finally, at the end of the carnival there came what everyone had been waiting for: Bellini's *La Sonnambula*. Despite the fact that it was presented late and regardless of the envious ones and the ill-wishers, this opera did make a tremendous impression. In the few performances given before the theaters closed, Pasta and Rubini sang with the most evident enthusiasm to support their favorite conductor; in the second act the singers themselves wept and carried their audience along with them, so that in the happy days of carnival, tears were continually being wiped away in boxes and parquet alike. Embracing Shterich in the Ambassador's box, I, too, shed tears of emotion and ecstasy.

When we got home after each opera we would hunt out notes on the piano in order to fix special favorite passages in our minds. In a short while, Ivanov could sing Rubini's arias and excerpts from *Anne Boleyn* quite well, and later on he also managed to do *La Sonnambula*. I accompanied him on the piano and in addition would rather cleverly imitate Pasta by playing her aria on the

piano, to the great amazement and enjoyment of landlady, neighbors, and friends.

In this way the time passed quite agreeably, although we still
suffered somewhat in the winter months. Our little stove, in poor
working order, had almost no effect on the temperature that prevailed in our large room. At night we had to warm our beds with
the warming pan; we were comfortable at first, but this pleasant
warmth soon vanished and by morning both bed and bedding
were invariably cold and damp.

It was quite natural that as the winter progressed we had our
miseries—and our doctors. On the advice of Dr. Battaglia, who had
treated Shterich, I turned to his former colleague and friend De
Filippi. He had been with the Italian army at Smolensk in 1812.
A grave and serious man, he inspired respect. But I shall speak of
him later; I would like now to bring to mind some other acquaintances I made at about this time.

Not only did I enjoy Ambassador Vorontsov-Dashkov's box
at the Carcano Theater, I was also sometimes invited to his house
for dinner. He lived like a nobleman; through him I met Count
Pompeo Belgiojoso, who sang bass excellently and was most
clever at imitating the best singers of the day, especially Lablache.
His cousin, Prince Emilio Belgiojoso, and his younger brother,
Count Belgiojoso, were first-rate tenors; the first soon left Italy,
while the second sang to perfection duets with Pompeo Belgiojoso. It seems that at this same time I also became acquainted with
Marquis Visconti and then with a multitude of secondary artists
and lovers of music.

In March of 1831—alone, or with Ivanov? I don't remember—
I visited Shterich for Easter. We were then getting along fine
together, and my presence was a comfort to him—but I shall say
more about this later on. Soon after coming to Turin he had been
much attracted by a young dancer, Colombi; she was, in fact, a
very pretty girl, although too pale. Without wasting any time at
all he made all the right moves and achieved his aim, so that at first

the affair proceeded very nicely indeed. But gradually his mother, Serafima Ivanovna, who loved him to distraction, became uneasy and feared that a serious entanglement might develop between her son and the dancer which would endanger his future career. At the outset she made her disapproval known only through gentle hints and light banter, but before long she was exhorting, begging, and even reproaching—and, as always happens in such cases, all this simply bound her son more closely to his loved one. Finally, it fell to me to calm first the mother and then the son. I remember very clearly how once in Milan during a performance of Meyerbeer's *Crociato* (the music of which I had already heard in Petersburg, and never liked) Shterich spent nearly the whole time sobbing violently against my chest.

Back again in Milan, I recovered my spirits on the coming of the wonderful Italian spring, my imagination was stirred, and I set to work once more. By now we were known in Milan to a certain extent, and people would speak of us as the two *maestri Russi*—one sang, and the other played the piano.[8] Since we wished to preserve the little fame we had already acquired, I began to write some songs for the piano; I still didn't dare to try singing, because in all truth I could not consider myself fully acquainted with all the subtleties of the art ("tricks of the trade"). I began with variations on a theme from Donizetti's *Anne Boleyn* which I dedicated to Shterich. After that I wrote variations on two themes from the ballet *Chao-Kang*,[9] and these I dedicated to Count Vorontsov-Dashkov. They were later reprinted in a Parisian music journal. That same spring, I wrote a rondo on a theme from

[8] A. N. Strugovshchikov writes in his *Reminiscences* that "within a year of Glinka's arrival in Milan, passersby, on seeing him, would exclaim: 'Look! There goes the Russian *maestro*.'" In an article on Glinka, N. A. Melgunov, his schoolmate, also comments on this ready acceptance: "It is quite true. Our *maestro* was already one of the Milanese; his compositions were played and sung at all the concerts."

[9] The precise designation of Glinka's variations was *Two Dances from the Chao-Kang Ballet.* A. Tityus presented this ballet in St. Petersburg in 1832 to music taken from works by Romani, Rossini, and Spontini.

Bellini's *I Capuleti ed i Montecchi* and dedicated it to the Marquis Visconti's daughter.

As for piano music, I became acquainted with the compositions of Pollini in the spring of 1831 and soon afterward with Pollini himself. In my opinion he was one of the most remarkable of the Italian artists of the time, and, in all justice, *to him and to no other* is due the invention of the new method of playing the piano. Even Liszt agreed on this point; he told me, in fact, that he had written an article on the subject in some journal or other. But could Pollini have ever imagined that, in time, there would come from this product of his creative imagination that horrible, jerky, chopped-up piano music, played exactly as if the performer were mincing meat?

In 1831, Pollini was about eighty years old; he sustained himself by strictly observing his own special diet: he ate no meat—nothing but vegetables and milk dishes. Despite his advanced years, he still played even the most complex passages of his music —very clearly and smoothly, too, in contrast to nearly all the other *maestri* in Milan, who pounded the keys mercilessly. Pollini had a sincere love for his art; at first he wrote operas, which he showed to me, but noting that he had produced nothing of special merit in this line, he determined to try his skill along some other line and in so doing found success. In Milan he enjoyed the fame he deserved; he was respected by all and was widely acquainted in artistic and theatrical circles. Rossini was a good friend and once sang for him his entire opera *Otello*, without roulades. Nevertheless, art was not for him a means of making money; he made his living, and a good one, from a decoction (*rob antisyphilitique*) he had invented which he called *eau de M. Pollin* and sold for ten rubles a bottle.[10]

[10] The ruble was worth about fifty cents at that time. Some idea of the price equivalences of the Russian ruble and the French franc can be gained from the following information supplied by Professor Walter M. Pintner of Cornell University:

I recall this period of my life with satisfaction. In the spring-time I loved to walk about the city after breakfast, and although the surroundings of Milan are flat, the fields are well cultivated and in April and May the vegetation is lush. I went to Lake Como alone the first time, but later on I spent three days driving about the countryside with Ivanov, Eliodoro Bianchi, and our Italian teacher. We went first to Como, by ferry to Varenna the following day, and from Varenna by longboat to Lecco, where we spent the night. The third day, we passed through Brianza and Monza, and so back to Milan.

In the first part of June, I visited Shterich in Turin to say good-by before his return to Germany for the waters. In Turin, I found an old schoolmate, Sobolevsky (writer of epigrams),[11] and met Prince Elim Meshchersky.[12] Serafima Ivanovna was extremely vexed with her son and his dancer, and quite often Sobolevsky and I were witnesses to scenes that were partly ludicrous, partly distasteful. The dry heat in Turin and the perpetually clear skies

"In 1819 the inspector of a technical school got 1,200 roubles (paper) a year, teachers from 300 to 750 a year. A few years later it was proposed to give pro-vincial governors 6,000 a year in the largest provinces—the highest salary I have seen quoted. In 1835 the President of the Archangel Commercial Court got 3,000 plus 1,200 for board and lodging. His secretary got 1,200 and 400. In 1826 a mem-ber of the State Council—the highest governmental body—got 4,500.

"All of the above are in paper roubles (assignats), which were the most com-mon type of currency to 1839. Silver roubles also circulated at the time . . . *and should be multiplied by 3.5.* After 1839 all sums will be in silver roubles or silver rouble credit notes which were of equal value. *Before 1839* if silver is not indi-cated you are safe in assuming paper.

". . . but you can consider a silver rouble equal to 4 (French) francs. This is certainly true after 1839. . . .

"Just one qualification about the use of these salaries. High government of-ficials did not, and were not expected to live on their pay. They either had large income from their estates or supplemented their pay by various types of graft and theft or by borrowing from the state with no intention of repayment . . . ."

11 Sergei Aleksandrovich Sobolevsky (1803–1870), man of letters and biblio-phile, best known for his epigrams. He was a friend to Pushkin as well as to Glinka.

12 Elim Petrovich Meshchersky (1803–1844). An amateur poet, he published a collection of French verse entitled *Les roses noires.* He was an intimate of Hugo.

began to irritate my nerves. When I returned to Milan, the sultry heat there had intensified and, especially in the evenings, the suffocating air reflected from the hot stones and walls of the houses exhausted me; there was no chance of sleeping. The warm baths and the doses of opium prescribed by De Filippi did me no good.

I accepted an invitation from a family I knew (during my stay in Milan, I enjoyed hearty, sincere hospitality on all sides) to visit them at Ansano. This is a village not far from the well-known Plain of Erba, lying between Como and Lecco. In addition to seeing the lakes, I advise all visitors to Lombardy to travel about Brianza and the Plain of Erba, where there are roads everywhere.

In July, De Filippi sent Ivanov and me to the mineral waters at Trescorre, about fifteen miles from Bergamo. A few of these sulphur baths, with an admixture of other components, completely unsettled my nerves. I stopped using the waters, and after visiting the neighboring Lakes Endino and Lovere, or Sarnico, I returned to Milan, where the unbearable heat again drove me out. Back in Trescorre a second time, I no longer took the baths but simply enjoyed the excellent, pure mountain air. There was pleasant society to be had there; dances, promenades, excursions, and finally a brief trip to Bergamo and Brescia provided no little pleasure, despite my ill health.

On my return to Milan, if I am not mistaken, I tried the *eau de M. Pollin*, with Pollini himself supervising the treatment. After one or two bottles, a very severe *migraine* forced even Pollini to discontinue the cure.

In spite of the constant pain in my *solar plexus*, I enjoyed the frequent visits of my friends Pini and Besana. The latter had a fine baritone voice and later became a well-known dilettante. At this same time I got to know Dessauer, who had come to Milan from Vienna. Subsequently, Dessauer wrote a few pieces that were successful in Paris.

Once Sobolevsky brought Mendelssohn-Bartholdy to see me; I was sick, and he, I suppose, because of the not entirely merited reputation I had acquired as a first-class pianist, took a somewhat derisive tone with me. I did not play, but he, after much coaxing, played a light rondo, from which I could not judge the extent of his talent.

Ivanov had given up his lessons with Eliodoro Bianchi before our trip to the waters at Trescorre; we both noted that this teacher had compelled him to force his voice. In September we decided to go to Naples. First, however, we made a trip to Turin and picked up Shterich, who accompanied us to Genoa. Not without reason is this city called *Gênes la superbe*; it is set in an amphitheater and it seemed to me to be the realization of the description of Babylon with its hanging gardens. We stayed there for two days and saw all the worth-while sights. Finally came the day of departure. Shterich went out to the steamboat with us in the rowboat. This was our last meeting with him, for he died the next year in Petersburg soon after returning to Russia. Early the following day we were in Livorno, with beautiful weather—this was early October. From Livorno we went to Civitavecchia, also by steamboat, and from there to Rome, where we stayed about two weeks. At that time the Princess Zinaida Volkonskaya[13] was living there. Shevyrev,[14] well known now as a professor at Moscow University and whom I had met in 1828 in Moscow at Melgunov's, was tutor to the Princess' son. During my stay in Rome he was my *cicerone* and showed me all the sights, with explanations. I could not be convinced of the merits of St. Peter's, probably because even today I prefer Gothic and Byzantine churches to all others.

[13] Zinaida Aleksandrovna Volkonskaya (1792–1862), a fashionable patron of the arts (poet, composer, singer). Her salon played a major role in the artistic life of Moscow.

[14] Stepan Petrovich Shevyrev (1806–1874), critic, poet, journalist, author of several books on the history of literature, and Academician of the St. Petersburg Academy of Sciences in 1852. He was best known, perhaps, as co-editor, with M. P. Pogodin, of the journal *Moskvityanin* beginning in 1841. The "reactionary" views expressed here were challenged by Belinsky and Herzen.

Near the end of October we took the coach to Naples; on the way I was particularly delighted by the palms at Terracina and the cacti between Itri and Fondi. These places reminded me of my first youthful ideas of distant tropical countries, especially Africa. We arrived in Naples the morning of November 1. I was enraptured and could not admire enough the unusual, majestic beauty of the place; the transparency of the air, the bright, festive world—all this was new to me and certainly most delightful. From the reflected sunlight in the bay, as in a mirror, Capri and the distant hills of Sorrento seemed semitransparent, like opals, on that cloudless day.

The environs of Naples may be divided into the following four groups:

1. To the north, Pozzuoli and vicinity, the Carthusian monastery, the Bay of Baiae, and the island of Ischia
2. Vomero and Capo di Monte
3. Vesuvius, Pompeii, Herculaneum, and Portici
4. Castellammare, Sorrento, and the island of Capri

Since it was my intention to stay in Naples for quite some time, I was in no hurry to see all the sights, and I therefore never did get to Sorrento or Capri, an oversight which I deeply regret to this day.

I visited the Bay of Baiae and environs with three red-haired English ladies: a mother and two daughters whom I had met while taking the waters at Ems. When we entered Sybil's Grotto and reached the part where it is covered with water, we all suddenly found ourselves being borne pickaback by our guides. The English ladies, recovering from their astonishment, complained loudly in English, while the guides, assuming that they were just afraid of falling into the water, clutched them more tightly still; it was a funny scene.

Did I compose anything in Naples? I don't remember. It seems, though, that I did do a piano piece for some concert or other at the house of some English people.

Mikhail Ivanovich Glinka as a Young Man

The Finale of *A Life for the Tsar*

Ivanov had a letter of introduction from Prince Grigori Petrovich Volkonsky (son of the then court minister, Prince Peter Mikhailovich Volkonsky) to the well-known singing teacher Nozzari.[15] This *maestro* undertook to teach Ivanov gratis, despite the fact that love of money is just about the most conspicuous trait with present-day Italians. After acquiring a considerable fortune, Nozzari quit the stage, but he still had a voice with a range from low B Flat to high B Flat, that is:

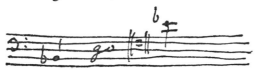

He did this with surprising smoothness and clarity, that is, in its way it was just as good as Field's range on the piano.

Madame Fodor-Mainvielle[16] (simply, Fedorova) gave away her origin; her appearance, her manners, her conversation in the purest Russian idiom, and even her way of carrying a handkerchief and frequently readjusting it—all this belonged more to a provincial Russian lady than to an Italian actress. She left the stage because of her poor health and settled down in Naples. We visited her quite often. Her husband, M. Mainvielle (a former actor on the French stage), who had married her in Petersburg, was constantly relating anecdotes that were supposed to have happened to him in Russia during the reign of Paul I. She herself, however, still sang very well and executed difficult passages as cleverly and as casually as, in Berlin, German women knit stockings during performances of one kind or another without dropping a stitch. She sang with Ivanov quite frequently and in correcting him adhered to the methods used by Nozzari, who had compelled Ivanov to sing Porpora's recitative in an unconstrained, soft, and distinct manner. If Ivanov strained his voice, Nozzari would make him

15 Andrea Nozzari (1775–1832), Italian tenor and teacher. A friend of Rossini, he sang parts in the latter's early operas.
16 Josephine Fodor-Mainvielle, the daughter of a French actor who played in St. Petersburg, where she passed her childhood and youth.

stop, saying that "strength of voice is acquired from exercises and time, but once delicacy is lost, it is gone forever." I think I am indebted more to Nozzari and Fodor than to all other teachers for my knowledge of singing.[17]

At the Fondo Theater I heard Tamburini in Rossini's *Turco in Italia*. He sang and acted very well. At the San Carlo, Ronzi di Begnis was singing, a good actress but with a voice already spoiled; Basadonna (tenor), on the other hand, was good. My favorite theater in Naples was the little Teatro San Carlino, where first-rate actors played in the Neapolitan dialect (*vago dialetto napolitano*).[18]

In Naples I met Karl Brullov and Bellini. I was at Donizetti's only once, if I am not mistaken, and this also was in Naples.

At one theater—the Teatro Nuovo, I think—they were presenting the comic opera *Il Ventaglio* in the Neapolitan dialect. This was quite an amusing piece, and the music greatly pleased the secretary of our embassy, Remer (a former schoolmate); I found it trivial, however, and did not seek an acquaintance with the composer, Raimondi. It now seems that this Raimondi was really a most remarkable contrapuntist; he enjoyed no particular fame at that time, however, although he was director of the Naples Conservatory. It was never my lot to study under strict contrapuntists.

Of my fellow countrymen, aside from those at the embassy, I often visited Kaisarov and Mikhailov, the latter married to a sister of Count Arkady Pavlovich Kutuzov. Princess Volkonskaya, wife of the court minister, often had Ivanov and me to dinner; her doctor, Pizzati, treated me.

[17] I had occasion to note the style that Ivanov had acquired from his singing lessons, so I bent all my efforts toward studying the difficult and delicate art of managing the voice, principally in order to be able to write for the various particularities of different voices. To this end I listened with the greatest attention to the most eminent professional and amateur singers. Nozzari and Madame Fodor were of the most help to me.—Glinka.

[18] All the well-known tragedies took on a Neapolitan character, thanks to Punchinello.—Written in the margin.

Soon after arriving in Naples I broke out in a rash, but none-theless, in December, Ivanov and I set out for Vesuvius to see the flow of lava. It had been raining a little in Naples, and when we started to climb the volcano, we ran into a heavy, Russian-type snowstorm. We found all rooms occupied at the building designed to shelter travelers. For my part, I wanted to go back; fortunately, we met up with a French party who were also forced to return to Naples. On our way down the high wind blew out the torches and we had to grope our way along in the dark, holding on to one another in order not to fall off the mountain. We finally got to Resina, entirely exhausted, where we found the carriage belong-ing to our French friends, which they had invited us to share with them for the trip back to Naples. We had not gone far, though, when a wheel broke and we had to walk about two miles. My rash secreted fluids and I fell ill; I soon recovered, however, and Ivanov and I set out again for Vesuvius soon afterward on a clear winter's night, and this time we were able to see the flow of red-hot lava quite satisfactorily.

In my last months in Naples I couldn't sleep at all; unhappily, instead of opium, local custom seemed to call for frequent, quite large doses of henbane (*hyoscyamus*), which so upset my nerves that I became unbearably weary and distraught and thus deter-mined to leave the city. On the other hand, our stay in Naples had done Ivanov a lot of good. He had had no fixed purpose when he first came to Italy, but the praise given his voice and the fulsome mention by Rubini, who found that Ivanov could hold a higher note than he, stirred his ego and he resolved to prepare himself for the stage. In Naples we had met a court painter who managed to present Ivanov at court, where he sang with success, and as a con-sequence he did, of course, make his debut at the Teatro San Carlo in *Anne Boleyn*.

I advised Ivanov not to request an extension of leave but to go to Russia and then, after spending a year there, resign and come back to Italy, but he ignored my advice.

In general, Ivanov was a *difficult* person, with an unfeeling heart and a mind that was sluggish and dull. His merit lay in the charm of his voice and in a certain instinctive faculty for imitative singing. We did not quarrel, but on the other hand we could not boast of any special friendship. Our parting in Naples ended all relations between us.

At the end of February, 1832, Remer, traveling as a courier to Russia, accompanied me to Rome, where I stayed a short while. I went on by coach through the Marche d'Ancona to Bologna. There I spent twenty-four hours, visiting the art gallery and the Campo Santo. From Bologna I went to Parma, Modena, and Piacenza, reaching Milan in the first part of March.

Signora Giuseppa Abbondio and Didina greeted me happily as one of the family. I was soon established in my old quarters, and since I was suffering severely from nerves because of all that henbane in Naples, they were very solicitous for me.

I believe I remember a slight earthquake at that time, and I acknowledge that even the little vibration I felt, in bed, was most unpleasant.

In the spring I revived again and started work on a serenade, based on a theme from *La Sonnambula*, for piano, two violins, viola, cello, and bass. I dedicated this piece to a young girl, one of Pollini's pupils, who performed it very nicely in July of 1832 accompanied by the best musicians in Milan. I had become acquainted with the family of a lawyer named Branca, whose eldest daughter, Cyrilla Cambiaggio, played the piano excellently, while a second daughter, Emilia, played the harp quite well. With them in mind I began writing a serenade on a theme from Donizetti's *Anne Boleyn*. In the beginning of summer, after having taken several artificial sulphur and iron baths, I felt blood flow to my head. This soon led to such serious nervous attacks that my doctor, De Filippi, thought it wise to take me out of Milan, where it had already become too hot. The doctor had a married daughter living in the village of Luinate, not far from Varese, between Lakes

Maggiore and Como. She was a very tall woman with a pleasant, expressive face. Moreover, she had been excellently educated, knew French, German, and English well, and played the piano so excellently that the best artists visited her, as, for example, Chopin, with whom she had often played the year before my arrival. After I had spent several days at Luinate, De Filippi, on the way back, introduced me to his friend Dr. Branca, a brother of the lawyer Branca. The Doctor, who took me into his home at once, was married and had a young daughter and two sons, Marchin and Min. Life had not been kind to him and discontent clearly showed in his face and in his sharp, gray eyes. I naturally visited De Filippi's daughter frequently—the similarity of our up-bringing and our passion for the same art could not but bring us together. Because of her interest in the piano, I began for her a *sestetto originale* for piano and two violins, viola, cello, and bass, but later on, after having finished it in the autumn, I was com-pelled to dedicate it, not to her, but to a female friend of hers.[19]

You see, I had to cease my frequent visits because they were exciting suspicion and gossip. De Filippi was not a little concerned at this, and in order to put a stop to the unhappy business a bit more smoothly, he purposely took me to see his daughter the last time; we rowed about Lake Maggiore for almost the entire day in rather unpleasant weather, which indeed more or less matched our low spirits. After our parting I composed a romance, *Ah, se tu fossi meco*,[20] to words by Felice Romani sent me by De Filippi's daughter. That same spring, one of Sobolevsky's friends sent me, at Milan, the words of two romances: Zhukovsky's *The Con-queror* and Koslov's *A Night in Venice*. I composed music to them at once.

Around Varese there were many villas belonging to wealthy Milanese, but they were not occupied in the summer, it being the

---

[19] In its published form this sextet was dedicated to Sofia Medici de Markesi de Mariniano.

[20] The romance to words by Romani is known as *Il Desiderio*, Russian trans-lation by M. I. Glinka.

custom to come to these places only in the fall and stay to the end of December. Most of the inhabitants were poor farmers, lacking in culture, whose talk was all of grain, silk, and grapes. Although Dr. Branca had been well educated, constant country living had insensibly coarsened him and there was something of hardness in his manner. It was my good fortune that the Doctor's niece, the elder daughter of the lawyer Branca, Cyrilla Cambiaggio, came to Varese with her husband, Isidoro Cambiaggio, a simple, kindly person. At the Cambiaggios', where there was a small piano, I went on with the serenade that I had begun, on a motif from *Anne Boleyn*, for piano, harp, viola, cello, bassoon, and horn. The arrival of Emilia Branca incited me to work still more; she was an unusually well-built girl and quite pretty. She pleased me, and it seems that she, for her part, did not find me unbearable, so that the time passed pleasantly in friendly talks, walks, and divers occupations. When my serenade was finished, we decided to play it on the terrace of Branca's home in Milan; we hoped for a tremendous effect, but the acoustics were bad and the sounds flew off in all directions. During the rehearsals, on the other hand, the piece had gone well—the top artists from the Teatro della Scala played the instruments. When I first heard the solo of my piece for viola, played by the famous Rolla, the purity and fidelity of the tone brought tears to my eyes, and yet he asked for my advice!

Rolla, the well-known violist, was one of the notable artists of his time. He was then eighty, but he still played with a very high degree of precision, faithfully and without any suggestion of charlatanism. As director of the orchestra at the Teatro della Scala, he himself went over all the parts (without glasses) and never on any pretext neglected his duties.

When I was in Milan, I often visited Pollini, who was fond of me, especially after I had dedicated a piece to one of his pupils, giving her the original manuscript, which was later lost on some journey or other. At his home I frequently saw Bellini, with whom I became fairly well acquainted. Although he had been born at the foot of Mount Etna in Catania, he was light haired, of fair complexion, had an agreeable expression, and was well proportioned; his manner and habits revealed a person of good society. We often talked about German composers, with whom he was very familiar. He wrote, as it were, by instinctive feeling, aiming primarily at the hearts of women.

I heard *Norma* in the spring of 1832 at the Teatro della Scala with Pasta, Donzelli, and Giulietta Grisi. The latter, just beginning her career, was not yet as fat as she was later in Paris and consequently she looked remarkably good, but she sang in a sort of caterwauling manner, that is, wishing to soften or modify a given musical phrase, she more or less miaowed in her nose. *Otello* pleased me more, both as music and as drama. In the last scene, Donzelli was so superb as to be almost terrifying.

Pini introduced me (I think this was in 1831, too) to his sister, an extremely ill woman but still pretty; in her pallor she seemed indeed like an exceedingly fine marble statue. Her husband (Pini's brother-in-law), by the name of Giulini, was a joyful and happy man, a merchant who had retired and was living with his family spring, summer, and winter in his own house in Milan and spending the autumn in a charming villa on Lake Como. They had a small boy, a boarding-school student, and two pretty, amiable, and well-educated older daughters—Luiggia and Carlotta. Luiggia, the elder, sang very charmingly, I must say, although she did not have a strong voice. Even the younger five-year-old daughter could give a brilliant imitation of Pasta in the last scene from *Norma: In mia man alfin tu sei.*

I often visited the Giulini family, where peace and happiness prevailed and where each guest somehow seemed in joyful spirits, despite the sickly state of the hostess, whose sufferings were alleviated by the solicitous attention and thoughtful care of her daughters, especially Carlotta, who with sincere childlike love supported her, led her to the table, and helped her get settled in her armchair. Pini had a fairly good tenor voice, Luiggia Giulini sang soprano, while her friend and her sister—the Contessina Cassera, a pretty little blonde—sang second soprano and contralto well. This Contessina Cassera and her mother, a pleasant and still beautiful woman, on one occasion made a trip to Paris; on their return I dedicated to the young Countess my variations (probably composed in that same year of 1832) on a theme from Bellini's *I Capuleti ed i Montecchi*: *L'amo, l'amo, e a me più cara*. While in Paris the Countess had often heard the famous Malibran, of whose singing she became enraptured, and she had also improved her own voice considerably; meanwhile, the trio from the second act of Rossini's opera *Le Comte d'Ory* went very well as performed by the older Giulini, Countess Cassera, and Pini. The "resident" *maestro* was Mauri, a very good voice teacher; at the Giulini's I also frequently saw one of the outstanding pianists, Trevani.

In Milan I had already become acquainted with the clarinetist Iwan Müller, who thought of himself as Russian, perhaps because he was by birth from the Baltic provinces or because, instead of Johann, he signed himself Iwan. The important thing was that by means of a multitude of valves he was able to play in all tones on the same clarinet; although with this novelty, instead of the full sound natural to this instrument, he produced sharp tones like the shriek of a goose, the inventor was none the less proud of his invention.

At the end of September, at Giulini's invitation, I went to visit him and his family at his magnificent villa at Tramezina in the center of Lake Como. Giulini was well off financially, and his home was lovely. He gave me a splendid room and entertained me as if we were in Russia, only more wisely, that is, there was enough of everything, but *in moderation*, not *in excess*. I recall, as if it were only yesterday, that for breakfast they gave me a piece of excellent beefsteak because they knew I was very fond of it. I spent nearly all of October with them, and this was without question the last agreeable time I had in Italy.

Aside from myself, another guest of Pini's was a painter from Milan who amused us with his low-comedy stunts. In the first part of the morning everyone did whatever he chose; I, for example, would take a short walk and then get to work on my sextet, for which I had already written the finale; before dinner we all gathered in the parlor, sometimes to sing, sometimes to talk. A little while after dinner we would generally set out for a stroll—a month would hardly have sufficed for seeing the lovely country roundabout. Some trees had already begun to lose their green coloring and the lilac-colored shade of the distance harmonized marvelously with nearer objects. I often cried out in delight, "O dio! Che tinte!" whereupon my host, Giulini, would always smile with a certain air of self-sufficiency. In the evenings the neighbors would join us, when we would play various games and sing, and whoever was able would amuse the group with stunts or tricks of one sort of another. Among these neighbors was the singer Tozi, who sometimes sang with us. Her voice was strong and high, but the middle notes were disappointing. She was to sing at the Teatro della Scala in Milan in the winter, making her debut in Donizetti's *Faust.* Since she thought there was no decent cavatina or prayer in the score for an entrance, she asked me to write one. I complied, and, it would seem, with success, that is, quite in the manner of Bellini (and as she wanted it) and, insofar as possible, avoiding the middle range of her voice. She liked the melody, but she was displeased that I had inadequately shown off her middle notes, which she thought were her best. I tried again to make some changes, but I could not satisfy her. Fed up with these *pretensions,* I then and there took an oath never again to write for Italian prima donnas.

I left Lake Como for Milan, traveling via Varese. The weather began to get worse, and along with it my health, too. De Filippi heated the nape of my neck with a lunar caustic, whereupon the pain became extremely severe and two large bumps the size of peas came out on the burned place, but no sores developed. The

mark left by this operation is still visible. On the advice of Dr.
Frank of the University of Vilna, who had settled in Borgovico
by Lake Como, at the end or middle of November I had a plaster
of camphor and diachylon applied to my chest. This evil-smelling
plaster ruined my nerves and brought me quickly to despair and
to those fantastic sensations which are called *Sinnetäuschungen*,
or hallucinations. In the first half of the winter my miseries were
still supportable, and I could go to the theater and visit friends. At
that time they were presenting an excellent fantastic ballet entitled *Masquerade*. I often visited the Giulinis, where I was received as one of the family. For Luiggia I wrote the *Beatrice di
Tenda* cavatina, words by Pini, and then for both elder sisters *Impromptu en galop* on a theme from Donizetti's *L'Elisir d'Amore*.
When the *sestetto* was finished,[21] it was performed at the home of
a girl friend of De Filippi's daughter. The father of this lady was
a bore well known in Milan, that is, he was a person who was able
to weary one constantly by his untimely visits and then *put down
roots* (he stayed too long). His daughter played my *sestetto* un-
satisfactorily, but the better artists accompanying her held up the
piece; even the flow of the basses in the finale very much delighted
Pompeo Belgiojoso. I remember that during the performance of
this piece the plaster benumbed my arms and legs to such a degree
that I had to pinch myself to see if there were still life in them. But
I was still struggling somehow with my miseries and discomforts
and wrote a trio for piano, clarinet, and bassoon.[22] My friends
the artists at the Teatro della Scala, Tassistro on the clarinet and
Cantú on the bassoon, accompanied me and on completion of the
finale the latter said in astonishment: "Why that is a thing of des-
peration!" And, in fact, I was in despair. At first the plaster was
kept on for a month, then three weeks, then two, while at the end
it dried out in twenty-four hours, or it was absorbed, you might

21 October 17, 1832.
22 As an epigraph to this *trio pathetique*, Glinka wrote: "Je n'ai connu l'amour
que par les peines qu'il cause."

say, by the body and had to be renewed every day, which caused my limbs to grow numb, stifled me, and deprived me of appetite and sleep. I fell into a state of utter despondency, which I voiced in the trio.

I decided to go to Venice for some recreation, hoping that, as quite often happens, the trip would improve my health. De Filippi approved of this, so at the end of February, 1833, I set off alone by coach.

My letters of introduction did me no good in Venice, but Bellini was at that time producing his opera *Beatrice di Tenda* and with his permission I went to rehearsals, where I often met Giovanni Ricordi, my Milan publisher and a very fine person, too. His music stores (Milan and Florence) were the best in Italy (and perhaps in the whole world in the number of operas he owned and published). I attended the last rehearsal and also the first performance. In spite of all that Pasta could do in the role of Beatrice, the piece was not a success.

Without losing any time, I went sight-seeing about the city, but of all I saw I can remember only St. Mark's Square, the Doge's Palace with Tintoretto's *Gloria*, paintings, Rialto Bridge, the Greek Mass, and the inhuman instruments of torture, which I saw not long before leaving Venice during the period of my own anguish.

Although on the way from Milan to Venice I had torn off the plaster, it continued its work, since it had saturated my body. Other harmful forces were added to this one, namely: the sea air, the sirocco, which raged violently during my stay in Venice, and the charcoal fumes, which often gave me severe headaches at night. From the combination of all these things my health went from bad to worse; finally, I was once so affected by the noxious charcoal fumes that I nearly died of suffocation.

If I remember correctly, it was at this time that Princess Gagarin, wife of our ambassador to Rome, with her children and their tutor were living at the same inn as I, and once I visited them.

Noting my suffering, she (it seems) recommended me to her doctor, who, attributing all my troubles to a stomach disorder, prescribed an enema which he said would give me some relief. Since the desired action did not result, he prescribed a second enema, of kitchen salt. This one had such an unexpectedly strong effect that I do not know how I remained among the living. Unbearably painful irritation in the abdomen with burning sensations and fainting spells, but without fever, along with a tormenting sensation of fear, or, more exactly, of *terror*, beset me. This attack lasted from late evening until morning. I stayed at Princess Gagarin's, where the tutor attended me constantly, taking me for walks and so forth, but the air did not help me much. The next day I started back to Milan; Ricordi and a woman he knew, about forty-nine, were passengers in the coach. They jointly looked after me and tried to calm me during my attacks, which commenced again on the second day of the journey. On our arrival in Milan, De Filippi found my pulse in such a state that he ordered blood to be taken at once from my left arm, but this was not of any great utility. I began to feel worse; my stomach, in fact, served me no good purpose whatsoever. They smeared an ointment on my back that took off the skin and then applied morphine right on the raw flesh. All this, and other remedies besides, proved to be quite in vain; my illness, or, rather, these severe pains, continued for about six weeks, that is, from the middle of March to the end of April. I was cared for by Didina, with the invaluable assistance of Signora Giuseppa Abbondio and the good Isidoro Cambiaggio, who would put me in my bath and also take me on walks. During my attacks, which were renewed every night, an old woman would come to act as bedside watcher. Along toward morning the irritation would gradually subside, leaving me exhausted and with a sort of false appetite, whereupon I would devour white bread and a melon-seed orgeat, superbly prepared by the Milanese nuns. No doubt this breakfast, which some instinct of self-preservation within me demanded as a sort of poultice, had a lot to do with my improvement. In the intervals between attacks my pains were not as sharp; I could sit at the piano and unconsciously extract weird sounds which reflected the fanciful sensations that were agitating me. However, this extreme irritation of my nervous system did not affect my imagination alone; my indeterminate and rather hoarse voice was suddenly transformed into a powerful, resonant high tenor with which I entertained the public for more than fifteen years, and indeed even now with *auxiliary means* I can once in a while manage two or three romances.

At the end of April, De Filippi sent me to Varese again to see Dr. Branca. It was hard for me to live there, although later on Cambiaggio also arrived with his wife. As was his custom, the Doctor showed no mercy in making me take walks, but sometimes he would hire a cabriolet and I would ride through the surrounding country with his sons, while occasionally I also rode horseback. My stomach trouble was somewhat lessened because of this, but the pains kept recurring. I went to Milan once in a while, but only for brief visits. I also went to Lake Como, where I again saw Sobolevsky, with whom I called on Pasta on her name day at her private villa. It was there, too, that a lady who had come with me from Venice advised me to take some Le Roy,[23] after which Dr. Frank applied a plaster of camphor and opium to me, and on my return to Varese, Dr. Branca also administered a medication of some sort. With all this, or perhaps because of it, my pain threw me into a deep melancholy, which in turn led to homesickness. Fortunately, in July I heard from home that my sister Natalya Ivanovna had gone to Berlin with her husband, Nikolai Dmitrievich Gedeonov.[24] This news made me want to join them at once, and since there was nothing to prevent me, I left Italy at the end of this same month—July, 1833.

[23] Simply the name of a medicine.

[24] Nikolai Dmitrievich Gedeonov (b. 1799), husband of Glinka's sister Natalya Ivanovna and cousin of A. M. Gedeonov, director of the St. Petersburg Theaters from 1835 to 1858.

I think it proper at this point to sum up briefly my experiences in Italy. I had suffered a lot, to be sure, but there had also been many pleasant and inspiring moments of pure poetry. My frequent association with first- and second-class singers and amateur musicians gave me a practical knowledge of the capricious and difficult art of directing the voice and of writing for it with some intelligence. Nozzari and Fodor in Naples had been for me representatives of that art carried to the highest degree of perfection; they knew how to create an improbable (for those who had not heard them) precision (*fini*) with unconstrained naturalness (*grâce naturelle*), which afterward I could never quite find anywhere else. I shan't speak of Rubini, but even in Pasta's singing there was a certain kind of excessive striving for effect.

I believe my work in composition was less successful. It was no slight strain for me to imitate the Italian *sentimento brillante*,[25] as they call the sensation of well-being which results when the body has been happily nurtured beneath the beneficent southern sun. We inhabitants of the North feel otherwise; either impressions or sensations move us not at all or sink deep into our souls. We are either furiously happy or weeping bitter tears. Love, that delightful sentiment which gives life to the universe, is with us always linked with sadness. There is no doubt that our doleful Russian song is a child of the North, and perhaps even sent to us in a certain way through the peoples of the East, for their songs are also mournful, even in happy Andalusia. Ivan Ekimovich once said: "Just listen a while to the coachman along the Volga—his song is plaintive, mournful—one hears in it the Tartar; well, they sang, they sing—very well!"

But to get back to my story! I could not work during the first half of 1833 because of all my aches and pains. I wrote nothing, but I did do a lot of thinking. All the pieces I had composed to please the inhabitants of Milan, published in de luxe fashion by Giovanni Ricordi, had only convinced me that I was not follow-

[25] Roughly, perhaps, "glittering or sparkling expression of feeling."

ing my own way and that I truthfully could not become an Italian.

Longing for home led me, step by step, to think of composing like a Russian.

Thus in July I left Italy. Dr. Branca accompanied me to Vienna over the following route: Como, Varenna, Colico, Sondrio Bormio (Valtelerina), then through Monte Stelvio (Ortler Spitz) in the Tyrol to Innsbruck. We traveled through all these places in a post chaise, changing at each station. From Innsbruck, we went through Salzburg and Linz on to Vienna. The Tyrol presented a sterner aspect than Switzerland, but the landscape was not as picturesque; between Innsbruck and Salzburg, however, we came upon more pleasing prospects.

After Italy, Vienna seemed more somber to me, especially because of the nasty weather there. I had frequent opportunities to enjoy the orchestras of Lanner and Strauss.

Dr. Branca took me to a wax display of anatomy, explaining everything, especially whatever related to my own illness, and thereby considerably lessened my tendency to imagine the worst.

We consulted with Dr. Malfatti, who promptly sent me to Baden, near Vienna, for the waters.

Dr. Branca stayed with me for a week, in which time my health visibly improved. When he left, he brought me a *lohn-lackey*, or valet, from the inn, Zum Wilden Mann, in Baden. The local doctor, a stout, healthy, rosy-cheeked type, entertained himself all day long by riding and dancing, but me he forced to drink the waters and bathe, a routine to which he later added showers.

The Baden waters, which consist of sulfur and a lot of alum, are very strong indeed. In a short time my nerves had become frightfully disturbed; finally, I began to be tormented not only by hallucinations, that is, delusions of the senses, but my legs and arms would not obey me completely and my valet had to lead me about.

For several days before this situation developed this fine servant had taken me, on our walks, to a Catholic priest who happened to have a piano. I began to improvise and, no doubt, very mournfully because the priest asked me in surprise, "How is it possible, at your age, to play with such melancholy?"

"What am I to do?" I replied. "You know, it's no joke being condemned to death, especially in the prime of life." I then told him briefly of my sufferings, and also that all the cures I had tried served only to further impair my health. The priest asked if I had tried homeopathic treatment, a question which I took to be in the way of a pleasantry. How could I imagine that those invisible, as you might say, atoms of medicine contained in such tiny grains could have any effect at all after the masses of matter in which I had been immersed or which I had drunk? However, he tried hard to convince me, saying at last: "You believe you are condemned to death, so isn't it all the same to you, in that case, whether you die from allopathy or homeopathy?"

One day I had fallen into such a fearful state that my good valet lost his head and sent for his wife, a woman of ripe years. She came at once and without more ado she and her husband carried me off to Vienna. My finances were in pitiful condition— the trip from Varese to Vienna, the expenses on the return trip for Dr. Branca, and the shockingly high cost of living in Baden had nearly exhausted my funds. My good Samaritans (I had no close acquaintances in Vienna) settled me in their apartment in a modest but clean little room and attended to me with unflagging care. As soon as I reached Vienna, I recalled the words of the priest in Baden and went to see the doctor he had recommended, one Marn-Zeller. The next day, on receiving a homeopathic remedy from him, I began at once to stand more firmly on my legs. In a short time, too, I came to feel generally more at ease, although unpleasant sensations continued to trouble me none the less.

After receiving some money from home I gladly settled accounts with my hospitable friends, but I retained my valet for a while and moved to the Kärtnerstrasse. This was at the end of August. I took to reading Schiller for diversion and copied out

Glinka (*at the keyboard*),
K. P. Brullov (*left*), and N. A. Kukolnik (*right*)

The Grand Imperial Theater in 1839

favorite parts, and for the same reason I rented a piano and learned Herz's variations on several themes. I had heard enough of Lanner and Strauss, did not even try to compose anything, but I do recall that at that time I worked out the theme I used later for the cracovienne in *A Life for the Tsar*, namely:

In September, Pavel Vasilevich Engelhardt[26] and his wife visited Vienna with my cousin Natalya Ivanovna and her husband, P. P. Ryndin,[27] and I managed to spend several pleasant days with them. Shortly before they left the brother of my brother-in-law Gedeonov, still in Berlin, Fyodor Dmitrievich, came to Vienna. He paid me a visit, during which he brought me to tears of laughter each morning talking to me in his rapid-fire German.

Understanding my great desire to see my sister and his brother, in the first half of October, with his usual organizing ability, Fyodor Dmitrievich promptly arranged everything for the journey. During the trip he fussed over me as though I were his own brother, and when I sighed, he would sing songs or tell stories to lighten my heart. I shall always be grateful to him for this.

When I met my sister and brother-in-law, I felt as if I had been restored to life. My sister was unusually kind and her "goodness," as we say, was unlimited. My brother-in-law was also kind and had a very open disposition, but he could also be irascible. My sister was being treated by the surgeon Diefenbach (world famous) and the royal obstetrician Hauke. My brother-in-law called the latter "The Whale"; when they introduced me to him, he asked in surprise, "Comment! Lui compositeur?"[28] referring, of course, to me. Afterwards, though, he gave a musicale for my brother-in-law and me. On this occasion there was a group of fif-

26 Father of V. P. Engelhardt, Glinka's friend who collected some of his manuscripts and eventually presented them to the St. Petersburg Public Library.
27 P. P. Ryndin was a relative of the Engelhardts and of Glinka.
28 "What! He a composer?"

teen German girls who sang several choral pieces at sight, mostly Spontini's.

Diefenbach prescribed gymnastics and the *Husarenleben*[29] for me, but neither had the desired effect.

In Berlin I met a schoolmate, Chirkov, an eccentric but charming and well-educated person with whom I had shared lodgings in Petersburg in 1828. After arriving in Berlin I first settled down with my sister and brother-in-law on the second floor of No. 10 Jägerstrasse.[30] Later on, I took a separate but similar apartment across from my sister and brother-in-law in the same building and on the same floor.

Some time after my arrival I met the voice teacher Taeschner,[31] whom I had known in Milan. He introduced me to one of his pupils, Maria, age seventeen or eighteen. She seemed to be of partly Jewish origin, tall and not yet fully developed, but with a pretty face that made one think of a Madonna. In addition to Maria, the family consisted of her father, mother, and two brothers. I began to teach her singing and wrote her *études* (from one of them I later worked out the *Jewish Song* for Kukolnik's drama *Prince Kholmsky*. I saw Maria nearly every day and insensibly felt an inclination toward her, which she, in fact, seemed to share.

This same Taeschner introduced me to a homeopathic doctor, Stuhler, who treated me constantly all the time I was in Berlin.

I am also indebted to Taeschner for my acquaintance with Siegfried Dehn, who is now custodian of the music division at the Royal Library in Berlin.[32] I studied with him for about five

[29] Equivalent to "the dashing life."

[30] Unfortunately, this house has now been rebuilt. 1856, June.—Written in the margin of the manuscript, presumably by Glinka.

[31] Gustav Taeschner (1800–1883), German teacher of voice.

[32] And indisputably the first musical *sorcerer* in Europe.—Written in the margin of the copy in Glinka's hand. The copy referred to here was made by Glinka's sister Ludmila. Although authorized by the composer, it suffered from several sad defects. For example, many details of family life were omitted, and many prominent persons were indicated only by their initials. Less important were some stylistic changes. Unfortunately, it was this copy that was used for

months. In a very short time he had discovered the degree of my knowledge and capacities and decided first to set me to writing three- and then four-part fugues, or, more exactly, skeletons, extracts of fugues without text on themes by well-known composers, requiring that I follow the rules adopted for this type of composition, that is, observance of exposition, stretta, and pedal. He put my theoretical knowledge in more orderly shape and wrote out for me in his own hand the science of harmony, or thorough bass, the science of melody, or counterpoint, and instrumentation—all in four little notebooks. I wanted to have them printed, but Dehn would not give his consent.

There is no doubt that I am more indebted to Dehn than to any of my other teachers; as a critic for the Leipzig music journal[33] he could bring some order not only to my knowledge of music but also to my ideas about art in general, and as a result of his lessons I began to work no longer in the dark, but with understanding. Moreover, he did not torment me with pedantic nonsense or overstrict reliance on systems—on the contrary, nearly every lesson showed me something new and worth while. Once he gave me a theme consisting of eight bars on which, for the next lesson, I was to write a skeleton of a fugue. This theme was more like a recitative than a melody suitable for a fugue, and I toiled over it fruitlessly. At the next lesson he again asked me to work on this theme, and again I struggled with it to no avail. At the third lesson Dehn appeared with a huge book containing Handel's fugue on this same theme that I was finding so troublesome. One look at it showed that the entire development evolved by the great composer had been based on the eighth bar, while the first seven bars appeared only rarely. This single conception alone showed me what a fugue was.

In addition to Dehn's lessons and Maria's lessons, I spent some

all editions of the *Memoirs* up to 1930. This translation is, of course, from Glinka's original, entirely intact and unabridged.

[33] *Allgemeine musikalische Zeitung.*

of my time composing. I wrote two romances, *Rustle of the Forest* (Zhukovsky) and *Say Not That Love Shall Fade* (Delvig), variations for piano on Alyabiev's theme *The Nightingale*, and also a potpourri for four hands on several Russian themes. The latter clearly showed a turning toward counterpoint. I also wrote a study for a symphonic overture on a roundelay (Russian theme), which, incidentally, was worked out in the German style.

These last two pieces, as well as most of my exercises with Dehn, should be in V. P. Engelhardt's collection of my compositions.

The idea of national music (I am not speaking now of opera) was becoming increasingly clear to me, and I composed the theme *When They Killed Mother* (the orphan's song from *A Life for the Tsar*) and the first theme for the allegro of the overture. The fact is that in my youth, that is, soon after leaving boarding school, I had done a lot of work on Russian themes.

Apart from my own exercises I did not hear much music in Berlin during this particular stay.

I remember, though, once seeing a performance of Méhul's opera *Une Folie*. Maria would sometimes play with a violin accompaniment. Taeschner introduced me to the pianist Berger, who had written some excellent piano *études*. Despite a nervous stroke which had paralyzed one of his arms, he could still play very well.

In this fashion we lived a quiet and happy life until the end of March. Once I took a trip to Charlottenburg with Chirkov; when we got back, my brother-in-law told me my father had died. This news shocked me all the more because although they had written me that my father was ill, I had had no idea that he was in danger. Since all of Dr. Diefenbach's art had done nothing for my sister, who had gone through several operations with the sweet patience of an angel, we decided to go home.

A seemingly unimportant event occurred at this time which had a singular effect on my future. A widow who had been attending my sister as maidservant and nurse was unable to make the trip because she could not leave her young daughters. In answer to a newspaper advertisement for someone to go with us, forty German girls showed up, among them one who, although quite a pretty girl, had extraordinarily long arms and legs. I remember very well saying to my sister: "Take any one of the lot, but not that one." However, we *did* take that one (Luisa) because all the rest refused to go to Russia.

In April, 1834, then, we set out from Berlin in a barouche: my sister, brother-in-law, Luisa, and I.

We traveled via Poznań, Königsberg, Tilsit, Jurbarkas, Kovno, Vilna, Minsk, and Smolensk.

We reached Novospasskoe at the end of April, but after that I don't remember at all how we passed the time until July; I suppose we lived a quiet and fairly satisfactory life.

In June I went to Moscow to see my friend Melgunov. He was living in the same house near Novinsky Street. I was given rooms in which, said Melgunov with some attempt at humor, "whoever lives here always gets married," as, for example, Shevyrev. Pavlov (later the author of some well-known stories)[34] lived on the entresol. He gave me his romance *Call Her Not Heavenly*, which he had recently written and which I set to music then and there. But more than that, I came upon an idea for a Russian opera. I had no words, but *Mary's Grove* was running through my head and I played several bits on the piano, some parts of which I later used in *A Life for the Tsar*.

I also wanted to show the public that I had not been wandering around Italy to no purpose at all. Melgunov's father was still living and several families belonging to the highest Moscow society had at this time gathered around him. This group included, among others, Bravura and Kireeva (nee Alyabieva), both very pretty

[34] Nikolai Filippovich Pavlov (1805–1864), author, well-known critic, and publicist. Himself the son of a serf, freed in 1811, in 1835 he wrote three stories attacking serfdom, but later on, in the 1860's, he joined the reactionary camp.

and well-educated ladies. I sang and played my compositions while, I believe, these two accompanied me on stringed instruments.

At this time I became friendly with the composer Hebel[35] and often heard his quintets and quartets, played well. I also saw Henisht (who wrote the romance *The Black Shawl* and the elegy *On, On, O Faithful Sail*). At the same time I met the well-known amateur singer Praskovya Arsenyevna Barteneva,[36] and together we ran through my romances. All in all, I spent my time in Moscow very enjoyably.

[35] Francis Xavier Hebel (1787–1843), German composer, pianist, conductor, and teacher. He moved to Moscow in 1817, took an active part in the city's cultural life in the 1830's, and was known especially for his organization of "evenings" of chamber music. His work clearly showed the Russian influence, a fact noted by Borodin.

[36] Praskovya Arsenyevna Barteneva (1811–1872), amateur soprano. She sang many of Glinka's compositions at benefit concerts.

# 7

*Novospasskoe, Moscow, and St. Petersburg.*
*Marriage. First Performance of*
A Life for the Tsar

Back in Novospasskoe again, I applied for a passport for foreign travel and was granted one in August. I planned to go directly to Berlin to see Maria, with whom and with whose family I had been in constant correspondence. My mother and my sister Elisaveta Ivanovna had gone to Petersburg after hearing that my brother Evgeny Ivanovich, who was then at the Artillery School, was seriously ill. My sister Natalya Ivanovna asked me to take Luisa to Berlin, and I readily agreed to do so.

So Luisa and I and the old servant Yakov left for Smolensk at the end of August, stopping there with my sister Maria Ivanovna and her husband, Dmitri Stepanovich Stuneev; we then started out forthwith on the journey to Vilna, where Yakov was to leave me. Here, however, we met with a difficulty: Luisa's passport had not been properly checked at the first provincial town on entering Russia, so the officials at Smolensk could not validate her passport for the journey—it would be necessary to go to Petersburg for that. It vexed me to abandon Luisa, since I had promised to take her along, nor did she herself want to go to Petersburg. The weather was excellent and Stuneev persuaded me to go on (he had arrived in time!); moreover, an added reason was my hope of reaching Berlin before winter. Fate decided otherwise.

In Petersburg I stayed with Aleksei Stepanovich Stuneev,

where my mother and sister were already. My brother had already died. The first person I saw when I arrived was Luisa, combing the hair of a pretty young girl. This was Maria Petrovna Ivanova, sister of Sofiya Petrovna, wife of Aleksei Stuneev. In Berlin my sister Natalya and my brother-in-law had said that my late father had sometimes, in jest, called her his daughter-in-law. I became involuntarily entranced with the loveliness and the somehow in-nate charm of Maria Petrovna, and did not speed my departure, although my mother had already bought a carriage to shield me from the raw autumn weather on the road. The German girl was jealous of Maria Petrovna—for indeed everything indicated that I would end up by marrying her.

My mother and sister went back to the village, while I stayed with Stuneev, who had turned his study over to me. Snow fell on the night of October 1; winter travel conditions were with us, and I definitely decided to remain in Petersburg.

Everything had been prepared for Luisa's return to Berlin, much to her vexation. The only difficulty, a slightly comical one, was that nowhere in Petersburg could she find boots big enough for her tremendous feet.

Aleksei Stuneev had a passion for providing doctors with pa-tients; he first gave me over to the care of one Volsky, with no good results. He took me next to the general-staff doctor, Gaev-sky, who found that I was in a magnetic condition and advised the use of mesmerism in order to correct the state of my nervous system (*pour me démagnétiser*).

The Dr. Lichtenstet selected for this operation agreed to it with reluctance, saying that he thought it worse than useless to try mesmerism. It is true, in fact, that during the mesmeric treat-ments I groaned and moaned from the pain and that after the third séance I had to stop the experiments because my nerves were so upset. I went back to homeopathy, and the then well-known Dr. Hermann was of considerable help to me here. I kept on with the homeopathic treatment for about two years, strictly observing the diet prescribed.

Aleksei Stuneev had a passionate love for music, particularly romances. We lived in a building that formed part of the Military Academy on Voznesensky Street, now belonging to the court of Her Imperial Majesty Maria Nikolaevna. Maria Petrovna paid frequent visits to her sister Sofiya Petrovna. It would happen quite ordinarily that A. Stuneev would sit at the piano and play romances, singing each verse in order, one after the other, without missing a single one, although there would be a lot of them. Maria Petrovna and I took advantage of his involvement with the music and whispered busily away on the sofa as Stuneev plunged ever deeper into his rapture. I must confess I did not behave too admirably, but he sang unmercifully through his nose and pronounced the words too precisely, as if cutting them out with an ax—nevertheless, I not only encouraged this singing of his but even helped him to learn some new romances. Sofiya Petrovna had a pleasant enough alto voice. I began to teach her singing, and also Maria Petrovna, who, without knowing a note, was soon singing short romances quite truly and sweetly.

Slowly, amateur singers began to visit me. Nikolai Stepanovich Volkov (now director of the Warsaw School of Fine Arts) was a cadet at the Communications School in 1824; at Bakhturin's, which he much frequented at that time, we called him "Kosha." During the winter of 1834–35 I found him to be a kind, educated, and talented young man who sang baritone well and sketched beautifully. I spent a lot of time with him on singing, and that same winter he made an unusually good portrait of me in water colors. I also quickly became acquainted with his brother, Matvei Stepanovich Volkov. He was studying voice with Belloli, and we would sing together at the Demidovs'; our friendly relations have endured ever since. This same winter Ivan Nikolaevich Andreev often came to sing with me as well—he is now in Warsaw and still has an excellent tenor voice. Sometime that winter I wrote my romance *Inezilia*, words by Pushkin, and the romance *Could I But Know You*, the latter for Maria Petrovna.

My friend Kopiev, a huge captain (now major general and commander of the Polotsk Hussar Regiment on active duty), a music lover who had an agreeable bass voice and who had composed several romances, once brought to me a small man in a blue frock coat and a red vest who spoke in a squeaky soprano voice. When he sat down at the piano, it turned out that this little fellow was the very sprightly pianist and later extremely talented composer—Aleksander Sergeevich Dargomyzhsky.

I was then living a stay-at-home life, the more so since my feelings for Maria Petrovna had insensibly intensified; despite this, however, I continued to visit V. A. Zhukovsky in the evenings. He was living at the Winter Palace, and each week a select group, consisting of poets, writers, and, in general, people interested in the finer things, gathered there. To mention a few, A. S. Pushkin, Prince Vyazemsky, Gogol, and Pletnev were there all the time. Gogol once read his *The Marriage* when I was present. Prince Odoevsky, Vielegorsky, and others turned up once in a while. Sometimes, instead of reading, there would be singing and piano playing, and sometimes, too, there were ladies present, but only those who were receptive to the fine arts.

When I mentioned my desire to undertake a Russian opera, Zhukovsky wholeheartedly approved my intention and suggested a subject: Ivan Susanin. The scene in the forest impressed itself strongly on my imagination. In it I found much that was original and characteristically Russian. Zhukovsky wanted to write the words himself, and as a sample composed the following lines:

> Oh, but 'tis not for me that blows
> The desolate, stormy wind.
> (From the trio and chorus in the epilogue.)[1]

[1] V. Zhukovsky, V. Sollogub, and N. Kukolnik took part successively in work on the libretto. Zhukovsky wrote the epilogue, Sollogub the text for the

His affairs did not permit him to carry out his plan, and in this matter he passed me on to Baron Rosen, a hard-working man of letters of German origin, then serving as secretary to His Imperial Majesty the Tsarevich.

My imagination, however, ran ahead of the industrious German; as if by an act of magic the plan of the whole opera was suddenly formed, and there came, too, the idea of counterposing *Polish* music to Russian. Many themes and even the details of arrangements—all this flashed into my head in an instant. I began to work, and in an entirely whimsical fashion, too, sort of back to front, as it were, that is, I started where others finished, with the overture, which I wrote for four hands on the piano with the instrumentation indicated. In the published edition of *A Life for the Tsar* this four-hand overture was preserved just as I wrote it then, except for the adagio, which was altered substantially later on. I wrote down in a special notebook the themes for the various sections of the opera, often with the counterpoint worked out, as I devised them.

At one of Demidov's concerts during the winter of 1834–35, I sang Rubini's part in the finale to Bellini's *Il Pirata*. At Count Vielegorsky's, during Lent, Beethoven's *Seventh Symphony* was performed with unusual success. The first violins were Lvov, Böhm, Romberg, and Maurer, and they all played with genuine enthusiasm. After the adagio, Soliva, music professor at the Dramatic School, and a distinguished theoretician, jumped to his feet, exclaiming: "E una cosa che fa stupore!"[2] As for myself, I was so stirred by the deep impression produced by this inconceivably wonderful symphony that when I got home, Maria Petrovna asked, with a look of concern, "What's the matter, Michel?"

"Beethoven," I said.

first act, but he broke with Glinka over interpretation of the second act; Kukolnik agreed to do it according to Glinka's plan, but his (Kukolnik's) departure from Moscow ended this project. Baron E. F. Rosen, a secretary at the imperial court, was called in when there was finally an insistent need for a librettist.

2 "It's astonishing!"

"But what's he done to you?" she said, so I had to explain to her that I had just heard a wonderful symphony. Music was not her strong point.

After the anniversary of my father's death I wrote a letter to my mother asking her blessing for my marriage and, receiving it, sent my reply to *her*. In getting things ready for the wedding, my bride often stayed with my mother on Peska Street, while my poet Rosen lived near by on Konnoi Square, so that when I visited Maria Petrovna, I would usually stop in to see him. During the spring, that is, in March and April, he wrote the words for the first and second acts, according to my plan. It was not easy for him: not only had most of the themes been set down, but the pieces had also been developed, and it was up to him to fit his words to the music, which sometimes demanded the most singular meters.[3] Baron Rosen showed courage here; I would ask, say, for so many lines of this meter or that, disyllabic, trisyllabic, or even something entirely unheard of—it was all the same to him—"come by in a day or so and it will be ready." Zhukovsky and the others made a joke of it, saying that Rosen always had his pockets filled with ready-made verses and that I had only to tell him what kind, that is, what meter I needed, and how many verses and he would pull out just the right number of just the right meter—and each meter would come from a certain particular pocket.

But when the meter and the idea were fitted to the music and made to harmonize with the flow of the drama, then my poetic fellow would show a quite unusual brand of obstinacy. He would defend his each and every single line with stoic heroism; thus, for example, take these verses from the quartet:

[3] According to V. F. Odoevsky's account, he was an active middleman between Glinka and Rosen during work on the text of *A Life for the Tsar*. Odoevsky would "take Glinka's single-voice melody and, with consideration of his intentions, would put the proper stresses on the notes, striving to give the meter some kind of form. It was to these meters and in accordance with these thoughts, expressed by the music, that Rosen wrote most of his verses."—V. F. Odoevsky to V. V. Stasov, 1857.

As thou for earthly life
My little spouse to be'est, *etc.*

To me, they did not seem to be quite right. The words "to be'est" and the Slavic, biblical, and even peasant "little spouse" struck me as being somehow crude and unpleasant. I struggled long and futilely with the stubborn Baron, but I had no chance of convincing him of the correctness of my observation—he talked a lot, and heatedly, and his thin, pale face gradually flamed to a bright red. He ended our little discussion by saying: "You don unnerstant! Dat iss de ferry pest potry!"

The idea for the well-known trio was inspired by my mad love of that time; one minute without my beloved seemed to me unendurable, and I really felt what I expressed in the adagio or andante *Pine Not, My Dearest,* which I had already written, in fact, in the village the summer before.

I was married around the twenty-fifth or twenty-sixth of April, 1835.[4] My father-confessor and law professor at the boarding school, Aleksei Malov, married us in the chapel of the Engineering School. The Privy Councilor Aleksander Vasilevich Kozodaev, my respected relative, was nuptial godfather, and my best man was Captain (now Major General, commanding the Third Carabineer Training Regiment) Peter Aleksandrovich Stepanov.[5]

In the first half of May, my wife, my mother-in-law, and I set out for Novospasskoe. We went first to Moscow to see my wife's relatives. I now had words for two acts, and I remember that in the carriage, somewhere beyond Novgorod, I suddenly wrote the *Bridal Chorus* in 5/4 time.

The details of village life at that time have slipped from my memory—I know only that I worked hard, that is, I was *writing down* the score already in mind and preparing the ground ahead. Each morning I would sit at a table in the large and cheery draw-

[4] Glinka was married on April 26, 1835.
[5] Peter Aleksandrovich Stepanov (1805–1891), commandant at Tsarskoe Selo beginning in 1872 and an amateur artist. He wrote reminiscences of his friend Glinka.

ing room of our house in Novospasskoe. This was our favorite room; my sisters, my mother, my wife—in a word, the whole family—milled about there and the more they talked and laughed, the faster my work went. The weather was lovely, and I often worked with the doors open onto the garden, drinking in the pure balsam air.

I had first written *Pine Not, My Dearest* in ¾ time and in the key of A minor, but I saw that I had too much even division of time in the first act, that is, the introduction, Antonida's aria, and Susanin's recitative with the chorus. I also recalled the words of Dehn, who once perplexed Spohr by asking him: "Why is your *Jessonda* all in ¾ time?" Not wishing to give them an opportunity to quibble with me about monotony, I wrote the same melody in ⅝ and B minor, which no doubt better expresses love's sweet, tormented longing.

Karl Fedorovich Hempel visited us for a while and was honestly happy about the good progress of my work. I believe he rewrote the G Major scene, in which the Poles come to Susanin in the hut, as it appears in the autograph score now in V. P. Engelhardt's possession.

In August I returned, with my wife and mother-in-law, to Petersburg, where I soon settled down on Konnoi Square in a private house which my wife and I occupied alone. My mother-in-law soon moved in with us. I should perhaps say here that Aleksei Stuneev did not approve of this, and more than once he had said to me: "Ah, Michel, never take a mother-in-law into your home!" On the whole, however, he was not really a participant in my marriage or in its aftereffects. Partly from self-conceit, partly from the laziness natural to an artist when it comes to household cares, and also out of submissiveness to my wife, I did admit a difficult mother-in-law into my family. Nevertheless, all went well, and so well, in fact, that my friend Stepanov, who often visited us, once said to me: "Your happiness makes my heart glad, and I congratulate you!"

"I will thank you more," I replied, "if you'll congratulate me ten years from now!"

I had met Stepanov (Peter) while at boarding school, at the home of one of our common relatives (we were distant relatives ourselves), Fyodor Stepanovich Kashtalinsky. Afterward, we met in a social way at Prince Khovansky's and at Astaviev's, my schoolmate who is now a major general on the staff of His Imperial Majesty.

My work continued to go along well. Each morning I would sit at my table and write about six closely spaced pages of score— the same one that is now at Engelhardt's. Evenings, sitting on the sofa in the circle of my family and sometimes with a few good friends, I would take but small part in the life around me; I was always absorbed in my work, and although I had already written a lot, there was still a great deal of hard work ahead. In fact, I had to drive myself to produce a well-ordered, harmonious whole. I wrote the scene where Susanin is in the forest with the Poles in winter. Before I began to put down this scene, I often read it aloud, with feeling, and I put myself so vividly in the place of my hero that my hair would stand on end and I would be taken with cold shivers. The development of this scene according to my plan was entirely the work of Baron Rosen. Lomakin,[6] whom I got to know at this time, lent his co-operation. He brought the singer Belikova (soprano) to run through the aria *'Tis Not for That I Grieve*, the ritornel of which Tikhmenev played on his flute.

Praskoviya Arsenyva Barteneva was in Petersburg. Through her, or through her son-in-law D. I. Naryshkin, an orchestral rehearsal of the first act of my opera was arranged at Prince Yusupov's. The orchestra,[7] although a bad one, performed fairly well.

[6] By his own never ceasing work and talent, Gavril Ekimovich Lomakin secured an honored place among the leaders in the world of music and was sincerely loved and respected by all who knew him.—Glinka.

[7] A serf orchestra.

99

The conductor was Iogannis, who was later an impresario in Moscow. The choruses were not performed, but somewhere or other, Barteneva, Volkov, and I sang, and despite this, the effect of the instrumentation proved to be satisfactory. This was Lent, 1836.

This same winter, that is, 1835–36, I became acquainted with Petrova[8] and Shemaev, then with other actors and actresses in Russian opera, and gradually began to rehearse my opera. My theatrical friends ran through their parts with me with quite evident zeal. Petrova (then still Vorobieva) was an exceptionally talented actress who would always ask me to sing each new piece of music for her a couple of times, and the third time she would know words and music by heart.

Despite the fine attitude of the artists, my dealings with them were not always free of petty rancor and silly quarrels. Theater Director Aleksander Mikhailovich Gedeonov wrote me a letter unjustifiably rebuking me for making my artists sing in smoke-filled rooms so that, he said, their voices were injured. I was annoyed at this, but went on rehearsing the parts.

In March of 1836, Count Mikhail Yurevich Vielegorsky made arrangements to rehearse the first act of the opera at his house.[9] The actors and actresses sang the parts, but I don't remember who was in the chorus, except that they were not of the court. Gedeonov attended this rehearsal, as did my mother, and it all went very nicely. Count Vielegorsky made two sensible observations: there was no coda in the introduction, so on his advice I added one later. In No. 3, in Susanin's scene, the principal theme of which I took from a Russian song I had heard at the near-by town of Luga (St. Petersburg Government), the chorus was not on

[8] Anna Yakovlevna Petrova, nee Vorobieva (1816–1901), contralto, was the first to play Vanya in *A Life for the Tsar*, and it was she who created the stage model for the part of Ratmir in *Ruslan and Ludmila*. She wrote her recollections of the first performance of *A Life for the Tsar*. Her husband was the opera singer Osip Afanasievich Petrov, who took the roles of Susanin and Ruslan in Glinka's operas.

[9] For which I shall be forever grateful to him.—Written in the margin in Glinka's hand.

stage before the arrival of the bridegroom, but stayed behind the scenes. The Count advised me to bring my chorus on stage crescendo and finish fortissimo, which I did, with good results, adding immeasurably to the solemnity of the bridegroom's entrance.

In the course of the work I became considerably indebted to Prince Odoevsky and to a lesser extent to Charles Mayer. Odoevsky was particularly pleased with a theme I had taken from the song of a Luga coachman:

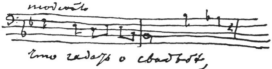

He advised me to recall this theme, which begins Susanin's part in his last scene in the forest with the Poles, and I was able to do so. After the words "There shall I take you, where the gray wolf runs not, where no black crow flies," there is a progressive fragment from this coachman's theme, namely:

In composing the beginning, for Susanin's replies I had in mind our well-known brigand song *Down the Volga, Down the Mother River*, using its first part with a repeated movement in the accompaniment, like this:

I sometimes consulted with Charles Mayer on instrumentation, especially in fortissimo; I also remember that he showed me notes for the accompaniment in the mazurka:

This figure is repeated in various keys by the different instruments and is quite effective.

In connection with my opera I became acquainted with Nestor Kukolnik,[10] who had been presented to me as our best dramatic writer of the time. He was willing to write the words for me, but left for Moscow and from there sent an outline of a scene, which proved to me that it was not possible to do such work when the collaborators were separated, especially since most of the music had been written and the words had to be fitted to it. On the other hand, Baron Rosen had entered spiritedly into the job, and out of consideration for V. A. Zhukovsky, I could not avoid his cooperation. In spite of this circumstance, when Nestor Kukolnik returned, my good relations with him not only continued but became even more friendly; he took a wholehearted part in my work and exulted, with sincere enthusiasm, at each newly created scene.

In the spring of 1836, my wife and mother-in-law went to Peterhof, where they stayed with her married brother Nikolai Petrovich. After Venice it was difficult for me to withstand the sea air, so I rarely visited my wife while she was at Peterhof. Moreover, after the rehearsal at Count Vielegorsky's there were malicious rumors and much unfriendly gossip, and I had a lot of

[10] Nestor Vasilevich Kukolnik (1809–1868), man of letters, chiefly a playwright of sorts. Glinka set several of his poems to music, particularly the cycle *Farewell to Petersburg*.

bothersome work to do to get my opera accepted for the stage.[11] I had been made to believe that the conductor, Catterino Albertovich Cavos, who had at one time successfully written music for an opera *Ivan Susanin*, was actively conspiring against me. The course of events proved the opposite to be true—he had been more effective than anyone else in persuading the director[12] to stage my opera, and he subsequently conducted the rehearsals zealously and honestly. Finally, I was obliged to promise not to demand any compensation whatever for my opera; I gave such an agreement, in writing, to Gedeonov's secretary, A. L. Nevakhovich,[13] in N. Kukolnik's apartment in Gavrilov's house at the Sinny Bridge. It was then up to me to finish rehearsing the parts and the choruses. I also had to complete the dances and plan some new ones at the suggestion of the ballet master, Tityus. Aside from the polonaise, the cracovienne, the mazurka, and the *pas de quatre* (A Major), I also had to prepare two other dances, one of them in E Major, in which there was a solo for Böhm, and the other in C Major, for oboe and cello.

Cavos began rehearsals at once with the quartet in rooms at the theater. Since the string instruments are the foundation of an orchestra and since there are incomparably more of them than there are wind instruments, he planned his program thus: he took two quartets with one bass for one rehearsal and for the next, the other two quartets with another bass, and carried on in this way, continually correcting mistakes until all performers were able to play their parts properly. He would then take the wind instruments alone and finally the entire orchestra—first in one of the practice rooms, then on the stage.

[11] Glinka's petition to the director of the St. Petersburg Theaters for *A Life for the Tsar* was dated April 8, 1836.

[12] Also an honorable man.—Glinka.

[13] Aleksander Lvovich Nevakhovich (1810–188?), secretary to Director of Theaters Gedeonov and later chief of the Theater Office for the Administration of St. Petersburg Theaters.

Cavos ran the rehearsals with his characteristic vigor and efficiency, but, as was also his custom, he did not pay attention to the nuances; the pianissimo, especially, never quite came off, but was something by way of a *mezzo forte*. In the same fashion, somehow he could not catch the true tempo, but always had it a little slower or a little faster than it should have been.

I do not recall exactly where it was or at what rehearsal, for the D Major polonaise or the C Major chorus, where the pizzicati of the stringed instruments imitate balalaikas, that the musicians, laying down their bows, loudly applauded me; they also applauded for some other number. I must confess that this approbation gave me more satisfaction than any expression of approval on the part of the public. It should be noted that at that time I knew very little about the people who were performing my opera. The orchestra was good, but not perfect. The second violins were, in comparison, very much worse than the first; there were few violas, and the basses were not at all good, except the first, Memel. Of the wind instruments, not all the horns were in tune, nor were some of the other second wind instruments. On the other hand, among the first violins there were some good artists, also four or five excellent cellists, and among the winds, the clarinetist Bender was distinguished by his unusual fullness of sound, while the flutist Zusman was unquestionably one of the best, if not the very best, artists in Europe.

The very brilliant and distinguished oboist Brod came to the final rehearsals. He played his parts exceptionally well on the oboe and on the English horn. A little while before the performance the tenor Charpantier arrived from Moscow and was given the stage name Leonov; he had the role of Sobinin.

Although Zhukovsky did not write for the libretto, he did not give up his zealous participation in my work. For example, he would tell the sceneshifter and stage setter, Roller, how to create most effectively the last scene, in the Kremlin, and together we would go to Roller's studio for a consultation. Zhukovsky would look at everything keenly and ask questions. Our efforts in this case were successful, and in the last scene the detached crowd, cut out of cardboard, created a fine optical illusion, appearing to be an extension of the live throng gathered in the foreground.

At the end of the summer I wrote the trio with chorus *Oh, But 'Tis Not for Me That Blows the Desolate, Stormy Wind* to accord with the capacities and talent of Madame Vorobieva. On the departure of Acting Councilor of State Pelikan, with whom Kukolnik had been living, the entire first floor of the house fell to him—and to his friends. In one room the host himself would be at his writing, for example, in another there would be conversation, while in a third Dr. Heidenreich would be completely absorbed in a game of chess, and so on. The trio and chorus I have mentioned (from which I took the adagio of the overture) were written in a happy frame of mind. I remember as if it were yesterday that we had about fifteen people around; Petrov (the actor)[14] was there, too, and I wrote this moving scene, or, rather, *composed* it, amidst the bustle and talk of my carousing friends. I first set down the accompaniment to this trio for violas and cellos, but later, on the advice of Prince Odoevsky, I arranged it for four cellos and one bass only. The Prince also gave me the idea of using violins divided into four and three parts in the introduction of this trio, *Ever the Same Weary Longing, etc.*

Perhaps it was because I had bathed in the sea on my last visit to Peterhof in the summer of 1836, or it may have been for some other reason, but at any rate I felt some agitation around my

[14] Osip Afanasievich Petrov (1807–1878), outstanding Russian operatic bass, first played the roles of Susanin and Ruslan, created the stage model for the role of Farlaf, and founded the Russian vocal school. Later on, he played leading roles in such productions as *The Barber of Seville, Der Freischütz, Robert le Diable, The Stone Guest, Boris Godunov,* and others. He became a close friend of Mussorgsky, who wrote the chief character in *The Fair at Sorochintsk* for him. He was the husband of Anna Yakovlevna Vorobieva Petrova.

heart, and indeed I began to suffer cruelly—first it was my nerves, together with an unbearable sort of numbness in my entire body. In a short while I developed a fever, accompanied by nosebleeds in the morning and in the evening by fits of burning, so that before long I found myself wasting away. Fortunately, I already knew how to use certain homeopathic remedies, and one dose of ipecac halted my fever.

My illness forced me to stay at home, and when, feeling somewhat better, I went to rehearsal, it was hard to recognize me, since I had become improbably thin and had turned a sort of greenish color.

We rehearsed in the practice rooms and on the stage of the Aleksandrisky Theater, since the Bolshoi Theater[15] was undergoing alterations. Before long, though (in the autumn), in order to test the acoustic properties of the hall at the Bolshoi Theater, we performed there the quartet *My Children! Let There Be Peace and Love Amongst You!* from the opera.

Since it had been decided to give my opera at the reopening of the renovated theater, we began auditions and rehearsals on the stage of the Bolshoi Theater. Workmen were busy dividing the boxes, adding candelabra and other ornamentation, so that the sounds of several hundred hammers would frequently drown out the conductor and the performers.

Not long before the first performance I had the pleasure of meeting the Emperor at one of the rehearsals. The hammers were silenced, and Petrov and Vorobieva sang the E Major duet, and, of course, they did it very nicely. The Emperor approached me and graciously asked if I were satisfied with his artists.

"Particularly with the fervor and zeal with which they carry out their assignments," I replied. This answer pleased His Majesty, and he passed it on to the actors.

[15] This the old Bolshoi Theater in St. Petersburg is often called the Grand Theater, possibly to distinguish it from the present Bolshoi Theater in Moscow.

Through the co-operation of Gedeonov I was granted permission to dedicate my opera to the Emperor, and instead of *Ivan Susanin*, it was called *A Life for the Tsar*.[16]

Because of illness, I was not present at the last rehearsal; as was customary, this one was in costume, with scenery and lighting. Since many persons had already heard excerpts from my opera and since the public had become interested, the theater was filled.[17] Following the dress rehearsal Prince Odoevsky calmed me in a letter assuring me that there could be no doubt as to the success of the first performance.

Finally, Friday, November 27, 1836, was set for the *première* of *A Life for the Tsar*.

It is impossible for me to describe my feelings on that day, especially just before the curtain went up. I had a box in the second tier; the first was entirely occupied by high court officials and dignitaries, together with their families. My wife and relatives were in a box, but I'm not sure whether my mother was also there.

The first act went all right, and the by now well-known trio was loudly and enthusiastically applauded.

The audience was very quiet during the scene with the Poles, from the polonaise to the mazurka and the final chorus. Greatly distressed by this silence, I went backstage. There, Ivan Cavos, son of our orchestra conductor, tried to reassure me, saying that this was only because the *Poles* were on stage. I was not convinced.

The appearance of Vorobieva, however, dispelled all my

[16] Glinka had named his opera *Ivan Susanin* early in 1835, when he was planning it for three acts only. In speaking of the renaming in the third person, Glinka may be emphasizing the fact that it was not he who made the change but that it was more or less pressed on him from sources at the imperial court.

[17] In a letter to A. Ya. Bolgakov on the day of the *première*, A. I. Turgenev wrote: "They're giving the new Glinka opera today, and everyone is trying to get seats, but they've been sold out for a long time."

"We are impatiently awaiting Glinka's opera," wrote Ya. M. Neverov to S. P. Shevyrev on November 17, 1836, and N. I. Kulikov noted that without influence it was impossible to get a ticket for the *première* of *A Life for the Tsar*.

doubts of success. The orphan's song, Vorobieva's duet with Petrov, the quartet, the scene with the Poles in G Major, and other numbers in the act came off with great éclat.

In the fourth act the chorus, playing the part of the Poles passing through the forest, at the end of the scene, fell upon Petrov with such fury that they ripped his shirt and he had to defend himself against them in all seriousness.

The magnificent spectacle of the epilogue, showing the people rejoicing in the Kremlin, astonished even me. As ever, Vorobieva was superb in the trio with the chorus.

The success of the opera was complete. I was in a daze and cannot remember to this day just what happened when the curtain came down. Right afterward, though, I was called to the imperial box on the side of the theater. The Sovereign first thanked me for my opera, then observed that it was not good to have Susanin killed on stage. I explained to His Majesty that I had not been to the last rehearsal because of illness and could not know how things had been planned there but that according to my program the curtain should have been lowered as soon as the Poles attacked Susanin and his death recounted afterward by the orphan in the epilogue. After the Emperor had thanked me, the Empress did so, too, and then all the Grand Dukes and Grand Duchesses who were in the theater.

I soon received an imperial gift for my opera: a four-thousand-ruble ring made up of a topaz encircled by three rows of the finest diamonds. I gave it to my wife at once.[18]

Even before the opera had been performed Kukolnik had helped me sell it, as a literary property, to Snegirev. The arrangement went very well indeed, especially at first, and I received a certain profit from it.

Despite the brilliant success of the opera, there were some carp-

---

[18] The four-thousand-ruble ring Glinka received was the usual presentation for an opera in those days, and the "Tsar's reward" was essentially an honorarium, given not in money but "in kind."

ing critics, of course, who fell upon it. Faddei Bulgarin had two long articles in the *Northern Bee* for December, 1836, or January, 1837.[19] These articles were curious ones, and they clearly defined the degree of the author's ignorance of music. Some aristocrats, in speaking of my opera, had exclaimed contemptuously: "That's music for coachmen" (*C'est la musique des cochers*).[20]

Notwithstanding all this, the opera was increasingly successful as time went on, the theater was always filled with enthusiastic crowds, and the printed songs from my opera were universally sold out wherever there was the slightest interest in music. Incidentally, Charles Mayer and I had transposed them for piano more correctly than they were printed by Snegirev. His paper was of the poorest quality; moreover, he did not even have the music ready in time to meet the public demand.

19 One should seek these out as a *chef-d'oeuvre* of musical galimatias.—Written in the margin of the copy in Glinka's hand. V. Stasov also added a note to the original: "This is not true. There were only three articles by Prince Odoevsky in the *Northern Bee*: the first on December 7, 1836, No. 280; the second, December 15, No. 287, and the third, December 16, 1836, No. 288. There were no others."

In one of these articles Odoevsky wrote: "This opera answers a question that is important for art in general and for Russian art in particular, that is: the existence of Russian opera, of Russian music. . . . With Glinka's opera there appears what has long been sought in Europe, and not found—new poetry in art and a new period in its history: the period of Russian music. Such an achievement . . . is the product, not of talent alone, but of genius."

And Ya. M. Neverov, friend of Stankevich, Granovsky, and Melgunov, wrote in the *Moscow Observer* on December 10, 1836: "Never has a stage production stirred such lively and thoroughgoing enthusiasm among us as *A Life for the Tsar* . . . the enraptured audience overwhelmed the eminent *maestro* with its applause. M. Glinka fully deserved this attention: the creation of a national opera —that is an exploit that will forever impress his name in the annals of our country's art. . . . Scarcely three weeks have passed since the performance of *A Life for the Tsar* and already its songs are heard, not only in the drawing rooms, where they have replaced conversation, but even in the streets—further evidence of the popular spirit of this opera."

Gogol also wrote in glowing praise of the opera, dwelling in particular on Russia's great treasury of folk songs and melodies and pointing out the interesting contrast between the Russian motif and the Polish mazurka motif.

20 That is all right, and even good, because in my opinion a coachman is a more sensible person than a gentleman!—Written in the margin of the copy in Glinka's hand.

In concluding this period of my life it is probably not necessary to cite here the verses composed in my honor at a party at Prince Odoevsky's[21] by Zhukovsky, Pushkin, Prince Vyazemsky, and Vielegorsky.[22]

[21] Get hold of and attach copy of the verses.—Written in the margin.

*Note:* I beg the worthy and, as I believe, a sincere friend of mine, Dmitri Vasilevich Stasov, to obtain a copy of these lines from Prince Odoevsky and attach them to these notes. Berlin, July 5/June 23, 1856.—Glinka's note.

[22] The verses of this "mock hymn," along with the music, were published in 1836 under the title *Hymn: Words by Pushkin, Zhukovsky, Prince Vyazemsky and Count Vielegorsky; Music by Prince V. F. Odoevsky and M. I. Glinka.* The lines appeared a second time in 1936 in a book entitled *Pushkin in the Songs and Romances of his Contemporaries.*

*A Life for the Tsar* evoked a flood of "patriotic" references, in verse and prose, expressing pride in this triumph of Russian art and frequently indicating a sort of ironical hostility toward the West and its slavish admirers in Russia.

*December, 1836,* то *June, 1844*

# 8

*Kapellmeister of the Imperial Chapel Choir.*
*Little Russia.* Ruslan and Ludmila. *Retirement from*
*Official Service. Dissolution of Marriage*

St. Petersburg, September 7, 1854

IN January, 1837, I was appointed Kapellmeister of the Imperial Chapel Choir. This came about in the following way.

In the winter of 1836, the director of the court singers, Fyodor Petrovich Lvov, died.[1] Since they were most kindly disposed toward me, Count Mikhail Yurevich and Prince Grigori Volkonsky utilized this occasion to talk up my capacities, for they clearly saw that aside from the other advantages associated with this appointment, the material help it would provide, such as the salary and government quarters with firewood, was in no way to be disregarded. The court minister ordered me informed through his aide, Panaev (author of the *Idylls*), that they had an appointment for me and would I kindly reply. I then inquired what my duties would be, and learning that I would be concerned only with matters of art, I agreed to accept the position. First, however, I asked who my chief would be and what my relationship to him might be expected to be. Panaev explained that the director would be supposed to handle only the business side, while to my question as to precisely whom it was planned to name, he answered that it would be either Prince Grigori Volkonsky or Count Matvei Yurevich. Although I might have guessed that whichever one

---

[1] Fyodor Petrovich Lvov (1766–1836) was director of the Imperial Chapel Choir, succeeding Bortniansky.

was selected would also mix into the musical part, I was happy to think of serving with either of them for they were agreeable persons and friendly toward me.

The evening of that same day, the Emperor, on catching sight of me back stage, came up and said: "Glinka, I have a request to make of you, and I hope you will not refuse me. My singers are known all through Europe, and consequently, it would be worth your while to concern yourself with them. I only ask that they don't become Italians under your direction." These kind words threw me into such a pleasantly confused state that I could only reply with a few respectful bows.

The next day, I went to see Count Matvei Yurevich Vielegorsky, who received me more cordially than was his custom. We were both happy to be working together and had already been thinking of possible improvements to make in the Imperial Choir. It turned out a few days later, however, that Aleksei Fedorovich Lvov had been named director. This disturbed me somewhat because my relations with him had altered just at that point, and for a reason which to me seemed very peculiar indeed.

Fyodor Petrovich Lvov, a man of advanced years, had visited me soon after my arrival in Petersburg in 1834 when I was living at Stuneev's, and this even though our apartment was on the very top floor. At that time he paid unusual attention to me; afterward, he sent me a letter accompanying his little book on Russian church singing that still further expressed his friendly feelings. I had once been in a box at some theater or other with my bride, Maria Petrovna, while in another box sat Fyodor Petrovich Lvov with his family. When he saw me and my bride, he turned from me with an air of displeasure, and from that time on we were not on bowing terms.

Nevertheless, Aleksei Fedorovich Lvov[2] received me with evi-

[2] Aleksei Fedorovich Lvov (1798[?]–1870), born in Estonia, was the son of F. P. Lvov—composer, violinist, and director of the Imperial Chapel Choir from 1837 to 1861—and was one of the first students of Russian national songs. In 1834 he wrote a brochure entitled *Singing in Russia*. He organized a quartet regarded

dent pleasure and we resolved to enter upon our new sphere of action in a spirit of complete co-operation. Soon after this decision Aleksei Fedorovich gave a qualifying examination. Many of the adult singers, that is, tenors and basses, proved to be very bad. Aleksei Fedorovich wanted to eliminate certain ones, but this was not done. I set to work teaching them music, that is, how to read notes and how to correct their intonation, in short, how to adjust or "true up" their voices, as we say in Russian. My method of teaching consisted in analyzing a scale, denoting the half tones, and then trying to determine why signs of augmentation or diminution were used. Later I would write short two-part problems on the blackboard, first having them make an analysis, then sing one, then analyze and sing the other part, and finally, all together, striving to educate the ear of my pupils and to adjust their voices. When I appeared for the first lesson with chalk in hand, there were few music lovers to be found; most of the important singers stood some distance off with a skeptical look on their faces, some of them even smiling. Paying no heed to them, I set to work so forcefully and, if I do say so, so adroitly that after a few lessons nearly all the important singers, even those who had been taking private or scholarship lessons, were coming to me for instruction.[3]

I saw Lvov often during this period. Throughout the winter

as one of the best chamber groups in Europe, wrote four operas, was an outstanding violinist—especially as a quartet player—and teacher, writing several worth-while handbooks in this latter capacity, as well as his memoirs. In 1833 he composed the Russian national anthem, assisted by Zhukovsky. M. Montagu-Nathan, in *A History of Russian Music*, writes: "The national anthem itself cannot be regarded as a particularly happy inspiration, for beyond its temporary lapse into the minor, it has no affinity either with Russian popular song or with the national character." Lvov also harmonized the traditional chants and tunes of the Russian church, which he edited in eleven volumes. He was a friend of Berlioz.

[3] In an article in the *Russian Musical Gazette*, 1899, K. A. Bulgakov recalled Glinka's years with the Chapel Choir: "He set to work with obvious zeal. . . . I delighted to hear the fruits of his efforts; he always said how much he enjoyed what he was doing, since he was confident it would be of service to his country . . . but A. F. Lvov, an untalented and envious musician, tormented by his own incompetence in the face of Glinka's bright genius, could not adjust his life to

and early spring of 1837, from time to time he invited Nestor Kukolnik and Brullov, with me, to his house, where he offered us friendly hospitality. This, of course, was in addition to music, which there is no need to mention (he played Mozart and Haydn excellently, and it was at his place that I heard Bach's trio for three violins). Moreover, wishing to attach the artists to himself, he did not begrudge a sacred bottle of some rare wine or other.

I also saw Zhukovsky and Pushkin quite frequently. At the end of the winter of 1836–37, Zhukovsky gave me a fantasy, *Midnight Review*, which he had just written. I had the music finished by evening and sang it at my place for both Zhukovsky and Pushkin. My mother was still with us, and she was truly pleased to see me with such distinguished guests.

When she left in March, my wife fell ill and was finally stricken with an inflammation of the lungs. Her doctor, S. F. Volsky, managed to save her, but she had a long convalescence. We were living in Fonar Lane at Merts', in the same apartment that Kukolnik and The Brotherhood[4] were to take over later.

My wife's illness shook my belief in conjugal bliss, and her capricious behavior afterward completely demolished it.

The first flare-up was so memorable that I shall give a detailed account of it.

Aleksei Stuneev was living in the same house on Voznozensky Street and was therefore close by, and Sofiya Petrovna[5] used to

---

the circumstances and began, as director, to annoy Mikhail Ivanovich with various acts of nasty pettiness. . . . Glinka was too fine a man to endure all this, so he left the chapel service, giving it over to Lvov to ruin, which he later did indeed do."

[4] "The Brotherhood," with Kukolnik as more or less the focal point, was a collection of writers, artists, and musicians of varied aims and points of views. Glinka enjoyed Kukolnik's company and appreciated his admiration, but he did not think too highly of Kukolnik's literary production: "He is a man of letters, not a poet . . . his verses are too heavy and graceless." Glinka delighted in the freedom and lack of restraint he found with The Brotherhood, in the praise he received there, and in the refuge from his family troubles that it provided.

[5] Sofiya Petrovna Stuneeva, nee Ivanovna, sister of Glinka's wife, was married to A. S. Stuneev. She was an amateur singer (contralto).

visit us often. One time in early spring when she was still not well, Maria Petrovna wanted to see her sister; the weather was terrible —a wild north wind was raging. I had asked my wife not to go because of the bad weather, but she was very determined and stubborn about it and ordered the horses harnessed. Seeing that my entreaties were futile, I felt compelled to use my authority and in a tone of command I ordered the coachman *not*, under any circumstances, to dare harness the horses. Maria Petrovna began to cry bitterly, while my mother-in-law, in a rage, let loose a stormy flow of abuse, her anger rising so in the process that it was hard to make out her broken Russian and I could hear only a whistling sound, like a samovar. The women quieted down at last, but I was deeply grieved by the ugly strife.

These scenes came to be repeated, and always merely because of trifles. In such cases the samovarish whistling of my mother-in-law and the sobbing of my wife would be heard in the house; as for me, I maintained a role of deep silence and walked, in a measured step, back and forth about the room, wheeling upon my right foot at each turn and carefully describing a left-hand semicircle with my leg, which indescribably annoyed my mother-in-law and, in fact, shut her up pretty quickly. I would then turn to her and ask if she had said everything she wished. She, of course, would go into a rage again, but not for long; sheer exhaustion would close her lips, and I, for my part, would slowly draw on my gloves, take my hat, and, politely bidding good-by to my ladies, go out to visit friends, where I would sometimes stay for several days, depending upon the specifically particular situation at home.

During Lent we moved into a rent-free apartment in the choir building. Soon after this the Smolensk nobility sent me some verses through the governor of Smolensk, N. I. Khmelnitsky, requesting that I compose a polonaise and chorus to them for a ball to be given when the Tsarevich passed through their city. When he returned to Petersburg, Zhukovsy brought my wife a

1,500-ruble gift from the Tsarevich for this polonaise,[6] a ring containing a ruby set off by diamonds. Also during Lent of that same year, 1837, the trio *Pine Not, My Dearest* from *A Life for the Tsar* was performed at a patriotic concert with extraordinary success. It was sung by Princess Lobanova, Andreev (who was superb), and Andrei Pashkov. The Tsar, who attended this concert, said to A. Stuneev at one point: "Glinka is a great master—it would be too bad if he only gives us this one opera."

In May we moved to the Lanskys' *dacha*, situated between the Black River and the Vyborg Road. The Odoevskys were also staying there at the time. I had often visited them, usually alone. The distress caused by the scenes at home led me to bitter reflections; it was not only my wife's character but also her lack of education that worked so surely against our chances for domestic happiness. The Princess had guessed everything, although I had carefully kept my family discord a secret and all others really envied my supposed bliss.

Andrei Petrovich Lodi,[7] son of a professor friend of Kukolnik's father, had returned from a trip he had undertaken to complete his musical education. He was introduced to me. He sang; his voice was so pleasant that Prince Odoevsky,[8] who had heard him from a distance, said: "What a delightful voice! That would be a great find for the theater!"

Others thought so, too, and later Lodi did decide upon a career

---

[6] This polonaise has been lost.—Written in the margin in Glinka's hand. Actually, the polonaise was not lost and is now in the Glinka Archives.

[7] Andrei Petrovich Lodi (1812–1870), tenor, voice teacher, and member of The Brotherhood.

[8] Vladimir Fedorovich Odoevsky (1804–1869), music and art critic, composer, and man of letters. He was an early student of the history and theory of music, especially of the origin and creation of folk music. Together with W. K. Kuchelbecher (Glinka's tutor), he published a collection of stories in 1826; subsequently, he wrote voluminously on musical subjects, both Russian and Western, and produced fairy tales and satirical writings. He was the first to critically acclaim Griboedov's *Woe from Wit* and was throughout the years a strong supporter of Glinka and a propagandist for his music. Later, he was close to Dargomyzhky, Balakirev, Tschaikovsky, and Rimsky-Korsakov.

in the theater. As his stage name he took Nestor, after Nestor Kukolnik.

During that year I often went to the city, mostly to visit the Kukolniks. Nestor was then publishing the *Art Journal*, and for that reason many persons from the world of art met at his house, and I was thus completely in my element there.

My work with the singers was highly successful. I could see the rapid progress of my pupils, who were already beginning to grasp the meaning of notes quite readily. I did not have to confine myself to this, however, and wished, in fact, to try church music. I wrote the C Major *Cherubim Song* and began work on a fugue with *text*, but without success.

I also became better acquainted with Professor Soliva of the Theatrical School; for him I had Sarti's double fugue for chorus rehearsed, which my singers did well. Although the assistant singing teacher Dmitri Nikitich Palagin had a lively understanding of his business in general, he was especially good with the younger pupils, that is, the sopranos and altos, but out of zeal for the work I often attended his classes anyhow.

At the end of the summer, Gedeonov, with whom I had become increasingly intimate after my opera was produced, asked me to teach singing to four girls he had selected at the Theatrical School. They were all pretty good, and moreover, one of them was the then well-known beauty Stepanova, who played the role of Peki in *The Bronze Steed*. It was not she, however, but another pupil, not so pretty perhaps, who gradually aroused tender feelings in my heart. It may be that the time I spent with these sweet half-children, half-coquettes was the best of my life; their playful chatter, their hearty laughter, the very simplicity of their modest dress, to which, nonetheless, they well knew how to give a very special grace—all this was for me new and captivating. Soon after I had started giving these lessons one of them always showed up a little better combed and dressed than the others, and when I entered the room, her fresh cheeks would suddenly flush; it would have been difficult to long withstand or oppose an involuntary expression of sentiment in such a case.

For the moment, though, I shall leave my nice young pupils and mention Lodi's preparation for the stage. Cavos had heard Andrei Petrovich's voice with me one time at the theater and was well satisfied with him. It was decided that he would make his debut as Pollione in *Norma*, a choice which I did not consider a good one but there was nothing to be done. Lodi had to be taught how to wear a Roman toga, so we girded the poor fellow in a sheet. He submitted with almost irreproachable good nature to the remarks of our entire Brotherhood, which persecuted him for a whole day.

I think it was about this same time that, at Petrov's request, I went to work on a supplementary scene for his wife in my opera *A Life for the Tsar*. In one place in the adagio I adopted a good idea Soliva had with regard to the movement of the basses, namely:

N. Kukolnik wrote the words for this additional scene in a very short time. Petrov assures me that I composed this scene in one day and that I delivered the part for his wife the next morning.

I sometimes went to see Soliva and had the intention of practicing with him in the *strict style*, but these plans were never carried out, and because of some kind of absurd gossip, we quarreled.

Petrov's benefit performance was set for October 19, 1837. Stepanova had fallen ill sometime before that, and, *by decision of the director*, the role of Antonida was given to Solovieva, who had always been distinguished by her absent-mindedness and her wretched memory. I taught her with all my power, but my efforts, which with most actors led to expressions of gratitude, only evoked manifest dissatisfaction in her, and for this reason.

The younger son of Gedeonov, Stepan Aleksandrovich, was courting Stepanova. She was singing well at that time, although later on Karl Brullov labeled her voice a *drafty wind,* and she was of course peeved when they gave her role to a rival who had it is true sung several parts—not at all perfectly, but, still, with admirable enthusiasm. The romance *'Tis Not for That I Grieve, My Darling* was repeated, to the annoyance of old Cavos. Even he, however, advised me not to take up Solovieva so zealously, but I, having once become involved in the business, did not wish to turn back. Gedeonov's children treated me coldly, then even quarreled with me, but I continued to frequent the stage and to teach at the school anyhow.

Aside from the supplemental scene I've already mentioned I wrote two romances in 1837, *Where Is Our Rose?* and *Night Breeze,* to words by Pushkin, and I believe I wrote them in Stepanov's apartment in Garnousky's house at the Ismailovsky Bridge.

The first idea of *Ruslan and Ludmila* was given me by our famous comic writer Prince Shakhovsky;[9] in his opinion, the role of Chernomor should have been written for Vorobiev.[10] At one of Shakhovsky's "evenings," Pushkin, speaking of his poem *Ruslan and Ludmila,* said that he would have changed a lot of it; I wanted to know just what alterations he proposed to make, but his untimely death kept me from finding out.[11]

[9] Aleksander Aleksandrovich Shakhovsky (1777–1846), playwright and director. He composed theatrical "fairy scenes" on themes from Pushkin's poems, featuring a combination of music, dances, and brilliant visual effects. He wrote many plays, mostly in the "classic" tradition, and also poetry, fables, and stories. He advised the actor not to "think of himself alone, but of the individual and particular effects of his role, of the general course of the play and of the others acting with him, of the success of the play as a whole, and of the laws of dramatic art." Late in life he directed an active serf theatrical troupe in the provinces. Some of his regulations for the imperial theaters remained in effect until 1917.

[10] Yakov Stepanovich Vorobiev (1766–1809), Russian bass, outstanding in comic operatic roles, in which he also demonstrated his talents as an actor. He made his debut in St. Petersburg in 1787; in 1803 he was appointed Inspector of Operatic Companies.

[11] Glinka says no more of this conversation with Pushkin. However, at a

Gaivazovsky, who visited Kukolnik very often, acquainted me with three Tartar melodies. I later used two of them for the *Lezghinka* and the third for the andante in Ratmir's scene in the third act of *Ruslan and Ludmila*.

Things were not going too well for me at home. My wife was one of those women for whom finery, balls, carriages, horses, livery, and so on were everything. She had a poor understanding of music, or, to put it better, with the exception of light romances she really understood nothing at all—then, too, anything of an elevated or poetic nature was wasted on her. Here is an example of Maria Petrovna's indifference to music: when I began to write *A Life for the Tsar* in 1835, she complained to my aunt (my father's sister), Maria Nikolaevna Zelepugina, that I was spending money on manuscript paper!

Nevertheless, sometimes friends came to us for dinner, among them Peter Stepanov quite often. Soon after the first performance of *A Life for the Tsar* I came to know Prince Mikhail Dmitrievich Volkonsky and, with pleasure, taught singing to Ostroumova, a protégée of his, whom he called after his own name, Mikhailova. One time in the midst of a lesson we noticed a fire at the palace. This was at night, and when the entire building was ablaze, I could read by the light cast into my rooms.

That same winter, there were so many parties at Kukolnik's that frequently total strangers would join in quite merrily. We all smoked so much that the air could carry an ax, as Plato Kukolnik put it. Only a group of very close friends would stay on for supper, though, so in order to get rid of the excess we would employ the painter Yakov Fedoseevich Yannenko. He and a few others, with hats in hand, would loudly and pointedly bid good

---

"literary evening" at I. I. Kozlov's in the winter of 1836, Pushkin did say, in talking about opera, that he would like to see one produced in which the arts of music, the dance, and stage design were all combined in a natural, graceful manner.

night to the host and the other guests—the latter would usually follow their good example, but in half an hour or so Yannenko and the others would come back for their supper.

During Lent of that same year, 1838, the eminent violinist Lipinsky[12] came to Petersburg. I did not like him at concerts, but his powerful playing of Beethoven's *Quartet* enraptured me. He played Beethoven's last quartets at Kukolnik's with surpassing excellence, while the cellist Knecht also did his part masterfully —one might have thought they had played together all their lives. The violinists Ole Bull and Vieuxtemps were also in Petersburg then.

I relaxed and found consolation, as it were, at the school and on the stage. Occasionally, I acted and sang; then unfeigned delight would illumine the face of my pretty pupil. The others would listen to me intently, and even the very young girls would crowd the doorways and listen breathlessly to my singing. Whenever I came to the school, these charming young things would run up, one after the other, curtsy, and say to me with a sweet smile: "How do you do, M. Glinka?"

Sometimes my special pupil and other students would take part in plays, to "adorn" them, as the director said. Of them all I best remember the ballet *Revolt in the Harem.* My pupil looked very attractive in military dress.

In 1838, at carnival time, I quarreled with Gedeonov through some misunderstanding or other and stopped giving lessons at the school. At the same time I wrote the romance *Doubt,* for contralto, harp, and violin (words by N. Kukolnik), for my lovely pupil.

At the end of April, 1838, I was sent, on the highest orders,

12 Karl Joseph Lipinsky (1790–1861), Polish violin virtuoso and composer of many works (now forgotten). He was Kapellmeister at Lemberg and later at Dresden and gave concerts in Italy, England, and Germany. He was at one time a close friend of Paganini, but their rivalry eventually parted them. In 1834, Schumann dedicated his *Carneval* to Lipinsky.

into Little Russia to engage singers. Soon after reaching Smolensk Government, I met Rimsky-Korsak,[13] who at my request wrote for me the romance *Always and Everywhere, Thou Art My Dear, Unseen Companion.* I wrote the music for this romance on May 20 or 21 of the same year, 1838, at Novgorod-Seversk and sent it enclosed in a letter to Nestor Kukolnik, to be delivered to my former pupil, whom I still remembered vividly. Later on, the words of Pushkin's poem *Flame of Desire* were set to this music.

For the trip, I was given a government carriage and travel money, as well as a sum for other expenses. Aides assigned to me were the assistant singing teacher, Dmitri Nikitich Palagin, the singer Nafanail Nikiforovich Sheinov, and the old servant G. Saranchin. Yakov was to serve as my valet.

At Chernigov we came upon several good voices. Our selections were made with great care. For example, we would go to the seminary classes, where children of the age we needed were studying. At first we took all those who had an ear for music and a good voice and then finally the best of these, so that out of forty youngsters we chose eight, and these we invited to our rooms. There we had tea and endeavored to put them at their ease while repeatedly testing ear and voice and getting them to follow Dmitri Nikitich on the violin. Some of them were endowed with such a fine ear that they could readily follow all possible intervals, even the musical nonsense that Palagin made up just to confuse them.

As our base of operations I chose the estate of a good friend of mine, a landowner of Chernigov Government, Borznen Council, Grigori Stepanovich Tarnovsky. To this place, then, we and the children selected at Chernigov all repaired. After leaving the main road in the little village of Monasyrishche, we made our way with difficulty through nearly a whole May day by oxen over muddy roads, banked up but nonetheless overrun by rivulets, and finally reached Icheni, where we stopped for the night. By dinner time

---

[13] Aleksander Yakovlevich Rimsky-Korsak (1804-?), active poet from 1820 to 1830 and a schoolmate of Glinka.

the next day we reached our destination, Tarnovsky's estate of Kachanovka.

Our host and his family happened to be off visiting at a neighboring estate. Our first impression of the place favored the owner: the several approaches led through rows of stately, pyramidal poplars. The large brick house stood on a rise. Around it spread a huge but charmingly laid-out garden with ponds and ancient maples, oaks, and linden trees—all this grandeur certainly pleased the eye. But after one looked about a bit, one's wonder was lessened: the house seemed somehow unfinished, nor had the paths into the great garden ever been completed. Well, never mind, the proprietor did have an orchestra, and not a bad one either, although not full and with wind instruments not all properly tuned. Even the conductor himself, the first violinist Mikhail Kalinich, was rather hard of hearing. For dinner that night they gave us a great quantity of dishes, but it seemed likely that the cook had not fully learned his trade. In a word, everything disclosed the excessive frugality of a childless householder, owning nine thousand souls and large amounts of capital.

When our host returned, he greeted us cordially and provided me and my assistants with shelter in the orangery next to the house. He also advised us, after we had rested a day or so, to go to Pereyaslavl, where the Bishop of Poltava, Gedeon, had a choir. We thought we could get there in time for Mass on Sunday. However, we did not reckon properly and reached Pereyaslavl on Saturday evening. The local mayor, apparently expecting an official on some matter of inquiry, repeatedly tried to see me to find out who I was and why I had been sent to Pereyaslavl. At my orders, Yakov replied only, "I dare not disturb His Excellency." The next day, Palagin and Sheinov went to Mass, giving themselves out to be merchants who loved church singing. They noted down the names of the best young singers, after which they even went to the Bishop's for breakfast, and there heard his singers once again. I myself, getting up a little late, had stayed in our rooms and was just starting to drink some tea when the mayor of Pereyaslavl asked to be admitted. He began by recommending himself to me in a rather comically pitiful way, bowing low and refusing to take any food, although I repeatedly urged him to. When I estimated that sufficient time had passed and that my assistants might already have accomplished their purpose, I asked my guest for whom he took me and, seeing that this threw him into even greater embarrassment, I finally explained who I really was and why I had come to Pereyaslavl. His happiness at learning the truth was quite evident, and he now sat down to take some tea, assuring me of his readiness to co-operate with me in anything and everything that might be required and of his dislike of Gedeon and the rest. I thanked him and said that no doubt my business had already been done.

And, as a matter of fact, we so mercilessly plundered that choir that for a long time afterward Gedeon went about complaining of me to his friends.

Leaving behind the singers we had selected, we went on to Kiev, where we secured Gulak-Artemovsky.[14] He was much loved by his friends, and when we took him away, they rendered him a tearful farewell.

We gathered up our singers at Pereyaslavl and returned to Kachanovka. All the young boys came under the watchful eye of "Uncle" Saranchin. They practiced their singing with Palagin, the assistant singing teacher, and also sang with the Tarnovsky Choir and went to Mass, where they, too, sang along with others.

We then went looking for more singers in Poltava, Kharkov, and Akhtyrka, picking up several very young ones.

Although we selected, in all, nineteen boys and two adults (aside from Gulak, who was not at Kachanovka all the time, since

---

[14] Simon Stepanovich Gulak-Artemovsky (1813–1873), Ukrainian baritone and composer, wrote a popular comic opera in 1863 and many romances. A protégé of Glinka, with whom he lived from 1838 to 1839, he was noted for his role as Ruslan and later as Don Juan in Mozart's opera.

he left to see his brother, with whom he arrived in Petersburg in the fall), our host was sincerely happy to have us all there, and, with the job of recruiting singers completed, we stayed on with him for quite a while. He was a very egotistical man, and the idea of court singers singing with *his* choir in *his* church quite obviously delighted him.

Let me say a few words about life at Kachanovka.

Grigori Stepanovich Tarnovsky was a swarthy, spare man of about fifty, who reckoned himself somewhere in the civil service hierarchy and with the social status of *Kammerjunker.* His wife, Anna Dmitrievna, was a small, exceedingly stout woman and a very quiet one. She loved to have her maidservants massage her legs. The proprietor was for one reason or another bringing up his cousins, for the most part young, well-behaved, and attractive girls who had a very pretty governess. The resident physician also had a lovely daughter. Of the cousins, the youngest, Maria Stepanovna Sadorozhnaya, about fourteen, was very charming indeed. At dinner she usually sat across from me and her roguish, twinkling (or winking?) eyes would involuntarily meet mine, for which she was often scolded by her aunt.

All the time I was in Little Russia our talented and very agreeable young artist, Shternberg,[15] was also a guest at Kachanovka.

Despite his sense of economy, our host received guests joyfully and did all he could to provide them with varied pleasures. Walks, rides to neighboring estates, illuminations, and dances—all these were employed for our diversion. Whenever several neighbors would come over, we danced. Tarnovsky himself encouraged the guests by his own example, especially in the "grandfather," in which he would execute the figures of the dance with extraordinary vigor. Sometimes a quartet would sing Little Russian songs,

---

[15] Vasily Ivanovich Shternberg (1818–1845), a landscape artist and genre painter, friend of T. G. Shevchenko. He was noted for his realistic paintings of Ukrainian peasant life, often with touches of biting humor. Sent to Italy to study at government expense, he died in Rome. His pictures are currently hanging in major Russian art galleries.

and sometimes Tarnovsky's neighbor, Peter Skoropadsky, would strike up some teamster's song, skillfully imitating the peasant accent. He was a remarkable man and, although our host called him a simple Cossack (very likely because P. Skoropadsky, a special friend of his, incidentally, did, in fact, in dress and manner follow the ways of simple Cossacks), he had actually been educated at Moscow University and was thoroughly cultivated and interested in the arts. He understood architecture, played the clarinet quite well, and knew good music as though by instinct.

In my portfolio were two numbers I had written (I don't know when) for *Ruslan*—the Persian chorus, *The Deep of Night Falls o'er the Field*, and the *Black Sea March*. I heard both pieces for the first time at Kachanovka, where they were done very well. In the *Black Sea March*, we replaced the bells with wine glasses, on which Dmitri Nikitich Palagin performed with consummate skill.

We played, and not badly at all, the entr'acte music from Beethoven's *Egmont*; *Clärchens Tod* made a deep impression on me —at the end of the piece I grabbed my arm, for it seemed to me that from the abrupt alternation in the tempo of the horns, my pulse, too, had stopped.

For Gulak-Artemovsky I orchestrated the elegy *Howl, Wind, Howl!*, music by Henisht. Gulak sang it well, but his pronunciation was indescribably bad.

A neighbor of the Tarnovskys, my schoolmate N. A. Markovich,[16] gave me some help with Finn's ballad: he shortened it, but also had to make up enough suitable new verses to round out the number.

I remember very clearly the time when I wrote Finn's ballad: it was a warm day and I, Shternberg, and Markovich were all together. I was writing down some verses I had already composed,

16 Nikolai Andreevich Markovich (1804–1860), Ukrainian historian, ethnographer, poet, and amateur musician (a pupil of Field). His five-volume *History of Little Russia* was published in 1842–43; he was also known for his studies of Ukrainian folklore and customs and for his collections of historical documents. He was a schoolmate of Glinka.

Markovich was gnawing on a pen—it was not easy for him to imitate Pushkin in the additional lines we needed—and Shternberg was happily working away with his brush. When the ballad was finished, I sang it many times, with orchestra.

The Little Russian poet Victor Zabella[17] also occasionally visited Kachanovka. I set two of his songs to music then and there—*Gude viter* (*The Wind Howls Noisily*) and *Sing Not, Little Nightingale*.[18] This Zabella was an unusual master of imitations; he did blind persons especially well. The first violinist Kalinich was once so impressed by such an exhibition that he cried out: "That, my dear sir, is utterly antique sorcery!"

Our host, who spoke with the same broken language as did his first violinist, was most regular and precise in his habits, and all our amusements or impromptu entertainments had to end unfailingly before midnight, or earlier, whereupon the host would politely bow and the guests would go their separate ways.

Not all of us, however, surrendered to sleep. Markovich, P. Skoropadsky, Zabella, and Shternberg would come to my orangery. Before very long Palagin would show up with his violin. Yakov would bring his bass, and there would be a cellist too. We played Russian and Little Russian songs, did imitations, and talked, sometimes until three or four in the morning, somewhat to the vexation of our more conventional host. These little parties were repeated frequently, and Shternberg successfully captured them on his canvas, just as he expertly caught Zabella's likeness.

As a souvenir of our life at Kachanovka he painted in oils for me a scene that often amused us: two boys in the domestic service of the proprietor would have their eyes bound and each would be

---

[17] Victor Nikolaevich Zabella (1808–1869), Ukrainian poet.

[18] Glinka's deep understanding of Ukrainian folkways led some critics to say that his music for Zabella's poems was not his own but simply folk music he had heard. In 1854, during journalistic arguments on this matter, an admirer of Glinka, P. P. Dubrovsky, received this reply to a query sent to the composer: "Yes, I really did write the music to the song *Gude viter* (words by Zabella), and if it is similar to a Ukrainian folk tune—that's not my fault!"

attached by a rope to a stake fixed in the ground so that they could each go a certain distance independently of one another. To one boy they would give two sticks, one of which was cut so that it would make a rattling sort of noise when rubbed against the other, while the second boy, armed with a knotted handkerchief, was supposed to catch his opponent and hit him with the handkerchief. All this naturally produced such amusing situations that not only our young singers but the adults, too, would laugh heartily. In Shternberg's picture (given to me personally),[19] on the left side, may be seen Kalinich, the regent and one of Tarnovsky's violinists, while some others look a little like some of the singers and our old servant, the *dyadka*.[20]

I ordered suitable clothing to be made for the singers and covered carts to be built. I myself went to the fair at Romna, and came close to drowning in the muck. Four of Tarnovsky's strongest horses had a hard time pulling me out of the thick, muddy river that had developed in the main street of the town. Before departure I visited Markovich's friend Korbe with a large group and, after finally leaving Kachanovka, visited Peter Skoropadsky for a while at Grigorovka, where I was variously entertained. Tarnovsky and his nieces, after having said good-by to me at Kachanovka, very trickily took a short cut so that I came across them again after a mile or so in a grove of huge oak trees, where we all drank a few farewell glasses of champagne.

At Grigorovka, Peter Skoropadsky entertained us with such abandon that when we left there was not a drop in the house to drink, nor any kind of poultry around.

At Orel the vice-governor, Semenov, showed me particular cordiality. The renowned General Krasovsky was also there; he

---

[19] I promised to give this picture to our talented actor, V. V. Smoilev, the idea being that he would eventually present it to the Imperial Academy of Art with a suitable inscription.—Glinka.

[20] Literally, of course, "uncle." This word has a multiplicity of everyday uses in Russian.

liked me and provided some first-class wine, from his own cellar, which lasted us all the way to Moscow.

My mother was in Petersburg when I got there, but she did not stay very long.[21] I do not remember too well whether the domestic scenes were renewed or not—I know only that my wife's demands forced me to published *A Collection of Musical Pieces,* printed in 1839.

It was not only difficult for me to collect these pieces but also extremely vexing;[22] I had a furnished apartment plus firewood and horses, and I received 7,000 rubles from my mother; in addition to that, my official salary was 2,500 rubles. With what I also earned from my compositions, I could, with a certain amount of prudence, live decently. I gave all the money to my wife, keeping for myself a mere nothing for small, unforeseen expenses, and although a team of four beautiful horses and a carriage were in our stable and shed, Maria Petrovna rarely showed them off, while I dragged about on foot or with some miserable hired coachman.

The singers I had collected had eye trouble, one after the other, on the return trip; when they had recovered sufficiently and been properly outfitted, I had the pleasure of presenting them to His Majesty the Emperor. This ceremony took place in the Hall of Flags near His Majesty's office. I arranged my singers in a semicircle and stood in the center of them in my uniform and sword, my three-cornered hat in my left hand and a pitch pipe in my right (A. F. Lvov was also present, and this was the way he wanted it done). The Emperor had on an old military coat with-

[21] Glinka returned to St. Petersburg on September 1, 1838.

[22] Glinka wrote N. A. Markovich on September 20, 1838: "I have been compelled to devise means of obtaining money in order to exist here in Petersburg—I am at present working on the album I mentioned to you back in Little Russia: there will be twelve of my pieces in it, ten of which are ready, and I hope not to have much trouble with the others. . . . These are trivial, harmless little things, but they do prevent me from getting on with *Ruslan* and I shall not hide from you that I am often sad, reflecting that I must use the poor muse as a means of existence."

out epaulets; he was accompanied by the court minister. The Sovereign addressed me pleasantly in more or less these words: "Oh! What fine young people! Where did you get them all just your height?" And then he asked me what I had in my hand. I explained what a pitch pipe was and how it was used. To His Majesty's question "What do your singers know?" I boldly replied (because D. N. Palagin had taught them well) that they knew all they needed to do their job. We knew from past examples how the Emperor examined new singers, and we had painstakingly prepared ours for the test. The Emperor began with *Save O Lord Thy People*, and His Majesty had barely given the key when nineteen boys and two basses burst gaily into song and gave a brilliant rendition of this chant (?). The Emperor was quite plainly satisfied, and had them sing something else—I don't remember what. As a sign of his pleasure, His Majesty made me a very low, playful bow in dismissal.

Expression of the royal good will toward me was not confined to this. Once, catching sight of me on the stage of the Bolshoi Theater,[23] the Emperor approached and, clasping me by the right arm, walked about with me for a while, conversing all the time, in the presence of the many others there, including, incidentally, the court minister, who offered me a very low bow.

On November 6 of that same year, 1838, I visited for the first time the church at the Anichkov Palace to attend the wedding of Aleksei Fedorovich Lvov.

After this I almost constantly attended the liturgies at Anichkov Palace Church and later went to the Winter Palace for large and small affairs.[24]

I was sometimes invited to Her Imperial Majesty's for the evening, where I was always very kindly received. Once, in speaking

[23] The Bolshoi Theater in *St. Petersburg*, of course.

[24] In letters to his mother during this period, Glinka constantly referred to this life: "I drove to the Anichkov Palace for Mass; from Christmas to the first week of Lent I was constantly 'under the whip': work with the choir, to the palace, dinners, suppers, and concerts."

of me to, I believe, Fraulein Barteneva, the Empress said: "Dites à votre ami de jouer ou chanter telle ou telle chose."[25]

When all the pieces, both mine as well as those of other composers, had been collected, I met with another unexpected difficulty: no music publisher had decided to buy the collection! I wept with vexation, but Plato Kukolnik, taking pity on me, arranged to have Peter Ivanovich Gurskalin, who had a store by the name of "Odeon," publish the collection for one thousand rubles.

About this same time I was given fifteen hundred rubles as my remuneration for engaging the singers.

This acquisition of funds quieted my relatives for the time being, but instead of using this sum to manage my household properly, I gave dinners and parties. At the latter, which were weekly affairs in the evening (I don't remember just which day we had them) there would be my friends, female friends of my wife, and relatives, artists, and literary men, chief among whom were Brullov and N. Kukolnik. Mikhailov and Artemovsky,[26] as my pupils, always came, too. (When he first arrived from Little Russia, Artemovsky stayed with me, and I discovered that it was not always easy to live with his temper.) Refreshments consisted of tea, rusk, pretzels, and so on, plus dessert; we did not play cards, nor did we dance—conversation and music, often singing with several voices together (*morceaux d'ensemble*), comprised our principal means of passing the time at these parties. Among the ladies who came were Countess Ekaterina Mikhailovna Saltiykova (our neighbor on the estate), now and then, and, more often, Elena Aleksandrovna Glinkina with her friend Krekshina. The pretty fourteen-year-old girl Nadezhda Andreevna Sodolskaya

25 "Ask your friend to play or sing something or other."

26 In his *Reminiscences of M. I. Glinka*, P. A. Stepanov tells of Glinka's parties: "They didn't dance, or play cards, but talked and played music. They would sing solos and *morceaux d'ensemble*, the latter frequently being made up on the spot, without any preparation. . . . The songs were always Russian. . . . They sang only three Italian songs, and no French or German at all."

(related to Sofiya Petrovna Stuneeva) was quite at home with us; she already played quite well on the piano—later on she married G. E. Lomakin.[27]

In addition to these people, we were sometimes visited—I in particular—at the evening parties and on other days, by the Shteriches, nieces of my late friend E. P. Shterich. The younger one, Polyxena, studied singing with me, while the elder—Princess Maria Alekseevna Shcherbatova,[28] a young widow—was charming: although not a beauty, she was a well-shaped and extremely alluring woman. They lived with their grandmother, Serafima Ivanovna, a woman not yet old but turned completely gray from the death of her adored son.

I was like one of the family, often dining with them and spending the early part of the evening (*l'avant-soirée*) at their house. I sometimes received little notes from the young, widowed Princess Maria inviting me to dinner with the promise of "a slice of the moon and a piece of fur." That meant that in the Princess' drawing room they would light a round chandelier of dull glass and that she would lend me her light sable cloak, in which I felt warm and comfortable. She would be on the sofa and I in an armchair beside her; sometimes conversation, sometimes pleasant, heedless dreaming provided me with agreeable moments. The thought of my dead friend was enough to keep my heart within the limits of a "poetic" but stimulating friendship.

We also went to see Count and Countess Saltykov, who received us with great cordiality and showed us many kindnesses. At their home I became still better acquainted with General

---

[27] Gavril Ekmovich Lomakin (1812–1885), active as director in Russian choral work. He was one of the founders, in March, 1862, of the important St. Petersburg Free School of Music, which served as a concert forum for the "Mighty Handful" and other budding composers and as a center for choral studies on an increasingly "popular" level, as opposed to the Imperial Music Society. Lomakin was Tschaikovsky's teacher at the School of Jurisprudence.

[28] Maria Alekseevna Shcherbatova, nee Shterich. Lermontov, captivated, dedicated his poem *For Worldly Chains* to her.

Leonti Vasilevich Dubelt,[29] whom I had met earlier in the director's box at the Bolshoi Theater.

Soon after my return from the village in 1838, Dmitri Stuneev[30] was appointed steward, and my sister Maria Ivanovna and her two children therefore moved to Petersburg, where they installed themselves in a rent-free apartment at the Smolny Monastery. I saw my sister and brother-in-law rarely at first because my wife and mother-in-law had managed to create friction between us, but later on Aleksei Stuneev persuaded me to go to see his brother, Dmitri. Thus in the winter of 1838–39 I did visit them quite often. I found them getting along very merrily; sometimes in the evening the school inspectors would bring some students with them to visit, and a few class superintendents would also come. The Stuneevs, I, Stepanov, and several other friends were glad to dance a little with the pretty young girls. Although the orchestra was not outstanding, it was always at D. Stuneev's disposal, while the bountiful supper, accompanied by excellent wines, was of course the thing to round out the evening. Even now I can distinctly remember how I sang willingly and from my heart on these evenings and how I stood out by my energy in the counterdances and waltzes and how, well, how—in a word—I really had a fine time.

My memories of how I wrote the opera *Ruslan and Ludmila* are not so clear. Aside from the pieces produced at Kachanovka, that is, the Persian chorus, the *Black Sea March*, and Finn's ballad, I had also worked on Gorislav's cavatina, *Resplendent Star of Love*. This was sometime in the winter of 1838 or 1839. I always wrote in the morning only, after tea, but I seemed to be constantly

[29] Leonti Vasilevich Dubelt (1792–1862), director of the Third Section (secret political police) of the Imperial Chancellery from 1839 until his retirement in 1856. General Dubelt was highly trusted by Nicholas I and Alexander II. An ultraconservative, he sought to ban Pushkin's work and to "make a serf" out of V. G. Belinsky.

[30] Dmitri Stepanovich Stuneev, Glinka's brother-in-law, brother of Aleksei Stepanovich Stuneev.

called away from this particular cavatina. I could hardly write a page, or possibly two, when my old servant (*dyadka*), a former noncommissioned officer, would appear, his arms stiffly at his side, and respectfully announce: "Your Excellency! The singers are here and are waiting for you." Who was waiting? Who was waiting? Who sent the old man? I still don't know; I know only that sometimes when I came into the rehearsal room I would find Lvov already there, holding out his hand to me with all cordiality.

I don't remember, either, when or where I wrote Ludmila's cavatina in the first act, *Sad Am I, Dear Father, etc.* (G Major). Barteneva sang it with chorus and orchestra at a patriotic concert in the spring of 1839.[31] I had expected a great success, and they did applaud, but with less enthusiasm than I was accustomed to. The eminent violinist, Lipinsky, standing beside me, listened to this cavatina with unfeigned interest, and at the end firmly pressed my arm and said: "That's really Russian, that music."

Aside from these five pieces, I was at the same time jotting down themes with contrapuntal ideas in a notebook given me for this purpose by N. Kukolnik. The notebook is now at P. Stepanov's.

I wrote the opera by bits and pieces. The idea for the subject, as I have already mentioned, came from Prince Shakhovsky. I had hoped to make up the plan in collaboration with Pushkin, but his untimely death made this impossible.

In the winter of 1837 or 1838, I once played with considerable ardor some excerpts from the opera *Ruslan*. N. Kukolnik, who always took a part in my efforts, kept spurring me on to do more work. Among the guests there at that time was Konstantin Bakhturin.[32] He undertook to make a plan for the opera, and sketched it out in half an hour, while drunk, and—how about this?—the opera was written according to that plan!

[31] Glinka is frequently a year or so off in his dates. For example, Ludmila's cavatina was written early in 1838, and P. A. Barteneva sang it at a concert on March 23, 1838.

[32] Konstantin Aleksandrovich Bakhturin (1809–1841), poet and son of Aleksander Nikolaevich, who was a member of the Transport Council.

Bakhturin for Pushkin! How did this happen? I haven't the faintest idea myself.

About this same time I was introduced to Captain Vasily Fedorovich Shirkov[33] of the Tsar's suite, a man said to be fully capable of writing the libretto for my new opera. He was, in fact, a very well-educated and talented person who was always drawing things and writing very facile verses with the utmost readiness. At my request he wrote, *as a sample*, Gorislav's cavatina *Resplendent Star of Love* and part of the first act. The experiment turned out all right, but instead of first contriving the whole and fixing the plan and course of the development, I set to work at once on the cavatinas for Ludmila and Gorislav, not worrying in the least about the dramatic action, supposing simply that all that could be worked out later.

On the third day of Holy Week I visited Odoevsky and from there went to see my sister Maria Ivanovna Stuneeva. On the way I suddenly felt a severe nervous upset coming on, which made me very jumpy, and when I got to my sister's, I had to keep moving back and forth from room to room. It was here that I saw E. K.[34] for the first time. She was not well, and a look of suffering or torment showed in her pale face. As I continued my agitated pacing, my glance involuntarily came to rest on her; her clear, expressive eyes, unusually gracefully shaped figure, and a special kind of charm and dignity that she revealed in her entire person attracted me more and more. After I had been somewhat restored by a hearty dinner and helped along by a good glass of champagne, I contrived to talk with this charming girl and, as I recall now, was able to express my feelings most artfully.

However, despite all my efforts to vanquish them, my nervous troubles became worse; since I wished to free myself of them as rapidly as possible, I thought—so what if it should be to my own

[33] Vasily Fedorovich Shirkov (1805–1856).
[34] By the initials "E. K.," Glinka denotes Ekaterina Ermolaevna Kern, daughter of Anna Petrovna Kern.

harm?—of resorting to camphor alcohol. This treatment irritated my nerves in a most frightful manner and I was deprived of sleep and appetite, and groaned from the pain. Finally, Prince Mikhail Dmitri Volkonsky took me to a Dr. Whering, who cured me in two weeks by the homeopathic use of sulphur and gold.

During my illness Lvov came to see me once and rather preached to me, suggesting quite pointedly that I did not care for the *Service*, in the most polite and friendly turns of expressions, it is true;[35] I kept quiet, but when I was well again, I visited the singers *less often than before*.

In the spring, Prince Mikhail Volkonsky and I arranged a concert for Artemovsky. Bilibina[36] took part in it, and so did the two Princesses Lobanova and Andreeva, for whom I orchestrated the aria from Halévy's *Guido et Ginevra*. My wife also sang the duet from *A Life for the Tsar* with Artemovsky, and Bakhmetiev[37] played some of his own compositions on the violin.

This concert was held in Prince Yusupov's hall with as full an orchestra as we could arrange for.

In the summer of the same year, 1839, Artemovsky went abroad on the money collected at this concert.

At the end of May we moved into a dacha at the Forestry Institute. I did not go there often, on the pretext of being busy in the service, but stayed in the city at Kukolnik's in Merts' house in Fonar Lane, from which base I more or less regularly visited my sister at the Smolny Institute. In order to conceal the real reason for my frequent visits, I used the excuse of having business with the orchestra they maintained there. This consisted of two rotten

---

[35] There are a number of documents indicating that Lvov, behaving like a petty bureaucrat, continually interfered with Glinka's work with the Imperial Chapel Choir. The worsening of their relations led Glinka to submit his resignation in a letter to Lvov dated December 8, 1839.

[36] Aleksandra Yakovlevna Bilibina (b. *ca.* 1820), well known as an amateur soprano in the 1840's and 1850's.

[37] Nikolai Ivanovich Bakhmetiev (1807–1891), violinist and composer of church music. He was director of the Imperial Chapel Choir from 1861 to 1863.

first violins, one second, one viola (I don't remember whether or not there was a cello), a bass, flute, clarinet, horn, trombone, and Turkish drums; when they played, a gray-haired civil servant by the name of Menshchikov, with a cross in his lapel, kept time very energetically, all the while waving a roll of paper about.

Although this orchestra was very bad, I did manage to bring it into some kind of shape. I first transcribed for it Labitsky's G Major *Waltz* and, taking account of the musicians' limited capacities, wrote another G Major waltz which I later dedicated to Her Royal Majesty the Grand Duchess Maria Nikolaevna.

Meanwhile, my romantic sentiments were soon fully shared by the lovely E. K., and my meetings with her became more satisfactory. On the other hand, my relations with my wife became worse all the time. She seldom went to see my sister at Smolny. One time there, though, my wife—apropos of what I don't know —in the presence of E. K. and Katerina Stepanova (daughter of my nurse, I. F. Meshkova, who had taken care of my sister's children), said to me scornfully: "All poets and artists end up badly; for example, look at Pushkin. He was killed in a duel." I answered her at once in a firm voice, saying: "Although I don't think I'm a wiser man than Pushkin, I shall not get myself shot for my wife." She made a face and turned away from me.

That summer we lost a horse out of our team of four. I wanted to see in this a reason for keeping only a pair of horses. When I explained this plan to my wife, she went out of her mind and, turning pale with anger, threw her arms on her hips and, stamping her foot, said in a haughty tone: "So, I am a merchant's wife, am I, to ride about with one pair? If you don't love me, then I'll leave you!"

She made such threats twice, and twice I answered her, mildly: "Maria Petrovna, don't say that again. If you leave me, I'll get along, but if I leave you, things will not go so well for you."

Each time Maria Petrovna went out, she was, as it were:

"A blending of roses and lilies."[38]

But how did she look at home in the morning?

When she got up, she would put on one of my dressing gowns, and, unwashed, with sleep-stained eyes, uncombed, with slippers on bare feet, with a cigar holder between her teeth and abuse on her tongue (when she dealt with the servants), she would stride about from room to room issuing her orders. Instead of roses and lilies, the prematurely withered face of my proud spouse was a sickly bluish-gray as a result of her immoderate use of cosmetics.

I was not often with Maria Petrovna at the dacha.

Everything in life is a *counterpoint*, that is, contrast. I realize myself that I am going beyond the limits of an unimpassioned chronicler. I'm guilty, but don't expect me to alter my present way of writing.

It was bad for me at home, but on the other hand, how much of life and enjoyment there was elsewhere! My ardent, poetic feelings for E. K. were now fully understood and shared. Then there was the unrestrained life with the happy and talented *Brotherhood*, as we called the society we had founded back in 1835 or 1836 at Kukolnik's, and which later fused into one grand, friendly family. Plato Kukolnik was our host and leader. He had torn down part of the wall separating a dark room from one of his corner rooms in Merts' house on Fonar Lane. Out of this room we formed an alcove in which we put a very wide oilcloth divan[39] stretching all along one wall of the adjoining well-lighted room. As host, Plato lived in a separate room. The rest of us, though, that is, Nestor Kukolnik, I, Chevalier Bobo (Vlad. Iv. Bogaev, a zealous government functionary) took up lodgings on the divan: each of us had his own place, but there was still room to give sanctuary to friends who, having stayed late, wished to spend the night. K. Brullov and Yannenko accepted this open invitation

---

[38] From the romance *Call Her Not Heavenly.*—Penciled in the margin in the hand of V. V. Stasov.

[39] One writer, in discussing Kukolnik's group, called it a "Turkish divan."

more often than the others, but Heidenreich, Lodi, *et al.* visited us frequently, too.

In the morning we all drank tea, after which the rest of the day was for each to use as he saw fit. I often visited my sister Maria Ivanovna. In the evening we got together again, when idle stories were told. Sometimes we had supper, and then this was a feast, not of food and wine (we could not afford such things), but of all manner of lively talk. Generally speaking, The Brotherhood consisted of the same group, but strangers and casual guests came, too, although always people of talent—Petrov with his mighty bass voice, or Peter Karatygin,[40] who had an inexhaustible store of puns *of his own invention*, or there would be someone or other from the world of letters; the conversation moved along in lively fashion, skipping from one subject to another, and time flew by rapidly and agreeably.

When we started singing, some who had had minor roles in the conversation would come to the fore: for example, Yannenko and Danchenko (Koko). Yannenko could imitate pizzicato supremely well, not only bass, but violin, too. In securing one of his better effects he would usually sneak up to some newly arrived guest and when it came his turn for the *solo dei pizzicati* he would suddenly pierce the guest through and through with those pizzicatos of his so cleverly that it seemed that he, the guest, had in fact turned into a bass. It was not only the astonishment of the guest, now become an instrument, that was funny; at the same time, Danchenko would become pizzicato all over! His eyes did it, his shrugs and grimaces did it, and so did even his *smile*.

Of all other songs, we liked this one best: *Goblets Wand'ring o'er the Table . . . etc.*[41]

---

[40] Peter Andreevich Karatygin (1805–1879), actor, playwright, and vaudevillian, noted for his playing of the comic role of Zagoretsky in Griboedov's *Woe from Wit.* He wrote about seventy light, humorous plays, most of which were successful, as well as his *Recollections* and his *Memoirs.*

[41] The reference is to Toropka's song from Verstovsky's opera *Askold's Tomb.*

The verse: *I Wonder, I Wonder, Shall I Marry Her?* was usually sung pizzicato piano, which was really effective.

Nestor Kukolnik sometimes made up couplets (*de circonstance*) for us; we would select music to go with them, or I would compose some especially and then rehearse and direct our choir.

The same fellow (Kukolnik) described our Brotherhood, or Committee, rather well in lines such as these:

> Now enters for a moment
> Andrei Petrovich Lodi,
> A nondrinking drunkard he, hoarse
> from younger days.
> He hurries to the water closet
> where, enthroned, he asks for soda,
> And sings an aria, an offering
> to his friends.
> From deathly sleep near *done*,
> Danchenko is waked up,
> He's slept three days in *one*!
> With a lecherous smile, hee! *hee*!
> He joins our Commit*tee*.

This "lecherous smile" was very funny to see, and contributed quite a good deal to the general merriment.

Here's what Kukolnik wrote about Heidenreich, who was almost always sitting at the chessboard:

> There's the pink-faced doctor,
> He's German and he's lean
> Sits at the chess board, he,
> Rooted like a tree.
> Nothing tempts him, no!
> Not pipe, and not cigar;
> Beer and Rhine wine, though,
> Tempt almost every one!

Chevalier Bobo (Bogaev) rarely left his desk when he came back from work, toiling and moiling there on his affairs with admirable constancy. He was in love with a young widow who lived with her mother, also a widow. Kukolnik wrote of him, among other things:

> Where have you been? At the widow's.
> What did you do? I was amorous.

Chevalier Bobo once said to Lodi, indicating the widow: "Look how sweetly she smiles." V. I. Bogaev is now married to his love and has a very good position. During the year in question I was often at the Stepanovs and became friends with Nikolai Alek.,[42] our well-known caricaturist.

I attended *ex officio* the betrothal and marriage of Her Imperial Majesty the Grand Duchess Maria Nikolaevna. During dinner they played music, the tenor Poggi (Frezzolini's husband) and the court singers sang; I was in the choir stall at this time and the clatter of the knives, forks, and plates intrigued me and gave me the idea of imitating it in the introduction to *Ruslan*, which, in fact, I later did as well as I could manage it.

I didn't work on the opera at all in 1839, but I wrote a waltz (G Major) and a polonaise (E Major) for orchestra which I dedicated to the Grand Duchess Maria Nikolaevna. E. K. looked through Koltsov's works and picked out the romance *If I Should Meet You*, which I set to music. I also wrote a waltz fantasy for her, although as a matter of fact the printed copies were dedicated to D. Stuneev.[43] For my sister, Elisaveta Ivanovna, now with her half-deaf nephew Sobolevsky in Petersburg, I wrote the nocturne *La Séparation* (F minor) for piano. I also worked on another nocturne, *Le Regret*, but did not finish it, although I used the same

[42] Nikolai Aleksandrovich Stepanov (1807–1877), caricaturist and artist. With the poet Kurochkin, he was co-founder and editor (1859–69) of the journal *Iskra (The Spark)*, a rallying point for a group of liberal, revolutionary poets. Stepanov had no formal art training, but he was a master of realistic, satirical drawing. Living in St. Petersburg from 1836 and moving in artistic and literary circles, he became famous for his sketches of Glinka, his caricatures in the journal *Eralash*, in Nekrasov's *Illustrated Album* (1848), and in the *Musical Album with Caricatures*, published together with A. S. Dargomyshky. He produced much patriotic art work during the Crimean War.

[43] Glinka's brother-in-law.

theme in 1840 for the romance *Ask Not the Songstress for a Song*.

In August my brother Andrei Ivanovich died. He was sixteen years old, a fine-looking boy of exceptional intellect and with a particular bent for mathematics. He could solve geometry problems without help from his professor. He was also first in riding at the Military Academy. One time, returning from camp, he had stayed with me at the dacha for a week or two and I got to know him very well. I last saw him alive and healthy at the home of my sister Maria Ivanovna. As I was going back to her place that day from Kukolnik's apartment, a black dog had followed me, barking and raging, from Spalernaya Street right up to the Smolny Institute. He threw himself on me, and me alone, so savagely that I nearly had to climb onto the coachman's shoulders, and all this despite the fact that there were a lot of carriages and carts in the street at the time. I found my brother altered in appearance. To my question, "What's the matter, André?" he replied "Oh, well, nothing; my head aches."

My sister wanted to play some cards; in getting things ready for this, my brother placed a chair for me next to E. K. After we had played for a while, my sister thought she would write some letters. At the time there were two candles burning on the table, but to get better light, she lit still another candle in a small candlestick. E. K. observed that it was not good to have three candles on the table. Not heeding this warning at all, my sister went on writing, without extinguishing the third candle. About two weeks before that a friend visiting Sofiya Petrovna[44] had told my fortune at cards; when spades kept coming up every time, she finally started hiding them from me. The day after I left my sister's this time, my brother became worse, and on the third day he died from an inflammation of the kidneys that developed into gangrene. His death shocked and saddened me terribly. I took a twenty-eight-day leave in September and went with my sister

[44] Sofiya Petrovna Stuneeva, sister of Glinka's wife, wife of Aleksei Stepanovich.

Maria Ivanovna and the old servant Ivan Andreevich to see my mother in the village. I felt very bad while I was in Novospasskoe, as I did on every subsequent visit to the village.

On the eve of my departure from Novospasskoe my brother-in-law Yakov Mikhailovich Sobolevsky said something—in what connection I don't remember—about my wife's unfaithfulness, and in such a positive manner that I blew up. I told him forthwith that if what he said were true I would leave my wife—which he ventured to doubt I would do. All the way back to Petersburg I was in a feverish state. Hurt ego, vexation, anger tormented me without letup.

In Petersburg I got out of the carriage and went home with a hired coachman, thinking of coming on my wife unawares, but they were expecting me and it was apparent that my ladies had taken precautionary measures.

On the pretext of illness I spent the night in my study, where my wife's brother, Aleksei Petrovich Ivanov, was living at that time. He was a naval lieutenant and a fine fellow. My wife's behavior greatly distressed him, for he sincerely liked me and in my absence had often spoken to his mother about his sister's outrageous connivance.

My wife and mother-in-law could not help noticing the changes in me. The former begged me on her knees to protect her from scandal, and although I tried to calm her at this time, I did not give up the plan I had resolved upon: to catch her in the act. All my moves led to nothing, however, and, in a state of torment, I consulted a wise and experienced distant relative, Aleksander Vasilevich Kazadaev.[45] He had been a friend of my father and was a devoted and helpful confidant to our family, one who had many times helped us with his good advice and, indeed, had had considerable influence in the management of our affairs.

Here again, though, everything was in vain until, as it were,

[45] Aleksander Vasilevich Kazadaev (1774–1854), senator, author of historical works, lover of music. He was a distant relative of Glinka.

chance served me better than all my schemes or the advice of others.

Exhausted by my worries, I once fell asleep in the presence of my mother-in-law and my wife. I can sleep soundly through loud noises and clatter, but a rustle or a soft whisper will wake me up at once, and this was precisely what happened. An old Finnish servant woman of my mother-in-law came into the room and quietly whispered something to her in German. I pretended I was asleep, and even began to snore a little, all the time trying to catch every word of this stealthy conversation. Finally, I heard with my own ears how my mother-in-law and the old woman were arranging a rendezvous for my wife and her lover. This was enough for me; without saying a word about it I took leave of my wife the next day and went to Nikolai Stepanov's, who knew all about my plans.

Aside from this particular bit of deceit I had good reason to be annoyed with my wife for her disrespect to my mother, who had always treated her very kindly, often even giving her presents. For example, while I was in Little Russia in 1838, my mother had gone to Petersburg on business and had stayed in my apartment. My wife and mother-in-law were then in Revel. When they came back, instead of being nice to my mother and taking care of her, they went so far as to remove even essential pieces of furniture from her room!

After considering everything, I decided to announce my intention of leaving my wife in a letter, which I sent to her on the evening of November 6. The letter went about as follows:

> Reasons, which I think should not be discussed, compel me to leave you, but this should be done without quarrels or mutual recriminations. I pray that Providence will keep you from fresh misfortunes. I, of course, shall take all measures to try to order your lot satisfactorily, and so I plan to give you half my income.[46]

[46] Very much like a letter to his mother, dated November 8, 1839, which contained a copy of this letter.—Written in the margin in the hand of V. V. Stasov.

This letter did not have much effect on Maria Petrovna. But the next day, when I ordered my own serfs to leave the apartment, to bring the horses given me by my mother, to remove my sister's needlework from the furniture in the parlor, and to get other things of sentimental value, since they had been given to me by good and faithful friends (all the rest, such as diamonds, furniture, carriage, and so on I left to my wife), well, then Maria Petrovna began to weep in earnest; it was even said that the tears destroyed her make-up.

All the females in Petersburg, commanded by Countess E. M. Saltykova and E. A. Glinkina, rose against me and there was no limit to their calumnies. To avoid disagreeable encounters, I admitted no one save a few of my most devoted friends, became ill, and because of that stayed fast in Stepanov's apartment in Garnovsky's house at the Ismailovsky Bridge. A few days after the break with my wife, Senator Sumarokov (who had been fond of Maria Petrovna and me) invited me to visit him at noon the next day. As was my custom, I arrived a half-hour early. This visibly disturbed the Senator and he kept saying that he had asked me to come at exactly twelve o'clock. I suspected his designs against me and I was not mistaken; at exactly twelve o'clock, the door opened and, with an air of importance there entered the priest who had taught me and married me, Aleksei Ivanovich Malov.[47] Everybody began urging me to make peace with my wife or, at the very least, to live with her, even though apart, but anyway under the same roof. This last proposal was the Senator's own idea.

For a whole hour I stubbornly and skillfully defended myself and finally so successfully destroyed all their arguments that they were forced into silence.[48]

After this I did not leave the house for a month; I went to see

[47] Teacher of religion at the Blagorodny School until 1827.

[48] Richard A. Leonard writes of Glinka's separation in his *A History of Russian Music*: "It would be hard to place the blame on either party, for while the composer would have been a trial for any woman, being undependable, indolent, and a libertine, his wife Maria was extravagant and frivolous."

Lvov just once—to tell him I was not up to working any more. He persuaded me to stay for another two weeks, though, in order to advance to the next rank. On December 18, 1839, I left the service with the rank of collegiate assessor.

At this time E. K. became dangerously ill. My sister Maria Ivanovna, who had frequently visited me at Garnovsky's house, had kept this from me for fear of distressing me.

It was not too bad living at Stepanov's. I made sketches with his younger brother, Vladislav—mostly of trees. In addition, among our constant visitors were Captain Tilicheev[49] of the Life Guard Hussar Regiment, a very clever and cultivated man; the regimental doctor Sadovsky; Sergei Nikolaevich Muraviev (Timei), who had taken an ardent interest in philosophy; and, finally, Yannenko. We had no piano, but at least there was a lot of lively, agreeable talk.

Peter Stepanov was away and so for the time being he had lent part of his apartment, specifically, a room covered all over with caricatures and vivid diabolical drawings on a black and white field like a chess board, created by Nikolai Stepanov himself, to an officer of the Life Guard Hussar Regiment. He had a bulldog which behaved so badly that every morning a currycomb had to be used to clean the room and then the currycomb itself fumigated to destroy the foul smell.

At times, such well-known literary figures as Filimonov,[50] Benediktov,[51] and Bernet[52] also came to Stepanov's.

---

[49] Igor Tilicheev, friend of Glinka, subsequently governor of Orel Government.

[50] Vladimir Sergeevich Filimonov (1787–1858), lyric and comic poet. His poem *The Dunce Cap* was well known.

[51] Vladimir Grigorevich Benediktov (1807–1873), Russian poet, for the most part of nature and of love—usually with an erotic tinge. Belinsky attacked him as the "poet of the bureaucrats, of society balls and dances . . . completely lacking in irony or any depth of thought." An intimate friend of Nestor Kukolnik.

[52] Bernet, a pseudonym of poet A. K. Zhukovsky.

# 9

## *First Performance of* Ruslan and Ludmila

THAT winter my mother came to stay with my sister and later I myself moved in with them. E. K. had recovered, and I wrote for her an orchestral waltz in B Major. Then, for one occasion or another, I did Pushkin's romance *I Recall That Wondrous Moment.*

In February my first cousin Sofiya Ivanovna Nolde (the same one with whom I had become friends while I was still in boarding school) arrived. She had two daughters and one son. The elder, Evgeniya Karlovna, was about fourteen; she had an interesting face and was even at that time a good musician. She later married P. P. Ryndin.

At the end of February my mother and I went to the village, going first to see my sister Ludmila Ivanovna Shestakova at her husband's estate Logachevo, situated about a mile from Novospasskoe. There I warmed myself a little by the stove in a corner room and then went home.

All during my stay in Novospasskoe,[1] that is, from the first of March to the end of April, I was sick. Loss of sleep, loss of appetite, and nervous distress brought me to such an agitated state that I was not up to traveling alone and so I persuaded K. F. Hempel to accompany me to Petersburg, which we reached in good order

1 Development of the *Kamarinskaya.*—Penciled in the margin in Glinka's hand.

in early May. Hempel and I took a small room at the Revel Inn in Novy Lane.

There I learned that even snoring has its virtuosi. Hempel, as I have said before, was a good musician, but at snoring he was outstanding. He would start by sniffling, then pass to gentle snoring accompanied by whistling; next, he made smacking noises, all this *crescendo*, and finally, he would emit pitiful groans and the concert would usually end in a fierce, penetrating cry, waking up both the virtuoso himself and me. He was fat and plethoric, and choked at night.

Hempel did not stay long in Petersburg. After he left I remained only a little while at the Revel Inn and then moved in with my sister Maria Ivanovna and my brother-in-law, plus their children, in Troitsky Lane. I had a bedroom and a large, airy study with a private exit.

On my name day, that is, May 21, while I was walking from the Revel Inn to Stepanov's, where I passed most of that day, the melody of the bolero *O Beautiful Maid of Mine* came to me.

I asked Kukolnik to write some lines for this new melody and he agreed, at the same time offering me some other romances he had written. It seems that it was this that gave Plato the idea of the twelve romances, published afterwards by P. I. Gursakalin under the name *Farewell to St. Petersburg*. I had several spare melodies, so the work went along very well, I must say.

Meanwhile, in early spring the state of E. K.'s health became very uncertain. Her doctor told her she was threatened with tuberculosis and that she would have to leave Petersburg for a warmer and more salubrious climate. This upset me very much but I determined, no matter what, to help E. K. I decided to persuade her and her mother to go to the south of Russia, where they had relatives, and in the meantime I asked my mother to send me seven thousand rubles, promising not to bother her again for a whole year.

I often went sketching in water colors with Shirkov, but without any great success. At his request I began to write the *Kamarinskaya* for piano, three hands, but it came out as such rubbish that on the spot I tore up what I had written.[2]

From the bolero I constructed an entire piece for piano. Herman transposed it very successfully for his own orchestra, along with the waltz fantasy in B minor. Both these pieces were very popular with the public.[3] On this occasion our Brotherhood stayed several days in Pavlovsk, where we very gaily passed the time.

My mother sent the money in Sobolevsky's name (I had kept my plans secret). Without losing any time, I set to work with the seven thousand rubles, that is, I bought a carriage for E. K. and her mother, who were not in any too sound a financial position. I also ordered a carriage for myself—I wanted to leave Petersburg (hence the collection of romances called *Farewell to St. Petersburg*). I was not really ill, yet not really well either; my troubles were a heavy weight on my heart, and vague, gloomy thoughts crowded my brain unasked.[4]

By the middle of August everything was in readiness for the ladies to leave for the south of Russia. The Kukolniks and all the Brothers—sincere friends all—did not want to part from me, and perhaps for a long while (as I surmised) had planned in secret a display of their affection. The Kukolniks had arranged a farewell

[2] Glinka thought of treating the *Kamarinskaya* theme in 1840, but it was not until eight years later that he completed this symphonic "scherzo fantasy"—one of his best pieces—based on two Russian themes mingled together, a wedding tune and a dance tune. Tschaikovsky said of the *Kamarinskaya*: "All Russian composers who followed Glinka, including myself, continue to this day to borrow contrapuntal and harmonic combinations whenever they have to develop a Russian dance theme."

[3] The B minor waltz fantasy was written in Pavlovsk in 1839. It was popularly called the *Pavlovsk Waltz*, and also the *Melancholy Waltz*.

[4] Glinka wished to go abroad with Mlle. Kern but decided against it, partly because of letters from his mother trying to break up the affair.

evening for me for August 10, to which, aside from good friends
and the family, they also invited some artists and writers.[5]

I sang a farewell song with exceptional spirit, our Brotherhood

[5] The farewell dinner for Glinka had the following program (devised by
Kukolnik):

### Ceremonial Send-Off for M. I. Glinka

#### Act One

*Introduction.* The guests assemble at 4 o'clock and converse as much as they
like and with whomever they like; *tête à têtes* permitted.

*Chorus.* Dinner. *Tête à têtes* prohibited from soup to end of party.

*Aria, with chorus.* Mikhail Ivanovich drinks his coffee and smokes his pipe.
The chorus accompanies him.

*Cavatina.* Mikhail Ivanovich sings:

    1) Rizzio's Romance.

    2) Jewish Song.

    3) The Lark.

    4) The Steamship.

*Chorus.* Drinking *pousse-café*, laughing; anyone who wants to can cry, and
this may be done *a parte* . . . and return to the portrait gallery with a happy
expression.

#### Act Two

*Overture.* Mikhail Ivanovich, Palagin and Yakov make a big fuss about performing something on piano, violin and bass. . . .

*Chorus.* Drink tea.

*Aria.* Mikhail Ivanovich sings:

    5) Barcarole.

    6) Cradle Song.

    7) Konya.

    8) Lodesko.

*The chorus sings.*

    9) To Ilinishna.

The *finale* of the Second Act is improvised by guests designated by selected
Minoses.

#### Act Three

*Overture.*   9) Chivalrous-type romance, with accompanimamament.
        [Kukolnik's faulty numbering here indicates
        how lightly the whole thing must have been
        regarded.]

*Aria.*     10) Romance from Bürger (*Ask Not the Songstress
        for a Song*).

*M. I. sings.* 11) Bolero.

The chorus has supper and works up a *finale* according to their inspiration,
starting off with

    12) The Good-By Song.

Choir sang, and in addition to the piano we had two clarinets and a bass. Although this evening was supposed to be of an "artistic" and friendly type, it was not without laughter. Someone stole a drink from Yakov, and in his distress he drank one glass of Madeira too many. At that point he became dissatisfied with being merely a listener and decided to take part in the farewell chorus. With all possible confidence he grabbed Memel's bass and started to play, but his arms would not move and he just stood there looking all about in astonishment.

On August 11, I left Petersburg. E. K. and her mother were at Gatchina, where I met them and accompanied them to Katezhna, where we parted, they for Vitebsk and I for Smolensk.

At my mother's I began to mull over my plans. You see, I had no passport and no money. Moreover, for several days before leaving Petersburg, E. K., in a fit of jealousy, had grievously distressed me with wearisome and undeserved reproaches. Still, I gradually began to get back to my normal self, thanks to the combined effect of planning for the future and remembering the past.

I set to work and in three weeks had written the introduction to *Ruslan.* I had begun it at Novospasskoe and finished it at the estate of my brother-in-law Nikolai Dmitrievich Gedeonov (with whom I had stayed in Berlin in 1834).

I caught a chill on the way back to Petersburg the night of September 14–15. I asked for tea at a post station (Gorodets, if I am not mistaken) and after warming up a bit continued my trip. I was in a feverish condition all night long, my imagination became inflamed, and that night I got the idea (and also thought it out pretty well) of the finale which later served as the basis for the overture to *Ruslan and Ludmila.* In Petersburg I stayed with the Kukolniks. Nestor was living in a separate apartment. Sometimes I visited the Aleksandrov family, which consisted of the father, mother, two sons, and three daughters, the youngest of whom I taught singing. Plato was courting the elder, whom, as a matter of fact, he later married. I was more often at home, though;

as an aftereffect of my cold I had a dull but tormenting pain in my right side that began to bother me every day about sunset. When the Brotherhood broke up, Yannenko stayed with me more often than with the others. To loosen his tongue a little, I once asked him to tell me about his life and marriage. Well, he then told me in detail how he had been a tutor with the Stepanovs' father, at that time governor of Omsk Government, and of how he went to Siberia, where, feeling sorry for the lonely English governess also with the Stepanovs then, he married her. This Englishwoman (Kristina Ivanovna) returned her thanks to him by supporting him in the last years of his life.

Despite my illness I went to work once more, this time on Ludmila's scene in Act IV. Soon afterward, at the request of the Kukolniks, I wrote the overture, the interludes, the song *The Wind Is at the Gate*, and the romance *Rakhili's Dream* for Nestor's[6] new drama, *Prince Kholmsky*. My music was played quite well, but the play was not successful and had only three performances.

In November, I became dangerously ill when a burning fever suddenly developed No doubt it came from a cold I had caught the evening before going home on foot without my galoshes. That evening, however, I felt nothing special and had sat for an hour or so with Plato, *arguing*, as always, and we even sat drinking a bottle of *church wine*[7] (which is what we called the cheapest *Médoc*) each. The next day, everyone was up and ordering tea, but I was still in bed when Plato came in and said, "Mischa, time to get up." I tried, but could not. He then examined me carefully, took my pulse, and sent for my doctor, Shering. They induced me then to move into Plato's room—he gave up his bed for me and all during this illness and recuperation took very good care of me. Shering managed to control the fever in three days with homeo-

6 Nestor Kukolnik, of course.

7 In Russian, "church wine" (or, more properly perhaps, "sacramental wine") can also mean simply "red wine" in nonreligious contexts.

pathic powders—*Nux vomica, Belladonna,* and *Dulcamara*—in doses of one of each kind once a day. I was very weak for a while afterward, though, and a rash broke out all over my body. On my left side, near the heart, it ran together into a single mass. No doubt one of the principal causes of this rash lay in my long-continued afflictions of various kinds. Despite Shering's constant care the rash stayed with me for several months, and when it had gone, yellowish, liverish spots lingered for a long time on my skin.

When I felt better, I began again on *Ruslan* and at the same time wrote *Tarantella* at the request of Myatlev.[8]

Despite the sad state of my finances I was living well enough without being a burden to others. Yakov could make a wonderful soup from sour cabbage and gruel. P. P. Ryndin, with whom I became very close at this time, did not disdain such meager offerings and gladly came to dinner with me, when we would also have a bottle of our church wine. I was often at Pavel Vasilevich Engelhardt's,[9] for his wife, a good-looking woman and still young, frequently invited me. After my illness they would send a fur-lined carriage for me, as well as a fur coat to still further protect me from the cold. Sofiya Grigorevna loved music; for her I wrote the romance *How Sweet to Be With You,* words by P. P. Ryndin, and I often played for her excerpts from my new opera, especially Ludmila's scene in Chernomor's castle. My cousin Sofiya Ivanovna Nolde and her children were living at Pavel Vasilevich's. It was thus very pleasant for me there: at dinner the hostess would seat me next to her, with the ladies, and they themselves would entertain me—while there was no end at all to the jokes and stories. From time to time I also went to see the widow, by which I mean

[8] Ivan Petrovich Myatlev (1796–1854), poet and humorist, author of the book *Sensations and Notes of Mme. Kurdyukova abroad, dans l'étranger* (1840–44), in which he poked fun at the Russian aristocracy in its slavish imitation of foreign customs. Turgenev used the first line of Myatlev's poem *The Roses* in his prose poem *How Fine and Fresh the Roses Were.* Myatlev's song *The Lanterns* was widely popular.

[9] Pavel Vasilevich Engelhardt (d. 1849) was the father of Vasily Petrovich Engelhardt, Glinka's friend who had custody of many of his music manuscripts.

the charming family Mollerius, and I would also drop in on the Aleksandrovs.[10]

About this time the elder brother of the Kukolniks, Pavel Vasilevich,[11] arrived from Vilna, where he was a professor of history at the university. His presence among us enlivened things. Nestor wrote a chorus for him, I wrote and played music with him, and all in all, we received him in grand and festive style. On this occasion, too, Nestor wrote some verses, beginning thus:

> All Praise, P. V., to you!
> All Glory is yours, too!
> Here now is your honored seat,
> Pray sit you down and eat!

I don't recall the music. I think it was a solo for Lodi to sing.

Pavel Vasilevich was a very fine fellow and a lover of society, especially the society of women. He was amiable, he could sing, and he knew how to perform various stunts at parties. For example, he did a beautiful imitation of Jews in a synagogue. His ruling passion, however, was writing tragedies dealing with the early Christian era. When any of his work was read, he would be thrown into such rapture that he would cry out suddenly, often alarming his audience.

In the early part of 1841, I wrote an E Major graduation chorus at the request of the inspector at the Ekaterinsky Institute, P. G. Obodovsky,[12] to his words. I sometimes attended rehearsals at the Institute, where the chorus performed very well. For this work His Imperial Majesty the Emperor gave me a ring, an emerald set with diamonds, which I immediately sent to my mother. Because of the Empress' illness, dances and concerts were being held at the palace rather than at the Institute. I was invited, but I couldn't

---

[10] Timofei Aleksandrovich Aleksandrov, lawyer, acquaintance of Glinka, and father-in-law of Plato Kukolnik.

[11] Pavel Vasilevich Kukolnik, who died on December 9, 1848, was proprietor of the estate Novosiltsev.

[12] Plato Grigorevich Obodovsky (1805–1864), writer, dramatist, and inspector of the Ekaterinsky Institute in St. Petersburg.

go because I was notified too late to be able to buy the necessary shoes, silk stockings, and white gloves.

At Easter time I moved in with the Stepanovs, who had complained that I was favoring the Kukolniks. Nikolai lived in a separate apartment. Peter Stepanov gave me the famous room plastered with caricatures and devilish drawings. At night, when the lights of passing carriages would strike the room for an instant, strange figures would flitter, one after the other, and it seemed to me that the death's head sitting on the oven would grin at me in a mocking way. At any rate, I often thought it was laughing at my sufferings, and at such times I slept poorly, often giving in to sorrowful reflections on my fate. Despite the sickly state of my spirit I continued to work on the opera. Dr. Sadovsky came one time, lit up a cigar, and, looking at my work, said to me with a self-sufficient expression: "I think if I should perhaps flog you a bit, brother, you might write better."

Pasta, who came to see us in Petersburg in October, 1840, went to see my opera *A Life for the Tsar.* When Petrova began to sing *Oh, 'Tis Not for Me That Blows the Desolate, Stormy Wind,* accompanied, of course, by four cellos and a bass, Pasta turned to me and said: "How wonderfully those cellos weep!"

In early spring my brother-in-law Yakov Mikhail Sobolevsky arrived in Petersburg with his son (the one who was half-deaf) and my sister Elisaveta Ivanovna, who had assumed the upbringing of her nephew. They were going to Paris to try everything possible to cure the boy. My mother, from whom the sickly state of my spirit had not been kept, wished me to go with them, and in point of fact sent the money for the trip.[13] I did not go with them, however, for this reason.

---

[13] Glinka wrote Shirkov about the proposed trip on March 29, 1841: "You are right; I am going reluctantly, really under compulsion. I have done everything I could to go to Little Russia instead of Paris, but her relatives and my mother's wish (she is good, but perhaps too cautious) have destroyed my hopes. I must go, I must sacrifice myself for my mother and, it may be, also for her [E. Kern's] own happiness."

Not long before the arrival of my brother-in-law with his son and my sister a rumor was aired about town that Maria Petrovna had got married. This apparently absurd story was, in fact, warranted: it also seemed that the St. Petersburg Consistory had been informed of this illegal marriage. Moreover, written proof of the illegal tie between my wife and V[asilchikov] had come into my hands. After I had reflected for a while I requested dissolution of my marriage[14] and then went at once to my mother, with whom I spent about four days. Returning to Petersburg in June of 1841, I occupied myself with the business of ending my marriage. Maria Petrovna remained in isolation for a long time, feigning illness, but at last she presented herself at the Consistory. At the confrontation I restrained my anger and stood quietly. Maria Petrovna wept. After the usual threefold admonitions I declared that I could not give up my intention, that I was compelled to this by family circumstances, and that I was not prompted by malice, as proof of which I begged forgiveness of my wife for any suffering I might involuntarily have caused her.

Confrontation with Maria Petrovna's lawyer, someone by the name of Fedorov, was less difficult for me. I listened in silence to his accusations and in my turn repeated only that I stood by my first testimony. Despite all the unpleasant fuss in connection with the dissolution of my marriage, at the end of the year I began to work again.

Yakov Mikhailovich, with his son and my sister Elisaveta Ivanovna, returned from Paris at the start of the season. All attempts to help the half-deaf nephew had been fruitless. My brother-in-law remained for a short while in Petersburg and then went on to the village. My sister and I, with my nephew, moved into Shuppe's house (formerly Varvarin's) across from the Opekun-

---

[14] Glinka's divorce decree was granted on May 15, 1841. The process was handled in instances: the Consistory (up to 1843) and the Synod (1843–47). The whole affair gives a picture of bureaucratic delay, red tape, and harassment, at a time when Glinka's musical genius should have been at its peak of expression.

sky Council[15] in Meshchansky Street. My sister and nephew took a comfortable apartment, where we ate all our meals. I lived alone on the same floor in two small but very well-lighted rooms. Even before the end of summer I had felt an extraordinary inclination to write music, and this feeling was still with me. Moreover, I had begun to study sketching, mainly *landscapes*, with Solntsev,[16] a student at the Academy, and was doing well enough to copy a number of scenes for my friends. On one of my drawings K. Brullov wrote: "Not bad at all."

I would have dinner at my sister's and sometimes stay for a while afterwards, when she would play the piano, I accompanying her on the violin in, among other things, Beethoven's F Major *Sonata.*

She had a young girl (a serf) in her service who had learned to make dresses at a milliner's and had been assigned by my mother as a maid for my younger sister, Olga. This girl was eighteen years old, very well built, and quite pretty. She dressed very simply, however, but neatly and becomingly. I was frequently entertained by her very amusing, unexpected remarks. For example, she called my opera *Ruslan and Ludmila* "her" opera. (Yakov Ulyanov also, in speaking of *A Life for the Tsar*, usually referred to it as "our" opera.) In a word, she could in all fairness be called a *grisette*, and in a short time I had become quite accustomed to her:

> Habit turned to feeling,
> Feeling, to many happy days, *etc.*

I was indebted to her, as a matter of fact, for many, many pleasant moments. I was so content at home that I very seldom

[15] The Opekunsky Council controlled orphanages, most female educational institutions, poorhouses, and homes for the deaf and for deaf-mutes. As an organ of the "Administration of Institutions founded by the Empress Maria" it could issue decrees within its field of competence, had the close protection of the imperial family, and disposed of considerable funds—much of which was said to have been appropriated by Council members for their own use.

[16] Fyodor Grigorevich Solntsev (1801–1892), artist and archaeologist, a pupil of K. P. Brullov.

went out, but by staying at home I worked so earnestly that in a short time I had finished most of the opera. Looking it over, however, I found that the parts of my new opera were not interconnected, that is, they had no unity or common bond. In order to remedy this I invited Nestor and Mischa Gedeonov to dinner. Not only had I made peace with them, as well as with their brother Stepan Aleskandrovich, but we had become quite close in the process. Another guest at this dinner was Vladislavlev,[17] at that time staff officer on active duty with the Corps of Police. He loved art, painting, and, in particular, music. I was on friendly terms with him and had borrowed his silver and table linen for my dinner.

Because Shirkov was leaving for the Ukraine, Kukolnik and Gedeonov got busy helping me with the difficult job of making a whole out of the separate and diverse parts of my opera. Kukolnik wrote verses for the finale and Ratmir's scene in the third act, *Burning Heat and Scorching Sun*. Gedeonov wrote a little duet for Finn and Ruslan, *Thanks Be to Thee, My Wondrous Protector*, to follow Finn's ballad; Finn's recitative in the third act, *Warriors! Trait'rous Naina! etc.*; and the prayer for four voices which ends the third act. I myself wrote the scene between Farlaf and Naina and Farlaf's rondo, as well as the first part of the third-act finale. Thus it happened that the verses for the libretto, in addition to those taken from Pushkin's poem, were written by Markovich, V. F. Shirkov, Kukolnik, Mischa Gedeonov, and myself.[18]

[17] Vladimir Andreevich Vladislavlev (1807–1856), police official. He published a literary almanac, *Dawn*, from 1839 to 1843.

[18] In a foreword (February, 1872) to a collection of Glinka's letters to Shirkov, V. V. Stasov discussed the composer's work on *Ruslan*: "The consideration of the problem of each character and scene is with Glinka . . . so painstaking, detailed, and attentive . . . that once and for all the reproach that he concerned himself only with the musical side and handed the libretto over to casual and alternating librettists must be discarded [Glinka himself seemingly encouraged this erroneous view when he returned from abroad in the 1850's]. . . . But au-

My mother and younger sister Olga arrived at Easter time, 1842, to spend the year in Petersburg so that Olga could finish her education. She was then sixteen or seventeen. Soon after they arrived we moved into Davidov's house on Gorokh Street. My mother, along with the sisters and my nephew, occupied the first floor, while I found two rooms on the courtyard—with a kitchen.

Before long the opera had reached the point where the remainder could not be written without taking into account the settings and without working along with the ballet master and set designer. And so (in April of 1842, if I am not mistaken) I presented myself to the director, Gedeonov, with the score. Without any discussion at all he accepted my opera, ordered at once that arrangements be made to stage it, and, according to my wishes, instead of a single payment of four thousand rubles agreed that I was to receive pay for each performance, that is, 10 per cent of two-thirds of the total taken in at the door. Soon after that my score was given to the theatrical music office, and when the parts of the principal actors and the choruses were ready, I set about rehearsing my music.

I had to work out certain things with the ballet master, Tityus, a man of extremely limited talents. To ease the way, I contrived

thentic documents now published, plus letters and programs written in his own hand irrefutably demonstrate just the opposite: *no composer has ever occupied himself with a libretto and all its details* from the most important down to the most trivial more than Glinka, nor has any composer ever left anything to the arbitrariness and taste of his librettist less than Glinka."

It has now been fairly clearly established who wrote what parts of *Ruslan.* Of twenty vocal numbers, Shirkov wrote most of the words for twelve. Of the rest, one entirely (the Persian chorus) and another for the most part (Finn's ballad, treated by N. Markovich) belong to Pushkin. The other six were divided up as follows: the scene between Farlaf and Naina and Farlaf's rondo, as well as the first part of the finale in Act II to Finn's recitative (the *Patter Song*), were written by Glinka himself; Mikhail Gedeonov wrote the last part of the third-act finale and the short duet between Finn and Ruslan in Act II. N. Kukolnik wrote a recitative and chorus, a duet for Ratmir and Finn, and the Act V finale. Finally, Shirkov wrote Ratmir's scene in Act III, and Ratmir's romance is by Pushkin.

to give him a dinner (he loved to eat) and in order to humor him further I ordered his favorite dishes from a French restaurant, the Legrand. In addition to Ballet Master Tityus, I invited the Gedeonovs, Kostya Bulgakov[19] as a gay and agreeable conversationalist, and Pavel Pavlovich Kamensky, translator in the office of Director of Theaters Gedeonov, because, in our opinion, he was very good at the *lezghinka*. Since I had based the music for the fourth act on Eastern melodies, I wanted Tityus to do the dances themselves, as far as possible, in the Eastern manner, and for the solo in this dance, which I called the *Lezghinka*,[20] I had selected the dancer Andreyanova II, who was at that time a special protégée of the Director of Theaters. The dances in the third act, however, I left entirely up to Tityus. The dinner was a success, and the wine surely served its purpose: after dinner Kamensky danced the *lezghinka*, which did not suit the Frenchman Tityus too much, but in any event he did agree to stage the dance as I wanted it.

There was plenty of wine, so that when the Gedeonovs and Kamensky came in after the theater I could ply them with the very best sherry and lots of it.

Later they composed a sort of epitaph for me which included these lines with reference to this little party:

> He loved music and women
> Strangers, for him, would
> Stuff his pipe with Vakshtaba.
> He made his home at Davidov's,
> Not harming any one,
> Except for bottles of sherry.

For the time being I'll leave the theater and the opera to recall Liszt's visit to Petersburg.

[19] Konstantin Aleksandrovich Bulgakov (1812–1862), son of the Moscow postmaster and a Guards officer. He was a singer who had much success with Glinka's romances.

[20] Glinka's bold use of dissonance in the *Lezghinka* was so disturbing that the piece was often cut in early performances of *Ruslan and Ludmila*.

His appearance in February, 1842, caused a tumult among all the dilettantes, and even the society women. As for me, who had been living a secluded sort of life since the break with my wife, that is, from November, 1839, I was forced to come out among people again. Thus it was that a Russian composer, forgotten by almost everyone, had again to appear in the salons of our capital at the behest of a famous foreign artist. In spite of the general enthusiasm—partly my own, too—I can still give a full account of the effect Liszt's *playing* had on me. He played Chopin's mazurkas, nocturnes, and *études* and, in a word, all brilliant and fashionable music very nicely but with terribly affected "elegant" touches (*à la française, c'est avec exagerations de tout genre*). Less satisfactory, though (in my opinion), was his playing of Bach (whose *Clavecin bien tempéré* I knew almost by heart) and a Beethoven symphony which he himself had transcribed for piano. In Beethoven's sonatas and in classical music as a whole his execution was not of the requisite quality, and his way of striking the keys was jerky, as if he were chopping cutlets. His playing of Hummel's *Septet* suggested something close to contempt, and I thought that Hummel had played it incomparably better and *more simply*. Liszt played Beethoven's E Flat Major *Concerto* much better. In the last analysis, I cannot compare his manner of playing with that of Field, Charles Mayer, or even Thalberg, especially in the scales. I saw Liszt at affairs given by the Countesses Rastopchina and Palibina,[21] as well as the Counts Vielegorsky and Count Odoevsky. At Odoevsky's, Liszt played *à livre ouvert* several numbers from *Ruslan* from an autographed score of mine, not known to anyone before, and to the general astonishment he didn't miss a note.

Liszt's habits and manners could not but seem odd to me because I had not then been to Paris and knew of the *young France* only by hearsay. Aside from his very long hair, in society he

[21] The Countess Palibina was an amateur pianist.

sometimes resorted to a sort of dainty affectation and at other times to an arrogant self-confidence. For the rest, despite a certain patronizing air, he was generally well liked, especially among artists and young people; he gladly and wholeheartedly took part in the general merriment and was not at all loathe to carouse with us.

When we met in company, which happened fairly often, Liszt always asked me to sing him one or two of my romances. Best of all he liked *My Heart's Aflame with Desire*. He, in his turn, played some Chopin for me or some fashionable Beethoven.

At Easter, 1842, I became acquainted with the Tabaravsky and Serov families. Aleksander Nikolaevich Serov[22] was then a very young man, well educated (he had studied at the School of Law), and a very fine musician; he played the piano, and a little on the cello. He showed particular verve when playing at sight.

Our meetings in Merts' house came to an end—The Brotherhood dissolved. The first to move out and into a separate apartment was Nestor Kukolnik. Nevertheless, he remained a good friend of mine and at my request wrote some verses for my new opera and edited some I had already contrived myself. Whenever I told him I had written a scene or a number for the opera he would be overjoyed and would display an uncommon eagerness to hear the new work as soon as possible. He was, in general, one of the most agreeable conversationalists I ever knew in my life. It was impossible to be bored with him; he could talk wisely and wittily about everything. One evening he gave me a particularly clear and detailed account of the history of Lithuania, and when

[22] Aleksander Nikolaevich Serov (1820–1871), an outstanding Russian composer and music critic. He became acquainted with Glinka in 1842 and in the 1850's regularly attended his "musical evenings." He did much to promote Glinka's music and his position as the founder of Russian national music. In 1860, Serov wrote his reminiscences of Glinka. He was an intimate of V. V. Stasov and of "The Five" and also a propagandist for Wagner's music. In 1866, he began work on a ballet, *The Night Before Christmas*, and an opera, *Taras Bulba*, but completed neither.

РУСЛАНЪ И ЛЮДМИЛА.
ОПЕРА М. ГЛИНКИ
ИЗДАНІЕ П. ЮРГЕНСОНА ВЪ МОСКВѢ.

The Title Page from an Edition of *Ruslan and Ludmila*

Glinka at the Piano

I expressed my amazement, he smiled and said, "If the Tsar commanded, I could be an obstetrician tomorrow." And should I express an opinion contrary to his, he would simply say: "Mischa! I find I do not agree with that; let's have a drink." This meant, of course: let's have another glass of church wine.

V. I. Bogaev got married; Plato Kukolnik moved into the Aleksandrovs' house. Here he occupied the entire first floor, which was very nicely decorated, while the Aleksandrov family was lodged in the mezzanine. Most of The Brotherhood met at his place for parties, and he really knew how to give lively ones. There was singing, piano playing, dancing. At times, Nestor would read his latest work, or there would be agreeable conversation, and at the end, a tasty and ample supper still further disposed us all to that good feeling.

Not so frequent, but also very pleasant, were the parties at Vladislavlev's, where Russian and foreign artists sometimes met. Here, too, there was dancing and singing in the evening and a lot of gaiety. Later at night I often visited Mischa Gedeonov, who had started giving after-theater parties. He and his brother Stepan Aleksandrovich disposed their father so greatly in my favor that when he left for Moscow he permitted me to arrange production of my new opera according to my own ideas.

As a consequence of this agreement, Gaidukov (administrative clerk at the St. Petersburg Theaters Administration) and I examined the tremendous wardrobes belonging to the Administration and together determined which costumes had to be made over entirely and which could be renovated or altered. The costumes for the principal roles were made under Karl Brullov's direction. Brullov also gave his ideas on the sets to Roller, who had already made sketches in oils of the sets for *Ruslan and Ludmila*. These sketches are now in the possession of Nestor Kukolnik. Right after my dinner for Tityus (that was in the summer) he summoned me to dine with him at a dacha on Krestov Island, where he entertained me royally. Afterward he began to work on the dances, and I went willingly to school in order to understand his requirements and to make any changes that might be necessary. Thus it was that I had to introduce several rather stupid phrases in the third-act dances so that the dancing would be more vigorous.

Before Tityus began to create the dances for *Ruslan*, he indulged in some bragging about himself. "All dancing masters now are seated masters," he said, meaning that they taught sitting down; he, however, and one other ballet master, in Paris, were the only ones who could teach *standing*, that is, who could themselves dance. Then, with a violin in one hand and a bow in the other, he went into various steps and, gradually working up enthusiasm, finally executed an *entrechat* and other tricky maneuvers. All this was in the presence of pupils, dancers, understudies, and musicians, and seemed awfully funny.

I was leading a most agreeable life at that time: in the mornings I would revise some of the dances and work on a few unfinished parts of the opera; around noontime I would go to rehearsal at the theater or to the school,[23] and often be taken home from there in the theater's carriage along with the actresses. I had dinner at my mother's and afterward passed an hour or so with the family; at night I usually went to the theater, where I spent most of the time backstage. When I got home, my sister Olga would meet me with a laugh, and to my question "What are you laughing at, Oline?" she would reply: "You've come home—that means we'll have some fun!" And really, it wouldn't be a quarter of an hour before my sister and mother were laughing!

On August 10 my new opera was first tried by a quartet in my mother's apartment. Present were: first violins, Mes and Albrecht,[24] replacing old Cavos, who had died; second violin, Weitz-

23 School of Dramatic Arts.

24 Karl Frantsevich Albrecht (1807–1863), concertmeister and later conductor of the St. Petersburg opera.

mann; viola, cello, Shubert;[25] and bass, Memel.[26] Gunka[27] and Ral[28] were also there, the latter of whom I had given the job of orchestrating my war music. At this rehearsal I played the parts of the wind instruments on the piano; we had no singers. It was a great success, though, and when it was over my mother gave us all some wonderful refreshments while we talked pleasantly and laughed for a while at Weitzmann's funny tricks.

Rehearsals began in the fall—first in theater rooms, then on the stage. It was soon found that many numbers would have to be cut down; for example, Bayan's second song, *There Is a Desert Land,* had to be taken out of the introduction, and the final development (*développement et péroraison*) of the main theme

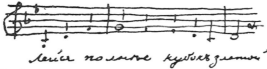

had to be eliminated later on.

The B Major chorus to Lel in ⁵⁄₄ time in the first-act finale was shortened.

In the second act, Finn's ballad was long, but I did not shorten it, and later the public became used to hearing it as I had orig-

[25] Karl Bogdanovich Shubert (1811–1863). A German by birth, he had a successful career as a cellist in Europe but moved to St. Petersburg in 1835. He was a soloist with orchestras of the St. Petersburg Theaters Administration, inspector of music at the School of Dramatic Arts, conductor of the St. Petersburg Philharmonic Society, and a member of the quartet composed of Venyavsky, Pikkel, Veikman, and Shubert. He composed many pieces for the cello and also a string quartet, *My Travels in the Kirghiz Steppes* (1862), which was the first attempt to use Bahkir, Tartar, and Kirghiz songs in Russian quartet music.

[26] Andrei Bogdanovich Memel (d. 1870), bass player with the St. Petersburg Theater Orchestra from 1822.

[27] Iosif Karlovich Gunka (1803–1883), violinist, music critic, composer, and teacher. A Czech by birth, he settled in Russia in 1823.

[28] Fyodor Aleksandrovich Ral (1802–1848), composer and conductor, chief of the Music Department of the St. Petersburg Theaters Administration (appointed in 1839); he was also in charge of military music for the Administration from 1842. In his latter capacity he made orchestral arrangements for several battle numbers in *Ruslan and Ludmila.*

inally written it. Golov's chorus, that is, the second-act finale, on which I had counted heavily, definitely did not go over and was actually sung so awfully that I myself couldn't stand listening to it.

In the third act, instead of the extremely difficult interlude I had written we had to begin directly with the chorus *The Deep of Night Falls o'er the Field*, the first couplets of which are sung off stage. In the finale, the trio *Why Love, Why Suffer?* had to be cut because it slowed down the action.

In the fourth act, Ludmila's scene, on which Stepanov had congratulated me when we were rehearsing in the theater rooms, did not go over at all on stage and this same Stepanov reproached me for not having properly gauged the theatrical effect!

A lot also had to be cut in the finale of this, and of the last act.[29]

In spite of all these developments, the stage director, M. S. Lebedev, guaranteed that the opera would go well.

I often worked on the overture directly for the orchestra in the stage director's office during rehearsals.

Gedeonov, back from Moscow, had some kind of a dispute with Roller. This had an important effect on the fate of my opera. The sets for the first three acts were good, although not entirely suitable for a Russian fairy tale.

I had counted most of all on the effect of the fourth act, laid in Chernomor's gardens. Of the magnificent and enchanting sets that could have seized the attention of the audience and made it forget the dramatic faults in the opera, Roller (probably out of pique) had made the most lackluster of all the sets in the opera. The castle looked like a barracks and the fantastic flowers on the sides of the proscenium were ugly and wretchedly painted in the dullest colors and merely smeared over with gold leaf.

Instead of a table laden with assorted choice viands for Ludmila, something in the nature of a pulpit rose up out of the ground, along with a queer kind of gilded, quivering shrub. In a word,

[29] There were some nasty surprises.—Written above this line in Glinka's hand.

this was not a set but a snare for the actors and the public; not even the best actress in the world, let alone Stepanova, could have played this scene effectively. You see, when the *clumsy* Chernomor appeared with his suite and the regimental band, there was no room for either musicians or dancers.

The last set in the fifth act was no better.

And now a new development added very considerably to my troubles.

Around 1840 or 1841, Bulgarin[30] was often at Nestor Kukolnik's place. I was on a friendly footing with him at the time, and even quite intimate. But then we quarreled—over trifles, nothing more. I don't see why I should conceal the reason for this tiff with Bulgarin. One time in Pavlovsk, Bulgarin was whispering at some length in Herman's ear while the public, meanwhile, was waiting to hear one of its favorite pieces; I said aloud, jokingly, to Herman: "Don't listen to him, he knows not a thing about music." Bulgarin got mad over this little joke. We were in the pavilion with the orchestra when Bulgarin started an argument. Since it was about music, it was naturally easy for me to explain to him, indeed to prove that he did not understand our art. This quarrel lasted for a long time and with quite a crowd around. Senkovsky,[31] with whom I was very friendly at that time, wishing to shield me from further unpleasantness, tried to make peace between Bulgarin and me. For this purpose he gave a dinner at Coulon's for the Belgian singer Merti and his mother (Merti later married the clarinetist Blaze,[32] who was with us for a long time and was much

[30] Faddei Venediktovich Bulgarin (1789-1859). A Soviet source describes him as a "reactionary and venal writer and journalist, an agent of the [counterrevolutionary] 3rd Division."

[31] Osip Ivanovich Senkovsky (1800-1858 or 1859), journalist, man of letters (he used the pseudonym "Baron Brambeus"), lover of music, serious Orientalist, and student of Arabic, Persian, and Turkish. Editor of several "reactionary" journals, he was an intimate of F. V. Bulgarin and, like him, was frequently attacked by Gogol and Belinsky.

[32] Arnold Joseph Blaze (1814-1892), Belgian clarinetist and professor at the Brussels Conservatory from 1842.

liked), Bulgarin, and me. We shook hands on this occasion as a sign of reconciliation, but I did not want to ask for his backing. When the talk came around to my opera, however, Bulgarin, with an air of mock commiseration, said: "It's too bad such a first-rate production has to be entrusted to *artists* who can't do it properly." To this I replied that I had written my opera knowing the artists who would perform it, that I had considered their talents, and that I was entirely satisfied with them.

A few days after this, at rehearsal, Leonov took me aside and told me the actors were mad at me. In point of fact, when I came on stage I could clearly see that they were indeed cool toward me and that everybody looked somehow upset. Petrova even flared up at me in anger and burst into reproaches, whereupon I learned that there had appeared in the *Northern Bee* an article maligning the artists and that the article had been attributed to me. I explained to Petrova that I had not read the article and knew nothing at all about the matter but that Bulgarin, in the article to which she referred, had printed precisely the words he himself had spoken to me during that dinner at Coulon's.

Since I saw I was convincing no one, however, I turned away from the excitable woman and left the stage director to get on with the rehearsal.

The musicians also (except for the respectable ones, such as Mes, Albrecht, Shubert, Memel, and a few others) were angry with me because of the Bulgarin article and began to play very sloppily, which was particularly noticeable in the overture and in the fifth-act finale.

Seeing all this, I asked the older musicians, namely the conductor, Albrecht, Mes, and Meingart, to try to persuade the young musicians to behave properly, "for if not," I added, "while I shall not be an informer, there will be others who would gladly tell the director that certain of the musicians are neglecting their work, and, as you know, a director is always glad for a chance to fire a musician."

"As for me, the way I feel," I concluded, "I think it would be a shame if anyone should suffer because of my opera."

At one of the last rehearsals Count Mikhail Yurevich Vielegorsky, after hearing the first half of Act V, turned to me and said: "Mon cher, c'est mauvais."[33]

"Retract those words, M. le Comte," I replied. "It may be that that did not produce an effect, but my music is most certainly not bad."

Subsequently, all this part of the fifth act was cut. I left all the cutting to Count Vielegorsky, who worked at it mercilessly, often eliminating the best parts and remarking with a satisfied expression: "I am, am I not, a master at making cuts!"[34]

November 27, 1842, was set for the first performance of *Ruslan and Ludmila.* Petrova[35] was ill, and the role of Ratmir had to be taken by the understudy Petrova,[36] who was a talented but nevertheless completely inexperienced and untried artist. No change could be made at this point, however, especially since the director did not like the elder Petrova.[37]

---

[33] "My dear fellow, it's bad."

[34] Aside from the cuts made in *Ruslan* by Mikhail Vielegorsky, Bayan's song, published separately as early as 1840, was banned by the censor because it had been dedicated to the memory of Pushkin.

[35] Anna Yakovlevna Petrova, nee Vorobieva, wife of O. A. Petrov.

[36] Anfisa Petrova, contralto, understudy to the *other* Petrova.

[37] Bulgarin's article, published in No. 250 of the *Northern Bee,* 1842, was intended to make trouble between the artists and the composer and to turn the former against the new opera; in this Bulgarin was quite successful. About a week later, however, V. F. Odoevsky had an article in the *St. Petersburg Herald* (No. 260, November 15, 1842) entitled "A Lover of Glinka's Music, of Truth, and of Moderation," a reply to Bulgarin. Of the impending *première* he wrote: "There are not many such musical talents as Glinka's in Europe, nor in Russian art are there many such subjects as Pushkin's *Ruslan and Ludmila.* . . . Those persons who already know how this significant combined musical-poetic production is being realized are delighted and enraptured. Those who as yet have no such knowledge fear they will be disappointed by the performance. They are perfectly right to be concerned about their own enjoyment of an opera, but with respect to the completeness and authority of this work, it would seem that they may be entirely reassured."

Despite the sick feeling that always came over me at first performances of my dramatic works, I had still not lost hope of success.

The first act went all right. The second act was not bad, except for Golov's chorus. In the third act, in the scene *Burning Heat and Scorching Sun*, the understudy Petrova was most unimpressive and the audience notably cooled. The fourth act did not have the anticipated effect. And at the end of the fifth act the imperial family left the theater. When the curtain came down, they began to call for me, but the applause was really not very enthusiastic and there was some active hissing, mostly from the stage and the orchestra.[38] I turned to General Dubelt in the director's box and said, "They seem to be hissing. Shall I take a curtain call?"

"Sure, go ahead," replied the General. "Christ suffered more than you."

Returning home from the theater, my mother and I hid our disappointment and cordially received the friends who had come in for supper. For my labors, my mother gave me a silver service for twelve.

The second performance was no better than the first. The elder Petrova was able to make the third performance, however, and she showed such feeling in her third-act scene that the audience was thoroughly enraptured. There was loud and long applause, and first I, then Petrova, was called out triumphantly. These calls continued through seventeen performances.[39] More than once Petrova became angry with me in this connection. During her

---

[38] Some witnesses thought the hissing was directed solely at Bulgarin because of his article affronting the artists. During the intermission, Bulgarin strolled through the theater condemning Glinka's opera, during which performance he was publicly rebuked by Kukolnik, who declared in a loud voice: "*Ruslan* may, perhaps, be bad, but Bulgarin is a scoundrel."

[39] After the *première* the increasing success of *Ruslan* was due not only to the appearance at the third performance of the great A. Ya. Petrova as Ratmir but also to S. S. Artemovsky's assumption of the role of Ruslan. O. A. Petrov, who had created the stage model for Susanin, and later Farlaf, was not good as Ruslan.

scene I would not be listening to her, since I was generally whispering with one of the pretty pupils in the wings, and so of course I was often late for the curtain calls.

During the winter, or, rather, from November 27 to Easter, the opera was performed thirty-two times. After that, it had a total of fifty-three performances in St. Petersburg.

Bulgarin did not confine himself to that article written just before the first performance. No indeed. With all possible malice he criticized the music and words and, what was very funny, carefully picked out primarily the words that I myself had written. It is common knowledge that Senkovsky defended me constantly and with great cleverness and wit. Prince Odoevsky also wrote a very kind article about my opera.[40] But when the talk would come around to *Ruslan*, Count Vielegorsky always said: "C'est un opéra manqué."[41] Another critic, in referring to the director, Gedeonov, once said: "What a pity you spent so much on producing Glinka's opera—it won't go over, you know."

"Not at all," replied Gedeonov. "I'm not sorry. I'm sure it will go over beautifully, and as for you, kindly try to write better."

Face to face, Gedeonov made fun of me, saying that I wasted

[40] Bulgarian seems to have been alone in his efforts to mislead the public and to destroy Glinka's opera. For example, O. I. Senkovsky had a long article in the December *Biblioteka dlya chteniya* in which he wrote: "With this opera M. I. Glinka has placed himself among the first composers of the entire world and alongside the very foremost of them. *Ruslan and Ludmila* is one of those magnificent creations which will never perish and to which a great people can point with pride in their art."

F. A. Koni, editor of the *Literary Gazette* also referred to *Ruslan and Ludmila* with deep respect, noting particularly its national essence and character. Then, hailing *Ruslan* as a work of musical genius, he wrote: "There was a time when everyone cried: '*Ruslan and Ludmila* is tiresome and boring'; now, most have become reconciled to it, and the time will come when it will be greeted with universal delight. Many are complaining that it has no tunes and that none of it sticks in the mind, but just wait! Before a month is out people will be dancing quadrilles, mazurkas, galops, and waltzes to these 'motifs,' and within a year, hurdy-gurdies will have carried this grand music to the masses of people all over Russia."

[41] "It's an opera that didn't quite come off."

musicians because there were times when some of them were not playing and that I should not write so learnedly; elsewhere, though, he always defended me vigorously.

# 10

---

## *Trip to Paris*

AT Easter time I received from the Theater Administration as my percentage three thousand silver rubles, which I gave to my mother to keep.

Liszt came to Petersburg for a second visit and during his stay often went to parties with us, along with the Gedeonovs (I had dedicated my opera *Ruslan and Ludmila* to Mischa) and Count Arkadi Pavlovich Kutuzov,[1] a most engaging and amiable conversationalist.

Liszt heard my opera and showed a true understanding of all the key passages.[2] Despite the many defects in *Ruslan* he reassured me as to its success. According to him, not only in Petersburg but also in Paris, my opera, which had thirty-two performances during the winter alone, could be regarded as having been well received. Rossini's *Guillaume Tell*, for example, had had only sixteen performances in its first winter.

I talked with him frankly about my views on art and my opin-

[1] Arkady Pavlovich Golenishchev-Kutuzov (1803–1859), amateur singer and friend of Glinka.

[2] The *Literary Gazette* had this to say of Liszt's attendance at a performance of *Ruslan and Ludmila* on April 18, 1843: "Liszt made no comment at all . . . and left the theater with an expression of astonishment and complete satisfaction on his face. It is strange: the opera did not seem long and dull to the No. 1 musician of Europe. Just judge for yourself now those who criticize *Ruslan and Ludmila* [a reference to Bulgarin]."

ions of composers. I said I thought Karl Maria von Weber was most disappointing (even in his *Der Freischütz*) because of his immoderate use of the dominant seventh in its first position. To this remark Liszt replied: "Vous êtes avec Weber comme deux rivaux qui courtisez la même femme."[3]

I remember very well the day of Liszt's departure. We had supper at Count Kutuzov's (I think). There was talk about my opera, and Count Mikhail Yurevich Vielegorsky said again: "Mon cher, c'est un opéra manqué." I was a little tired of hearing the same old thing, so I asked for the company's attention for a minute. "Gentlemen," I said, "I consider the Count to be one of the finest musicians I have ever come across." There was unanimous agreement to this. "Now then, with your hand on your heart, tell me, Count, would you have put your name to this opera if you had written it?"

"Of course, gladly," he replied.

"Then, please permit me, too, to be satisfied with my work."

Despite all these little attacks, inspired to some extent by *jalousie de métier*[4] (he was at that time writing his own opera *The Gypsies*), the Count was actually fond of me. In general, and today, too, he is very well liked by people and is always being carried away by fresh impressions and new sensations, just like a young man. When Rubini visited us (in March of 1843), the Count, tucking his chin under his outsize tie, said: "Mon cher, c'est Jupiter olympien."[5]

Ivan Ivanovich Rubini, as we called him, despite the cultivation of his voice and his assurance (aplomb), was *not* Jupiter but a ruin. I didn't like his voice even as early as 1830, in Italy; the first few times I heard it, especially, it sounded to me more like glass than like metal. Even in Italy I found his kind of singing artificial —this was in 1843—and I thought he carried exaggeration to a completely ridiculous height. He sang either with much too much

---

[3] "You and Weber are like two rivals courting the same woman."
[4] "Professional jealousy."       [5] "My dear fellow, it is Jupiter on high!"

strength or else you could hardly hear him; you might say he just opened his mouth while the audience sang his pianissimo for him, which made them feel good, of course, so they applauded with fervor. He gave several concerts at the Assembly Hall.

The parties at Mischa Gedeonov's got to be more and more lively and interesting. In addition to the Gedeonovs, these others were constant visitors: Count Kutuzov, Varlamov,[6] K. Bulgakov, P. P. Kemensky, Goronovich (Alisa),[7] Secretary to the Director Aleks. Lvovich Nevakhovich, Heidenreich, Dr. Bers, and my schoolmate Samarin.

We lived in perfect harmony and often had supper together, confining ourselves to the leftovers from the Director's dinner, and if that were not enough, we made up a sort of a pool and each would contribute whatever he happened to have. We broke up very late so that I rarely got home from Gedeonov's before five o'clock in the morning.

Samarin had written a romance, *I Love You, Lovely Rose,* which I set to music at K. Bulgakov's one night after the theater, as I remember it. About this same time I wrote a tarantella in A minor, ¾ time, for piano.

In 1843 also, if I am not mistaken, I wrote the romance *To Her,* translated from Mickiewicz' Polish by Prince S. Golitsyn.

My troubles and disappointments in the theater, as well as the breakup of my marriage, distressed me and I fell into a state of more or less indifference to everything. Although I had learned that Maria Petrovna had had a daughter by her second husband, I had no intention of persecuting her, rightly fearing further trouble, despite my mother's wish that I do something about it.

[6] Aleksander Egorovich Varlamov (1801–1848), teacher and composer of popular romances and songs. He published *The Complete School of Singing,* the first handbook for vocalists in Russian, in 1840. For ten years Varlamov sang in the Imperial Chapel Choir, became its Kapellmeister, and then went to Moscow as "composer of music" for the theaters there. Varlamov wrote more than 150 songs, some of which have become part of the national culture, music for *Hamlet,* ballets, choruses, and other pieces.

[7] Goronovich (Alisa) was a member of The Brotherhood.

In the spring my mother and my sister Olga Ivanovna went to the village, while my sister Elisaveta Ivanovna and her nephew went to the dacha at the Forestry Institute. I, staying at Davidov's house, usually had dinner and supper at Legrand's and there, out of boredom, I often caroused with friends. *Ce qui vient par la flûte, s'en va par le tambour,*[8] and so the money I had received for my opera did not last long.

E. K. had returned to Petersburg in 1842. I was seeing her less often now, and although we were friends, there was not that former glow and feeling to our relationship. She had got to know Maria Stepanovna K[rzhisevich],[9] who was then in Petersburg with her husband. At that time Maria Stepanovna was a pretty, gay, and attractive woman. Through her, or perhaps it was just by chance, I became very well acquainted with her relatives, the Tarnovskys.[10] Anna Nikolaevna Tarnovskaya was an utterly charming young woman. She became friends with E. K., and that summer, I passed some very agreeable time with Anna Nikolaevna, Maria Stepanovna, and E. K. The Tarnovskys' little boy called me "Unca Misa, tra-ta-ta."

In 1843, Ulybyshev[11] sent me his book on Mozart.[12] I read part

---

[8] "What comes with the flute, goes with the drum." Roughly, of course, "Easy come, easy go," or, in the Russian version, "As it is earned, so is it spent."

[9] Maria Stepanovna Krzhisevich (1824–1905), Poltava landowner, friend of E. E. Kern and Glinka.

[10] Grigori Stepanovich Tarnovsky (d. 1854), Poltava landowner, art lover, and hospitable host to poets, artists, and musicians. His wife, Anna Dmitrievna (d. 1854), was M. S. Krzhisevich's aunt.

[11] Aleksander Dmitrievich Ulybyshev (1784–1858), music critic, man of letters, and publicist. Born in Dresden, he was the son of the Russian ambassador to Saxony and himself served in the Russian Foreign Office from 1816 to 1830. In 1843, he wrote a three-volume biography of Mozart and in 1857 a critical study of Beethoven; he also wrote a number of plays and translated Dante's *Divine Comedy* into Russian. He had a good appreciation of Glinka's place in Russian music and supported the young Balakirev, early recognizing his musical gifts.

[12] The book Glinka refers to was Ulybyshev's three-volume *New Biography of Mozart, with a Review of the General History of Music and a Selection of Mozart's Principal Works*, published in French in St. Petersburg in 1843.

of it and studied anew all Mozart's operas from the scores. The remarks and criticism of Count M. Yu. Vielegorsky and this work I did on Mozart stimulated my critical spirit, which was further excited a little later on.[13]

In the summer of that same year, the eminent harpist De Vitte[14] arrived from Moscow en route to England, where he died the next year. He played with great precision and his compositions were not bad. I saw him constantly, now at his place, now at the Vladislavlevs', and finally one evening at the Tarnovskys'.

Soon after his departure I became ill, suffered for several months, and at last entrusted myself to Heidenreich, who cured me.

In the winter, Rubini, Tamburini,[15] and Viardot-García[16] arrived, and we had some Italian theater. Viardot was excellent, Tamburini also quite good, but Rubini sometimes sang indifferently, and then at other times his voice would fail him, which brought him to tears.

Among other things, they put on Mozart's *Don Juan.* All the principal roles were murdered; only Zerlina (Viardot) and Masetto (Artemovsky) were played well. Don Juan (Tamburini)

[13] Glinka's interest in criticism is indicated by his unfulfilled plan of publishing a music journal with V. F. Odoevsky and P. A. Vyazemsky. Not long before this, Glinka also thought—fruitlessly—of adding a music supplement to the *Northern Bee.*

[14] Nikolai Petrovich De Vitte (d. 1844), harp virtuoso and composer.

[15] Antonio Tamburini (1800–1876), Italian baritone, one of the great lyric artists of the nineteenth century. For ten years he sang with great success in London and Paris, at times with the famous Puritani Quartet, and also spent ten years in Russia. He was chiefly known as a singer of Rossini's music, but one of his principal parts was Don Giovanni.

[16] Michelle Ferdinande Pauline Viardot-García (1821–1910), mezzo-soprano, teacher, and composer. She was the daughter of the famous Spanish tenor and voice teacher Manuel del Pópolo García. The "Pauline" comes from Princess Pauline Golitsyn, one of her sponsors. Mlle. García had a highly successful singing career all over Europe and Russia, living first in Belgium, then in Germany (to 1871), and finally in France. Among her distinctions, she studied piano with Liszt. Turgenev wrote the words for operettas she presented in her little private theater, and Schumann dedicated to her his *Liederkreis.*

was insipid and dragged out the time unbearably. Rubini tried to
be a thunderer and sang the sweetish cavatina *Il mio tesoro* like a
pirate, menacing the audience and waving his right arm around.
I shall keep silence about the others, saying only that the German
conductor, Romberg (son of the celebrated Andrei Romberg),
acted as if he were conspiring against Mozart, whose masterful
(although not faultless) work he made the orchestra play pre-
tentiously and without fire. The public and even the papers took
up arms against the talented *maestro*, and to him, and not to the
incompetence and ignorance of music of most of the artists, they
ascribed the failure of the production of *Don Juan*. I wept from
chagrin and then and there took a dislike to Italian "songbirds"
and to fashionable Italian music.

Karl Brullov and then Yannenko also started coming to the
parties at Mischa Gedeonov's. Brullov had spent his youth in
Italy and for that reason loved Italian music. He used Gedeonov's
box, which suited him fine for he was a parsimonious man. He
talked wittily and with originality, though, so that he did a lot to
enliven our parties. He also went to Mischa's and Nestor's. At
this time, too, the Gedeonov's, especially Stepan, displayed a passion for imitating Rubini; Bulgakov and I were not far behind
them in this. Samarin and I, in our turn, acquainted our little public with anecdotes about Kolmakov and Oginsky. You might say
that we had our own theater. One time even Bulgakov and Nevakhovich very entertainingly put on *tableaux vivants*.

In the winter, my mother and my sister Olga came for the
marriage of my sister Elisaveta Ivanovna to Viktor Ivanovich
Fleri,[17] director of the School for Deaf-Mutes. During the ceremony my mother felt ill, but she forced herself to stay on anyhow.
A few days later I was at home (at Davidov's; my mother and
Olga were living elsewhere) enjoying the singing of my nightingale, who had flown out of his cage and perched on a fir tree I

[17] Viktor Ivanovich Fleri (d. 1856) was director of the School for Deaf-Mutes
in St. Petersburg and husband of Glinka's sister Elisaveta Ivanovna (1810–1850).

A Set Designed by A. A. Roller for *Ruslan and Ludmila*

Mikhail Ivanovich Glinka in His Later Years

had in the center of my parlor, where he was singing away, not only without any fear of me or my guests, but singing louder the more noise we made. Someone rang at the door, and Dr. Heidenreich came in. I invited him to look at my nightingale, but he explained to me at once that my mother was in danger, that she had a carbuncle, and that she would have to be operated on without fail the next day. Fleri and I made the necessary arrangements in secret and the next day at noon Heidenreich and the surgeon, Salomon, went to see my mother. The operation was a success, and neither my mother nor my sister was aware of the danger that had threatened her. My mother suffered some from the pain at first, but I stayed with her and kept her engaged in conversation, asking her about her youth and, in particular, about how she got married.[18] My sisters would come in the evening and we had a merry time. Heidenreich's assistant was the same girl, Lisette, who had been living with my sister at the time I was writing *Ruslan.*

In March my mother returned to the village, and my sister Olga went to stay with the Fleris. I saw my mother off in very cold weather and probably got chilled because right after that I experienced rheumatic pains. After my mother left, out of boredom I took to playing the violin before dinner to entertain my birds. I had sixteen of them, each of whom knew his own cage. In the mornings, though, they sang and flew about freely. After dinner I often went to see the Fleris. They would light a fire for me and when I had warmed up, I would play cards with Viktor Ivanovich's children (by his first wife). His elder daughter, Anyuta, about ten, was always cheating, and that made me angry.

Even before her departure my mother had decided to let me go abroad, to Paris, where I had never been before. The coming of spring dispelled my rheumatism and I began to get ready for the trip. Not wishing to go by myself, however, since I was then

---

[18] In his *Facts about M. I. Glinka and His Relatives* (1894), L. I. Shestakov tells of the romantic abduction of Evgeniya Glinka by Ivan Nikolaevich Glinka, with the co-operation of the composer's grandmother.

still very much indisposed, I asked Fyodor Dmitrievich Gedeo-nov[19] to go along with me. Once, long before, he had lived in Paris. Various little problems conspired to delay our departure. Meanwhile, summer came, and nearly all my friends had gone off to their dachas while I, in order not to pine away entirely, went to see Yannenko every day. General Astafiev, a schoolmate of mine, had built an addition on to a bathhouse belonging to his wife's father—Ponomarev—for Yannenko and his family. There was room enough here for them to live comfortably, and since on one side of the bathhouse there was a good-sized garden, it was very nice in the summertime. After tea in the morning I would go over to Yannenko's. K. Brullov would be there, and later other friends would join us. We dined and supped on contributions from everybody. They made a mask of my face at this time.[20] All in all, the time was passed pretty well.

By June everything was ready; a young French girl by the name of Adèle Rossignole was to accompany Gedeonov to Paris. I was at the Tarnovskys, as were E. K. and Maria Stepanovna. My carriage came for me, I said good-by to the ladies, went to pick up Gedeonov and Adèle, and we were off.

*Completed December 10, 1854*[21]

Not long before we left, that is, on my name day, May 21, Minister Bludov's[22] daughter had sent me an article by Henry Mérimée

[19] Fyodor Dmitrievich Gedeonov (b. 1797), brother of Glinka's brother-in-law, N. D. Gedeonov.

[20] From this mask, made by Ya. F. Yannenko and one of the Stepanov brothers, a bust of Glinka was fashioned, with the final touches given by K. P. Brullov. The original was broken, but the first copy from it is now in the Scientific Research Institute for Music and the Theater. Other copies, produced on the initiative of V. P. Engelhardt, are now found in music schools and museums throughout Russia.

[21] It is not known when the last part of this chapter, which follows, was written.

[22] Count Dmitri Nikolaevich Bludov (1785–1864), Russian government official under Nicholas I. In his youth (1815), he, together with Dashkov and V. A. Zhukovsky, organized the literary society *Arzamas*, to which Pushkin, Batyuskov, and others belonged. Bludov was in the diplomatic service in Sweden

(a cousin of Prosper Mérimée) which delighted me. None of my countrymen had, up until then, referred to me in such flattering terms.

The gist of the article is as follows:

M. Glinka's *A Life for the Tsar* is distinguished by a priceless originality—perhaps the first work of art which owes nothing to imitation. His talent has here been invested in such a simple and such a popular form. It is in its subject matter and poetry and music a most faithful summing up of all that Russia has suffered and has sung; here are her hates and her loves, her tears and her joys, her dark night and her radiant tomorrow. It is, first of all, a sorrowful lamentation, then a hymn of redemption so proud and so triumphant that the lowliest serf, if carried from his hut to the theater, would be moved to the depths of his being. It is more than an opera, it is a national epic, it is lyric drama restored to the noble purity of its original purpose, to a time when it was not a mere amusement or diversion, but a patriotic and religious act of solemnity. Although a foreigner, I have never seen this spectacle without a lively feeling of participation and understanding. (*A Year in Russia*, letters written from Moscow in 1840, published by the *Revue de Paris*, March, 1844.)

*Ruslan and Ludmila* was performed for the first time[23] on November 27, 1842. The performances through April, 1846, may be broken down as follows:

| | |
|---|---|
| 1842, November: 27, 29, 30 | 3 times |
| December: 1, 3, 4, 7, 9, 11, 14, 16, 22, 28, 30, 31 | 12 times |
| 1843, January: 2, 4, 7, 11, 15, 19, 25, 29 | 8 times |

and England and in 1826 received recognition when he was named to the commission investigating the Decembrists. In 1832, he became Minister of Internal Affairs and in 1837, Minister of Justice. In 1855, he was made president of the Petersburg Academy of Sciences and in 1862 chairman of the Imperial Council and Committee of Ministers. He was a close friend of V. A. Zhukovsky and I. M. Karamzin, helped edit the posthumous publication of the former's works and assisted the latter editorially with his twelve-volume *History of the Russian State*. His daughter, Antonina Dmitrievna, was close to the Slavophiles.

23 In the original manuscript, the entire page containing the data on the performances of *Ruslan and Ludmila* was written in an unknown hand. On the back of the page, however, in Glinka's writing, is the note "Appendix to the *Notes* of M. I. Glinka" and below this a sketch of a donkey.

| | |
|---|---|
| February: 2, 8, 12, 15, 17, 18, 19, 20, 21 | 9 times |
| April: 18 | 1 time |
| May: 2 | 1 time |
| July: 14, 27 | 2 times |
| August: 26 | 1 time |
| September: 8, 21 | 2 times |
| November: 14 | 1 time |
| December: 5, 20 | 2 times |
| 1844, January: 23 | 1 time |
| February: 2 | 1 time |
| April: 9 | 1 time |
| September: 17, 24 | 2 times |
| 1845, January: 6 | 1 time |
| February: 25 | 1 time |
| October: 7 | 1 time |
| November: 4 | 1 time |
| 1846, January: 13 | 1 time |
| April: 14 | 1 time |
| | *Total:* 53 times[24] |

[24] There are errors in this list of performances: in 1846, the opera was presented fifty-six times, and in that same year the Russian opera moved to Moscow, where *Ruslan and Ludmila* was presented for the first time on December 9.

*June, 1844,* to *May, 1854*

# II

---

## *Sojourn in Paris*

St. Petersburg,
January 25, 1856

WE have just returned from a short stay in the country. I
spent a few days with my mother in Novospasskoe, went to
Bezzabotie[1] to see Nikolai Dmitrievich Gedeonov, and then
passed through Smolensk en route to Warsaw. We traveled by
relays in the carriage I had bought in 1840. From Warsaw we
went to Berlin via Posnań. There I stayed several days with
S. Dehn (my old teacher of counterpoint). I had brought the full
scores of my operas with me, and Dehn was very pleased with
my terzetto *Do Not Tax Me, Father* from *A Life for the Tsar*.

From Berlin we journeyed to Cologne, still by relays, where I
left the carriage. We took the train to Aachen and lingered there
a few days; from Aachen we went to Brussels, then by railroad
to Mons, and finally on to Paris by coach.

We came into the city through the streets of the faubourg
Montmartre and rue Montmartre. The size of the seven-story
houses and the unfamiliar bustle in the streets were enjoyable
novelties to me. Théodore (Gedeonov), leaving me, Adèle, and
our luggage at the coach office, went out in search of rooms, and
we eventually established ourselves in the Passage de L'Opéra (de
L'Horloge) in a small but tidy apartment on the sixth floor. It was
now about the second half of July and the weather was hot. From

---

[1] *Sans Souci*, or "Kamp Kare Knot."

our windows we were able to see a good part of the boulevard. We took our meals in restaurants.

At this time among our compatriots in Paris were M. L. Nevakhovich (who later published *Eralash*)[2] and I. D. Norov, who was fairly well supplied with money (about eighty thousand francs). The former entertained me with his jokes and caricatures, while the latter insisted that I take part in all the *parties de plaisir* he arranged.

At the end of July came the celebrations commemorating the July Days (*journées de Juillet*), the contests on the Seine, and the illuminations; in our ignorance, we were swept along toward these festivities by the crowd and very nearly crushed to death. A Frenchman from St. Petersburg named M. Edouard rescued us, carrying me on his shoulders along the Champs Elysées so that I could get a better view of the brilliant lights.

In September, Prince Elim Meshchersky arrived in Paris and set about translating some of my songs into French. This difficult undertaking was not carried out, however; illness, and later the premature death of the Prince (in November of that same year) made it impossible for him to complete the task.

I made a point of seeing all the sights of Paris. Thus, for example, I went to Versailles with Prince Elim and Count Mikhail Yurevich Vielegorsky, who was spending a few days in Paris.

About this same time (September) I learned that Liszt was going to Spain. This news stirred my long-standing desire to visit that country so much that I at once wrote my mother, who did not immediately, or in fact, for some time, agree to my plan—out of concern for my well-being.

Without wasting any time, I began to take some preliminary steps. Prince Elim Meshchersky introduced me to a Spaniard, Souza, attached to the Spanish Embassy. Souza had previously been in Petersburg, knew music well, and had studied with the eminent composer Schubert; all in all, he was a person of culture

[2] Roughly, *Hodgepodge*.

who graced the society in which he moved. He recommended a Spanish teacher for me by the name of Biesma Guerrero (later tutor to the children of Louis Philippe). At the very first lesson he explained the characteristic features of the Spanish language; shortly after that, I translated *Gil Blas* from French into Spanish. At the next lesson he corrected my translation; I wrote it down again in that form, read it aloud a few times, and thus learned the correct pronunciation and accustomed myself to the turn of the Spanish phrase, learning nearly my whole translation by heart in the process. At the same time I was reading the Spanish comedy *El Sí de las Niñas* and various literary selections from an anthology, including excerpts from Cervantes' *Don Quixote.* By adhering to this very excellent system I soon began to understand Spanish, and even to speak it a little.

In September, Théodore, Adèle, and I moved to rue de Provence No. 5. Here we had a room of ample size; we ate our meals at home now and invariably set extra places for guests.

Dr. Schuster tried to cure me with iodine, but without the least success.

I lived a varied life and was genuinely happy with my friends until November. It then became quite cool and foggy, and I could no longer spend a great part of my time on the street, as I had done before. Some of my friends went away, while others settled down and began to stay at home more. I myself thought that perhaps I should be living a bit differently; thus I began visiting the small theaters, particularly the Chantereine, which was then in the rue de la Victoire, across from the home of the pianist Henri Herz.[3] Here young actors and actresses rehearsed and put on

[3] Henri Herz (1806–1888). Born in Vienna as Heinrich, he studied at the Conservatoire in Paris, virtually becoming a Parisian. Herz had a tremendous reputation in Paris as a pianist, teacher, and composer, doing very well financially with his compositions. His first attempt, with another entrepreneur, to manufacture pianos in Paris failed, and he made an extensive journey to the United States, Mexico, and the West Indies from 1845 to 1851 to recoup his fortunes (*Mes Voyages*, Paris, 1866). His second attempt to set up a piano factory by himself was successful, as was the concert hall in connection with it.

plays, in some of which they were really not at all bad. I noticed a few attractive young actresses, whom Théodore and I forthwith invited to our apartment.

So that the girls would be more disposed to visit us we would arrange supper parties. About eight o'clock we would round up the young actresses, as well as some fellow Russians and a few foreigners. These were pleasant affairs, with singing and dancing, and afterward tea, punch (a light one, of course), and finally a great sweet pie. Théodore planned everything very excellently, everyone had a good time, and moreover, we didn't have to spend too much. We were supposed to quit at eleven. If we danced much later the cooks and maids on all floors would soon appear and complain that we were disturbing their masters, each of whom always seemed to have a headache, migraine, a sore back, or some other ailment.

On one such evening, after a few waltz steps with a young actress named Adeline, I felt an unusually strong attraction toward her. I immediately began to pay my suit, haunting the Chantereine Theater whenever she played, and occasionally taking her home afterward. For a long time Adeline resisted to such a degree that I nearly lost hope. However, close to the end of December the affair was satisfactorily arranged.

Adeline was not a beauty, but there was great charm in the expression of her eyes and in her smile (a prime attraction in French girls). She was then about twenty-two, had a good figure, dressed tastefully, and was graced with many alluring qualities in her manner and way of speech. She was living with her young daughter and mother.

I moved to rue de Provence No. 22, and soon after that things worked out so that I ate all my meals at Adeline's, toward whom my feelings had not altered. In the morning I usually occupied myself with Spanish, letter-writing, and so on; I would then take a walk, visit friends, and finally dine at Adeline's. After dinner we would go to the theater, or else I would stay with her; at such times we would make a fire in the fireplace and play cards with her mother and brothers.

Adeline continued working at her dramatic art and as a matter of fact had a quite successful debut at the Montmartre Theater. I occasionally coached her in singing, but this project did not go so well, although she had previously studied music under a competent teacher. When Adeline opened at the Théâtre de Variété I sat in a box with her mother and brothers. From timidity—or perhaps just from habit—she sang so far off key that our neighbors kept crying out: "Ah, mon Dieu, qu'est-ce qu'elle a donc, cette femme!"[4] We all became quite red in the face, but there was nothing to be done about it.

That winter many of my fellow countrymen arrived in Paris. Among them was Prince Vasily Petrovich Golitsyn (the one I had lived with on the Black River). He and other friends[5] and some Russian ladies urged me to introduce my music to Paris, and I foolishly agreed.

Souza, whom I often visited, learned of my intentions and offered his services. He introduced me to Hector Berlioz, who was then planning a trip to Russia, counting on a rich harvest, not of applause alone, but also of rubles. Berlioz treated me most kindly (which was not the rule among Parisian musicians, who were usually unbearably arrogant and supercilious), and I called on him two or three times a week, talking frankly with him about music and especially about his own compositions, which I liked, particularly those of an imaginative nature, such as the *Scherzo, Queen Mab* from *Romeo and Juliet, The Pilgrims' March* from

---

[4] "Good heavens! What can be the matter with that woman!"

[5] Aside from those mentioned in his *Memoirs*, there were other friends of Glinka in Paris in 1844-45: Dr. K. Sokologorsky, artist B. T. Borispolets, A. Ya. and I. I. Panaev, L. K. Vielegorskaya and her daughter Anna Mikhailovna, I. V. Shirkov (brother of the librettist), a medical student, other Russian medical students Glinka met at K. Sokologorsky's, G. P. Volkonsky, and others.

*Harold, Dies irae* and *Tuba Mirum spargens sonum* from his *Requiem.*

As I say, I also saw Souza frequently; once I found a fifty-year-old Spaniard, Don Santiago, at his home. Souza introduced him as a man of honor and competence. After I had obtained my mother's permission to travel in Spain, I asked Don Santiago to accompany me, and up to the time of our departure he served me most actively as major-domo. I paid him one hundred francs a month for his services.

In March, Berlioz gave two prodigious concerts at the amphitheater on the Champs Elysées. He liked my *Lezghinka*, which I had transcribed for orchestra alone. Moreover, Berlioz and I asked Mme. Solovieva[6] (née Verteuil, married to M. Melchior), who was then in Paris, to sing the cavatina from *A Life for the Tsar—At An Open Field I Gaze*—to which she readily agreed.

When we started rehearsing, I soon found that French musicians are not very good at paying attention—they prefer to talk and chat with their neighbors. I also noticed that sometimes, especially in the heavy passages, they resort to their snuffboxes and handkerchiefs. This lack of attentiveness was clearly demonstrated at a concert given at the Paris Conservatory. They were playing Beethoven's *Sixth Symphony* (*Symphonie Pastorale*), and in such a bizarre manner that I could not recognize the music, and I cried out: "On m'a escamoté la symphonie!"[7] Moreover, the wind instruments sometimes failed—especially the horns and clarinets.

At Berlioz' concert in the amphitheater my *Lezghinka* did not have its hoped-for success because many of the effects had been designed to be played between two orchestras—one on the stage, consisting of wind instruments, and another below the stage (in

[6] Aleksandra Frantsevna Solovieva, soprano, performer with the St. Petersburg Theaters, 1837–43.

[7] "They've done away with my symphony!"

the orchestra) in which the strings predominated. Berlioz had a total of 150 musicians—consequently, they were spread out too much and the listener could not grasp the whole, but only hear the sounds of those instruments near him.

Solovieva lost her courage, faltered, and finally became completely disconcerted; nonetheless, I gave the signal to commence. Fortunately, when she heard the ritornel, Solovieva rallied and sang the aria well. Despite this, the aria did not produce the desired effect, either. Besides, the journal *Scharivari* wrote that the same note was repeated over and over again in this cavatina ("on entend toujours la même note"). At the time I was quite indignant at this, but I can see now where that critic was absolutely right: in the allegro of the cavatina *There Beyond the River* the quint of the main tone is heard too often and too sharply, which is, indeed, very Russian, but probably tiresome and monotonous.

The time came to prepare for the concert and we had much to do. Since I wished to please all tastes, I wanted, in addition to my own pieces, to include a few by other composers; some whom I invited agreed to take part. A very miscellaneous type of poster was gotten up: there was Rossini's overture from *Semiramis*, and *Variations on Russian Themes* played on the violin by Gauman, who also did another violin piece. The mighty pianist Leopold Meyer played two of his own compositions in the most chopped-up manner. The selections from my own music were the cracovienne from *A Life for the Tsar*, the *Black Sea March*, and the B minor waltz (*valse-fantaisie*) called *Scherzo*. Solovieva was to have sung the cavatina from *Ludmila* and *Doubt*, but she was taken ill and replaced by the very fine tenor Marras, who sang my Italian romance *Il Desiderio*, *Ah, se tu fossi meco*, and *Una furtiva lagrima* from Donizetti's *L'Elisir d'Amore*.

This concert was held in the Salle Hertz in April (I don't remember the day). The expenses were substantial, and I had to borrow 1,500 francs from Prince Vasily Petrovich Golitsyn. Although this concert was given to aid some society or other, the costs were high, and subsequently I had to repay the Prince the money I had borrowed.

Despite all this, the hall was filled: apparently the Russian ladies in Paris had agreed to adorn this concert given by their fellow countryman; they appeared in great finery, so that one paper, in referring to my concert, said: "Que c'était un parterre de fleurs."[8] Adeline sat in the third row, and when I came on stage to accompany Marras, she blushed prettily from excitement and concern.

The Parisian public could not, of course, really be made acquainted with my musical talent from the few pieces—and those not my best—that were performed at this concert. Nonetheless, I had a success (*succès d'estime*). Many papers wrote about me: the editor of the *Revue Britannique* wrote an extremely kind article about me, Maurice Bourge also wrote, and finally, Berlioz had a very long article with a brief story of my life entitled "Michel Glinka" in the *Journal des Débats*.

Melgunov had provided Berlioz with the data for this article. I have lost my copy but anyone wishing to read it can find it in the *Journal des Débats* for April or May, 1845.[9]

I often called upon Berlioz, for I found his sharp, even caustic conversation always entertaining. Naturally, I did all I could to make his forthcoming trip to Russia a success.

---

[8] "It looked like a garden of flowers."

[9] Most articles about Glinka in Parisian journals suffered from a certain lack of seriousness and genuine understanding, but Berlioz made a careful analysis of Glinka's creativity, and evaluated individual compositions: "Glinka's talent is distinguished by an unusual flexibility and diversity; his style is happily transformed according to the will of the composer to fit the demands and nature of the subject being treated. This is all done in simple fashion, even with some naïveté, but never degraded to the use of vulgar turns. Unexpected sounds appear in his melodies, and there are strange and charming periods. He is a great harmonist and writes scores for instruments with such pains, with such deep understanding of their most secret resources that his orchestra is one of the newest, most lively orchestras of our time." Of Glinka's two operas, Berlioz preferred *Ruslan*, believing that it showed a riper and more powerful talent: "*Ruslan* is unquestionably a step forward, a new phase in Glinka's musical development."

# 12

---

## *Spain. Return to Russia*

IN the middle of May, 1845, I went to Spain with Don Santiago and his twelve-year-old daughter Rosario. After dinner with Adeline, I bade her a tearful farewell and set off in a rented carriage to take the train to Orléans. Then, three days after leaving Orléans by post carriage, we reached Pau, where we stayed for several days. On the way, though, I had lost my passport. Don Santiago became quite excited about this, but I did not at all wish to give up my idea of visiting Spain. Santiago and I went to see the mayor of the department, where letters addressed to me, my seal, Berlioz' article, and, finally, the testimony of an actor who chanced to be in Pau and who had been in Russia, justified him in issuing me a temporary passport.

As they were getting my passport ready and after I had already paid a ten-franc fee to the local officials, my original passport was found as the result of a notice Don Santiago had had published. Without further delay we set off from Pau in a coach for the border village of St. Jean-pied-de-port, and went from there on foot to the Spanish customs at Val Carlos. I entered Spain on my birthday, May 20, and was completely delighted. We crossed the Pyrenees with three pack mules bearing our luggage. The first night we slept in Roncesvalles. The next day a thunderstorm and high winds overtook us when we were about three miles from Pamplona, which we reached the next morning. The Pyrenees here, where we crossed them, are not as picturesque as the Swiss Alps. At Pamplona I saw my first Spanish dance, put on by second-rate performers. From Pamplona we traveled by coach to Vittoria and then crossed the Ebro at Miranda de Ebro and found ourselves in the Pancorvo Gorge. This gorge looks like a bit of Africa. At Burgos we saw the cathedral. We had decided to spend the summer at Valladolid, where we settled down at Don Santiago's sister's in two pleasant rooms. I resumed my study of Spanish and in a short time began to speak it quite readily. We acquired a horse and rode every day with Don Santiago's brother-in-law through the outskirts of Valladolid, which were not bad. A nearby place called Espolon Viejo was very attractive, and then, too, there was a grove of silver poplars stretching along the Pisuerga River. The tops of the hills enclosing Valladolid were perfectly flat (*páramos*) and covered with aromatic grasses and plants such as sage, lavender, tomino, *etc.*

In the evenings, neighbors and acquaintances came around to sing, dance, and talk. Among them was the son of a local businessman, Felix Castilla, who played the guitar very well, especially the Aragonese jota. I kept this piece and its variations in mind, and later, in September or October in Madrid, I made from it a piece called *Capriccio brillante*. At Prince Odoevsky's suggestion the name was later changed to *Spanish Overture*.

In August, I went to Segovia with Don Santiago's family. This town is remarkable for its old aqueduct and for the Alcázar, where, aside from its exterior, the painted ceilings are also notable. The Alcázar was first used as a government prison but has now been made into an artillery school.

We were also at S. Ildefonso, or La Granja, where we saw the garden, orangeries, and, in particular, the superb fountains of crystal-clear water. But there was no general display here as at

Peterhof—these fountains worked only one after another in succession.

We returned to Valladolid for a short time and then, in the first half of September, went to Madrid. Don Santiago took along his daughter Rosario and a niece Mariquita. Several days after arriving in Madrid we rented a small but comfortable apartment, bought some nice furniture, and settled down in such a way that things were not bad at all for me, or for Don Santiago's family, either. Our apartment was in the very heart of the city, the Puerta del Sol, which is a small square from which six broad streets diverge.

I did not like Madrid at first, but when I got to know the city later on, I could evaluate it better. As before, I continued to study the Spanish language and Spanish music. In this pursuit I began to visit the Teatro del Principe, where Romea and his wife Matilde performed brilliantly in both tragic and comic roles. Sometimes they even put on classic dramas. Soon after arriving in Madrid I got to work on the *Jota.* When I had finished it, I made a painstaking study of Spanish music, that is, the songs of the common people. A *zagal* (mule driver on coaches) used to visit me to sing folk songs, which I tried to jot down and put to music. Two La Mancha *seguedillas* pleased me particularly and I used them later in my *Second Spanish Overture.* Don Santiago and I once took advantage of the pleasant autumn weather to journey to Aranjuez, where I was much impressed by an avenue of huge plane trees and pyramidal poplars. I also liked the little palace (*casa del labrador*).[1] In the great palace,[2] though, I did not particularly care for the porcelain and glass rooms.

Toledo—perhaps the most picturesque city in Spain—has been for the most part preserved as it was in the Middle Ages. In addi-

[1] A country house.

[2] Aranjuez was at one time a residence of the Spanish court. Its gardens are said to be magnificent.

tion to its cathedral (where I played the organ) and other architectural monuments, the city is marvelously situated.

Don Santiago and I also visited the Escorial, which did not
please me the first time, either.

I visited indefatigably all the principal sights of Madrid. My
first impression of a bullfight was of something rather wild and
strange, but I became accustomed to it and later found some attraction in this bloody drama, where each participant is in constant danger.

I visited the museum, that is the art gallery, with the talented
Russian architect Beine.[3] He was traveling about Spain with a
young Englishman, also an architect. Beine once took me along
to a benefit performance for the tenor Guasco at the Teatro della
Cruz—where, to my sorrow, they were doing Verdi's *Ernani*—
and forced me to stay through the entire performance.

Ballets were presented at the Circo Theater. There the dancer
Gui-Stefani beautifully (although affectedly) danced the *Olé*
and the *Jaleo de Xeres*; the music for this latter dance, although
composed by the conductor of the ballet orchestra, Skochdopol
(a Czech), pleased me and I kept it in mind. Gui-Stefani also
danced La Mancha *seguedillas* very well, in the costume of a
Spanish student.

For the most part I stayed at home during the latter part of the
fall. An acquaintance of Don Santiago's niece, Ramona Gonzales,
quite a pretty girl, often came to visit us and I made love to her.
She introduced me to a young man, Don José Alvarez, who
played the flute well and had a passionate love of music.

I made a number of acquaintances in Madrid, of whom I recall at the moment the glove manufacturer Lafin. His sister, Mme.
Gémissieux, of whom I always bought gloves in Paris, had given
me a letter to him. Letters of introduction are valued highly in

[3] Karl Andreevich Beine (1816–1858), professor of architecture at the School
of Art.

Spain. All the time I was in that country Lafin never ceased to be helpful, and I am indebted to him for many pleasant moments.

At the end of November I went to Granada with Don Santiago's family. It had been cold in Madrid, and all during the trip it rained—right up to the Sierra Morena. We passed through the most picturesque part of the mountains, the *despena perros*, in the nighttime. When we reached the summit of the ridge at Santa Elena we were already in Andalusia. Here, at the end of November it was a bit cool, the grass was quite green, and the live oaks made us forget that it was really winter. As we descended the Sierra Morena the climate became appreciably milder and the face of nature more agreeable. Soon we were surrounded on all sides by olive groves and here and there we saw the glistening agaves, used locally to hedge in plots of land.

At Carolina (a Swiss colony founded by Carlos III) we had a delightful breakfast and then went on to Jaen, where we ate very poorly that night. That same night and the next day, we traveled through beautiful, barren mountains, then passed into a narrow valley which adjoined a great valley called Vega di Granada.

We stayed at one of the best hotels, where rooms had already been readied for us by Dr. Jedor, to whom friends of Don Santiago had written from Madrid. Soon after we arrived in Granada a Don Francisco Bueno y Moreno came to see us. He was a man somewhat advanced in years, but still quite active, and had been given a letter of introduction to us by the Madrid glove manufacturer Lafin. He had first been a smuggler, but after accumulating a small fortune he decided to become a respectable citizen. He, too, had a glove factory, and also dealt in hides.

On the second or third day he introduced me to the best guitarist in Granada, one Murciano by name. This Murciano was a simple, untutored person who traded in wine at his own tavern. He played the guitar with uncommon skill, however, and with great precision. Variations on the national dance, the fandango, which he had composed and his son had written down, demonstrated his musical gifts. After spending a few days at the hotel, we moved into an apartment, but found it quite unsuitable. Meanwhile, we learned that not far from the Alhambra there was an attractive little house and garden on the mountainside, and we made up our minds to live there, as you might say, "in the country."

And so, for fifty rubles a month we rented this little two-story house with a belvedere; in the terraced garden there were several small fountains and a basin in the form of a huge bathtub. There were also a number of fruit trees, a tremendous orange tree, and flowers all winter, which in 1845–46 was so fine and warm that, except for three weeks out of the three months, we dined in the garden every day in summer attire. Don Santiago raised geese, ducks, and other domestic fowl, which would all come around at dinnertime and eat out of our hands.

I shall not describe Granada and the Alhambra, because all that is very well known. In the evenings I would go down into the city, where I passed the time pleasantly with friends of Don Francisco. We sang, danced, and made merry in various ways. Don Francisco introduced me to ladies with whom I could find asylum or solace. Beine arrived with his Englishman, Robinson (if I remember correctly), and we happily passed the time at my "refuges." Or again, I would stroll over to the Alhambra while the others sketched, and they in their turn would visit me, sometimes for breakfast and dinner, and so on.

Don Francisco found a pretty Andalusian girl for me, famed for her singing of folk songs. She was about twenty, small, with an interesting face and a build that was perhaps a bit on the sturdy side. Her foot was tiny, though, and her voice very pleasant.[4]

[4] The Andalusian girl to whom Glinka refers was Dolores García. Glinka wrote several songs about her—fandango couplets, a harbor song, and a student's song.

I could not manage things with her, however, without some trouble and danger, so I finally decided to take her to Madrid, which involved some difficulty, too. While in Granada I had, with the help of Don Francisco Bueno y Moreno, plus the co-operation of Murciano and his son, been able to witness all manner of local fetes and family celebrations. When we went to such things at night, however, they would accompany me because it was not entirely safe in Granada at that time.

Meeting a pretty Gypsy girl one time I asked her if she could sing and dance. She said yes, so I invited her and some of her friends to a party. Murciano made all the arrangements, and also played his guitar for us. Two young Gypsy girls and one swarthy old man, like an African, danced. The man danced with dexterity, but most indecently.

I tried to learn how to dance myself from a local dancing girl named Pello. My legs obeyed all right, but I couldn't manage the castanets.

I shall always remember our trip from Granada to Madrid. Don Santiago and his family went separately, while I and my songster, Dolores García, set out in a "galley" around March 15. This vehicle is not called a galley for nothing; it is like a big, high-wheeled Jewish cart with a canopy—of leather or cloth, I don't remember which it was. It has freight loaded all over it, and mattresses on top for the passengers to sit on, one across from another. It's so crowded that one can't move an inch. Opposite me sat a tremendous fat woman who was soon inflicting unbearable torture on my feet. We made about two miles an hour at our ordinary pace and stopped twice in twenty-four hours for three or four hours at a time, but we would travel or, rather, crawl, along for seven or eight hours continuously. I went a good deal of the way on foot.

On arrival in Madrid I soon found the same apartment I had occupied with Don Santiago before, and settled down in it with Lola (short for Dolores). At first things were rather difficult for my friend and me; we often went together to see my Granada friends, and no doubt they disconcerted her. Fortunately, they all left Madrid and then Lola altered visibly for the better so that toward the end we lived together in perfect harmony. Despite this, however, I could clearly see that she would never become a true artist, and I therefore decided to send her back to her mother, which I did in fact do in June, 1846.

In May of that same year, Don José Alvarez introduced me to a countryman of his, Don Pedro Fernandez,[5] who had come from Valencia to complete his musical education. Don Pedro had visited me occasionally when Lola and I were still living together. When she left, however, and he noted that I was sad, he began to come every day and to go with me on my walks. We usually went to the Retiro—the royal gardens.

At the end of June, Don Santiago and I took a trip to La Granja and Segovia. I had wanted to spend the summer there, but this turned out to be inconvenient.

When I got back to Madrid, I wrote Don Pedro. He came to see me, and learning that I wished to move in with him and his friends, demurred, saying that they lived very poorly indeed. I insisted, nonetheless, so Don Pedro moved to the house of his doctor, a person who rented rooms with board and maid service to students and young civil servants. These boarders of his were all fine, well-educated young people. Under my direction Don Pedro learned Cramer's *études* by heart. With our landlord, a friend of Don Pedro's, I read Calderón but not with great success; I thought the author's language very difficult. I knew the museum backward and forward. After dinner my friends and I would walk in the Prado; later on, acquaintances would gather at our place and we would sit around until long after midnight. I often took walks

[5] Don Pedro was for many years Glinka's inseparable companion, something between a secretary, servant, and friend. When he broke with Glinka in 1855, he took with him some manuscripts, including Glinka's Spanish diary, to which the composer frequently referred in his letter from Spain.

beyond the town before sunrise, returning about eight o'clock to drink some tea and go to bed.

In August, I went to the Escorial, and to avoid boredom, I invited along as my traveling companion a young, tall, and pretty Toledo girl named Cefirina. Notwithstanding the fact that my ladies sometimes quarreled, I had a good time at the Escorial. During our vacation there we breathed pure, fresh air, while promenades and donkey rides, the theater, and, most of all, the art treasures stored in the monastery provided us with very agreeable occupations.

Soon after our return to Madrid Don Pedro and I were invited to visit Don José Alvarez' elder brother in Murcia, where in September there was to be a fair and a children's theater.

One day toward the end of August we left Madrid by coach and the next day arrived at Albacete. From there we hired a *tartana* (a vehicle with two wheels, no springs, and a cloth canopy) with one mule and a driver. We dragged along slowly, passing the first night in the little town of Hellin, and the second in Cieza, where for the first time we saw palm trees. On the third day, soon after leaving Cieza, a smuggler asked us to take him and a ten-year-old girl along for about half the journey, to which we agreed, and which we did do. Murcia is of great interest to the traveler, but at that time the roads were worse than our country roads, and since there had been heavy rains, they were even substantially more unserviceable than usual. At one place before reaching Molina water had accumulated in a marshy spot to such a degree that the cart and its load of freight sank into it. Our smuggler was from Molina and he knew the country. After taking a good look around and selecting the best spot for crossing he carried us over the water on his shoulders and then helped the driver pull the *tartana* out.

We dined in Molina and then continued on our way, reaching Murcia that night. Don José Alvarez had already had quarters prepared for us at the home of one of his subordinates. There was a large living room, and a bedroom for each of us. A piano was found, and since the clerk at whose house we were staying was a family man, there were also daughters, who had cousins of course, and then, of course, *their* friends came, too. There were people in our living room every night—we sang, played the guitar, and danced—sometimes there were dances even when we weren't home.

We passed the time no less pleasantly with Don José Alvarez' family, with whom we took drives into the environs almost every day in a big *tartana*. The near-by mountains and cactus-covered *Monte Agudo* made for very nice scenery.

Murcia is famous for its irrigated bottom land, of which it has an area about three miles wide by thirty or more miles long. The principal product is the mulberry, but there are also occasional groups of date palms, which grow very well here, as well as lemon and other fruit trees. Quaint little cottages are scattered all through the valley. The bright green of the vegetation forms a pleasing contrast to the pink granite mountains close at hand.

The children's theater consisted of a presentation of Bellini's *Norma*—which had indeed been written to be performed by children—for the diversion of their parents. We went to a rehearsal and thought the children sang pretty well. The eleven-year-old in the part of Norma sang with enthusiasm—although not really adequately, of course—and was an excellent little actress, besides.

During the fair many ladies and young girls wore the picturesque national dress. The local Gypsies were better looking and richer than those in Granada—they danced three times for us, and there was one nine-year-old Gypsy girl who danced with special sparkle.

We left Murcia on October 21 and returned to Madrid in the *tartana*, hitched to one enormous mule. We went to Orihuela, then Elche—surrounded by groves of palm trees—and from there through Aspe, Novelda, Elda, and Villina, to Almansa. These varied, picture-like localities belong to the kingdom of Valencia.

Riding in our *tartana* tired me out and I sought to dissociate myself from driver and mule, but could find no suitable place in a coach for at that time people were streaming from all corners of Spain for the nuptials of the Queen and her sister. I had to go on in the *tartana* and so I reached Madrid exhausted but in good time.

We lodged this time with an Andalusian woman from Seville, quite old, but kind and friendly. She had a pretty daughter, nineteen, and a son, twenty. In addition to ourselves she also had another lodger, a lawyer from Tarifa.

We witnessed the festivities for the marriage of the Queen and her sister, namely: the procession from the palace to the Amory (Monastery), where the wedding ceremony took place and to which we could not gain entrance; dances in the squares on especially arranged stages; bullfights in the Plaza Mayor; and finally fireworks and the illumination of the Prado by varicolored lamps.

The autumn was cold, and in November I moved to the *Parador de las Diligencias*, an inn on Calle Alcalà, from which place Don Pedro and I set out for Seville at the end of this same month. We stayed in Córdoba a day or so, looked at the mosque—now a cathedral—and made several acquaintances, one of whom gave me a letter of introduction for Seville. In Seville we first stopped at the "Fonda de Europa," and then tried living at a boardinghouse;[6] when this proved to be unsuitable, we finally rented a small house just for ourselves in Calle de la Ravetta.

Soon after our arrival we found some old acquaintances of Don Pedro and, with our letter of introduction and also just by chance, we acquired a number of new, entertaining friends. Almost at once we had an opportunity to see a dance performed by the top

6 Here Glinka uses the Spanish *casa de huespedes* with the French *en pension* in parentheses.

dancers. Among them, Anita was unusually talented and ravishing, especially in the Gypsy dances, but also in the Olé. The winter of 1846–47 was a pleasant one for us; we visited the dance shows at Felix's and Miguel's, where during the dances the best local national singers would burst out in the Eastern manner, while the dancers would continue their intricate steps, so that it seemed we were hearing three different rhythms, that is, the singing went on by itself, the guitar separately, while the dancer would clap her hands and stamp her foot, as though entirely apart from the music.

The eminent although aging national singer Planeta visited us and sang for us. His nephew Lazaro also came calling frequently. Nearly every evening friends and acquaintances of both sexes would get together in our lodgings. One girl pleased me and I tried to *pelar la pava* with her, as they say in Seville (that is, talk with her at night through the window grating), but with no success; I made up for this failure with an inconsolable widow from Córdoba.

In the spring I raised some birds—fourteen, as a matter of fact. They flew about in a room especially allotted to them.

Orange groves stretch along the Guadalquivir from the Palace of St. Elmo; in February, when the fruit is ripe, it is a wonderful sight—and incidentally, these thick-skinned oranges are superlatively tasty.

In the spring the famous violinist Ole Bull came to Seville. He did, in fact, play powerfully and with great precision, but like most virtuosi, he was weak in music. During his six weeks in Seville he paid me a number of visits, so I got to know him to a certain degree.

In spring, too, Don Pedro and still another friend, Pepe Alebes (*labrador*)[7] arranged an "evening" with some Gypsy girls, who, although rather ugly, danced with distinction.

[7] A farmer.

With regret, we left Seville in the first part of May. Our friends were very sorry to see us go. The good Mariquita, our cook, fifty-five years old, bade us a tearful farewell.

The weather was blistering hot then. In the first stages of our trip we often saw agaves along the roadside, their leaves shining in the sun; most of them would bloom sometime during the summer and we could already see their great green trunks, some seven feet high and more.

In Madrid we stayed at the *Parador de las Diligencias* for about three weeks and then started back.

Among my friends in Madrid I remember the pianist Maria Kristina, Don Juan Guelbenzu, his friend Zabalburu, and his pupil Sofia Vela, who had a beautiful contralto voice and was generally an excellent musician.

We stayed for a few days in Zaragoza and then went via Tudela to Pamplona. Crossing the Pyrenees on horseback we passed through Pau and Toulouse en route to Paris, where we stayed for about three weeks. A few days before we left, a Colonel Komarov of the Ministry of Transport came to me with greetings from Peter Stepanov, who was then in Kissingen and wished to see me. We decided to go together and so set off, all three, for Cologne, thence along the Rhine to Biberach, then to Frankfurt, and finally from Frankfurt to Kissingen. Stepanov was very glad to see me and told me that my former wife[8] had received a large inheritance on the death of Vasilchikov. This news pleased me, because although I did not love Maria Petrovna I confess it would have pained me to see her in need.

During my sojourn in Kissingen in July, 1847, I had the good fortune of being presented to His Majesty the Tsarevich, now happily the reigning Emperor Aleksander Nikolaevich, who received me very kindly and presented me to his wife.

[8] I learned of the dissolution of my marriage to Maria Petrovna in Seville.— Glinka's note.

From Kissingen, Don Pedro and I went to Regensburg, and from there down the Danube to Vienna, where the councilor of our embassy, Fonton, and the secretary, Ubri, entertained us very heartily. On Fonton's advice we went to Warsaw, where he had arranged for us to get an old traveling coach.

We spent about six weeks in Warsaw very enjoyably, thanks to arrangements made by the ever obliging N. A. Novoselsky.[9] Before leaving I presented myself to the Prince of Warsaw and dined with him.

Don Pedro and I arrived in Novospasskoe toward the end of July.

[9] Nikolai Aleksandrovich Novoselsky (1818–1898), financier, lover of music and literature, member of the Petrashevsky intellectual circle. In his later years he was governor of Odessa.

# 13

---

## *Novospasskoe, Smolensk, Warsaw, and St. Petersburg*

MY younger sister, Olga Ivanovna, was betrothed to a young Life Guardsman from an Ulan regiment, Izmailov (cavalry captain).

My mother was in good health, but could not see very well; despite this, our life was cheerful at first. Close relatives dropped in, we went riding on horses and in carriages, took walks, and amused ourselves in various other ways.

I had come to Novospasskoe in good health, but I soon felt my appetite going and I had trouble sleeping as well. Wishing to restore myself if I could, for exercise I took to chopping down our excess lindens to give room to the oaks, elms, and other trees. No doubt I overdid it, for I began to feel pains in my stomach and on September 1, I had a severe attack of nerves. Nevertheless, I paid a visit to some close relatives one day that week. On the way home this nervous condition became much more intense and I was tormented by an unbearably painful sinking sensation in my stomach, accompanied by the fear of death, just as had happened to me in Venice in 1833. Without waiting for Olga's wedding I decided to go to Petersburg and put myself in Dr. Heidenreich's hands.

When I was leaving Smolensk [on the way back] my nerves flared up again and so severely this time that I was forced to retrace my steps and stay over in the city. I was unable to attend my sister's wedding. In October my mother and the newlyweds came to Smolensk for a time. From the very minute I had decided to stay there the local colonel of police, Romanus,[1] had lent me his grand piano. As a token of my gratitude I dedicated to him two piano pieces I wrote at that time: *Souvenir d'une Mazurka* and *La Barcarolle*, later published under the name *Greeting to the Fatherland*. At the same time, without Pedro and left alone in the dusk of the evening one day, I felt such a deep sadness that, sobbing, I prayed a little to myself and so improvised *The Prayer*, without words, for piano and dedicated it to Don Pedro. Lermontov's poem *Dark Moment of Life* was set to this prayer.[2]

We were living at the home of a relative, Ushakov, for whose daughter I wrote *Variations on a Scottish Theme*.[3] For my sister Ludmila I wrote the romance *Darling*, the melody of which I took from the jota I had heard so often in Valladolid.

In November my mother went to Petersburg; moved by sincere affection my sister Ludmila decided to spend part of the winter with me in Smolensk. In November, she, Don Pedro, and I moved to Sokolov's house at the Nikolsky Gate. We all got along splendidly together there, and in spite of my sufferings, life was good.

I generally stayed at home, spending the morning in composing. In addition to the pieces already mentioned I wrote the romance *You Will Soon Forget Me*. Under my guidance Pedro played, and learned by heart, Clementi's *Gradus ad Parnassum*. My sister read to me in Russian and French and Pedro in Spanish. Evenings, a number of acquaintances would come in and we soon had a delightful circle of truly devoted friends. I recall Dr. Stroganov, who treated me, and my old friend the druggist, Mero. The doc-

---

[1] Ivan Romanus, amateur composer, colonel of police in Smolensk.

[2] *The Prayer* was dedicated to "Don Pedro Nelasco Fernandez Sandino par son ami M. Glinka" and dated "Smolensk, September 27, 1847."

[3] The manuscript of the *Variations on a Scottish Theme* bears the words "Smolensk, 17 Décembre 1847" and the dedication "À mademoiselle Elise d'Ouchakoff par son parent Michel Glinka, l'auteur."

tor and the druggist often played preference with my sister—a performance that frequently afforded me much amusement. My sister played her cards rapidly, Stroganov skillfully, while Mero more often than not debated long and at length, and out loud, in an inimitable phlegmatic tone, whether or not he should take a card, and usually after such protracted reflection he would end up by saying: "Pass."

In addition to such regular guests as these, others came too; I may mention here the relatives of Ludmila's husband, the Shestakovs, whom we saw quite often.[4] A distant relative of ours, E. P. Zabella, a pretty and a merry young woman, was glad of occasions to visit me.

This quiet domestic life continued until January 23, 1848. The uncle of my brother-in-law Izmailov had always wanted most insistently to give me a dinner, without any doubt whatever, in order to put on airs and to push himself forward as my patron. The dinner ultimately took place despite my resistance to the idea. In charge of it were Commandant Liparsky and Goltsev, Izmailov's uncle. I was met in the hall of the Smolensk Nobleman's Council by local dignitaries, the chief and the principal senior civil servants, to the sound of an orchestra playing the polonaise from *A Life for the Tsar.* At dinner I was given the place of honor between the Governor and the District Marshal of the Nobility. The dinner was, in point of fact, magnificent. Colonel Romanus described it in detail in that year's *Northern Bee.*

To repay the obligations incurred by that dinner, however, I was obliged to give up my stay-at-home life. Each and every day I went to balls and parties, where I had to amuse the public repeatedly by singing and playing the piano. This hectic life, of course, still further upset my nerves, I fell into a strange despond-

---

[4] The family of Ludmila's husband, the seafaring Shestakovs, consisted of the father, Aleksei Antipovich; two sons, Dmitry and Illarion; and two daughters, Aleksandra and Maria (whom Glinka called "Marie aux beaux yeux"). Glinka was very close to this family and played and sang many of his romances at "evenings" with them.

ency and was impelled to ask my sister to take me to Warsaw. She informed my mother of my intention. When she (my mother) came back, in spite of the events of February in Paris, I applied for a passport for foreign travel. In the first part of March I set out for Warsaw with Don Pedro and my brother-in-law Vasily Illarionovich Shestakov,[5] who out of friendship had taken it upon himself to accompany me. We reached Warsaw safe and sound. Vasily Illarionovich left—and they refused me a passport. Once, while looking for an apartment, Pedro and I met Prince Paskevich, who was out horseback riding with an escort of Cossacks. Catching sight of him, I removed my hat, but Pedro, not knowing the Prince, looked at him and kept his cap on so that, noting this, His Most Serene Highness galloped toward us in a rage, nearly knocking me off my feet. This angered me and, as I remember, I wanted to leave Warsaw, but anyhow, everything came out all right eventually. Moreover, I got sick. My good friend at that time, Kastrioto-Skanderbek,[6] a fine musician, introduced me to Dr. Morris Wolff, whom I later came to know very well and who was always my doctor in Warsaw.

Kastrioto, who was married to a daughter of the banker Koniar, presented me to his wife's family. M. Koniar's daughter, Ekaterina, sang with great feeling, and in the early spring I spent many pleasant evenings with them.

We rented an apartment on Rymarsky Street, where I began raising birds behind a wire screen in half of an extra room. I had sixteen of them—nightingales, a blue-throated warbler, a redtail, and others.

Although we had an early spring that year, my illness had run its course, and around the first of May I found myself pretty much recovered.

[5] Illarion Vasilevich Shestakov (d. 1857), retired lieutenant, landowner in Smolensk Government. He was married to Glinka's sister Ludmila.

[6] Vladimir Georgievich Kastrioto-Skanderbek (1820–1879), composer, friend of A. S. Dargomyshky.

Meanwhile, also that spring, Prince Paskevich, realizing that he had almost run into me in a quite uncivil fashion and wishing to smooth things over, often had me for dinner and treated me with uncommon cordiality, seating me next to himself and supplying me with wines, especially the Kakhetinsk[7] variety of which I was so fond.

At the Prince's request I sometimes worked with his orchestra. It was not a perfect group, but nonetheless I found something of interest in it. I gave the Kapellmeister the *Jaleo de Xeres*, which His Most Serene Highness liked very much and frequently ordered played for his guests. Later, again at the Prince's orders, the *Jaleo* dance, set to this music, was presented at a Warsaw theater. Polens[8] shortened the *Jota* for this same orchestra and also arranged *The Prayer*, at my direction, with trombone obligato; thus arranged, it did have an effect.

At about this same time, I made up a potpourri from four Spanish melodies for orchestra which I called *Recuerdos de Castilla*. The Prince's orchestra did fairly well with this number. My many attempts to make something of the Andalusian melodies were fruitless, since most of them were based on Eastern scales, entirely unlike ours.

I rehearsed the polonaise from *A Life for the Tsar* and also *Les fureures d'Oreste*,[9] the celebrated chorus from Gluck's *Iphigénie en Tauride*. I thus heard Gluck's music played for the first time in Warsaw, and I began to study it from then on.

N. A. Novoselsky, constantly showering attentions on me, did everything possible to make my stay in Warsaw a pleasant one. At his request I began to teach singing to P. Konarskaya. She came to me three times a week and was soon singing fairly well; her voice (soprano) was agreeable, but a little weak and sometimes it slipped.

---

[7] A Georgian wine.
[8] Polens was a Warsaw Kapellmeister.
[9] There's a faultless work for you!—Written in the margin in Glinka's hand.

In June of 1848, when I was already feeling a little better, I was attracted once in a *café* (*kawiarnia*) to a well-built and quite pretty girl named Angélique. I won her over, and she came to live with me as housekeeper. Since she was clever, merry, and efficient, we got along fine.

In September, cholera broke out in Warsaw, and as a precaution I did not leave our rooms, all the more so in that every day many funeral processions passed by our house on Rymarsky Street. Staying at home as I did, I set to work and wrote the romances *Can It Be I Hear Thy Voice?* words by Lermontov, Pushkin's *The Toasting Cup*, which I dedicated to the widow Kliko,[10] and *Marguerite* from Goethe's *Faust*, as translated by Huber.

It was the censor in Warsaw at that time, P. P. Dubrovsky, who called my attention to the verses for these romances. I had already met him in 1847 when passing through Warsaw. He visited me regularly in 1848 and, with the kindness natural to him, often accompanied me on my walks—very often he read to me. In fact, he and I read many of the Russian writers and other authors, especially Shakespeare.[11]

Just by chance I found a connection between the wedding song *From Out the Mountains Tall,*

which I had heard in the village, and the generally well-known *kamarinskaya* dance. I suddenly had an inspiration, as one might

[10] Kliko—proprietor of French wine-making enterprises; "the widow Kliko" —a mark of champagne.

[11] In his *Reminiscences*, Dubrovsky writes of this reading together with Glinka: "We were then reading through the best poets. I couldn't help being astonished at his wide knowledge of European literature and art. He delighted me with his understanding of Spanish poetry and painting, not to mention music."

say, and instead of writing for the piano, I wrote a piece for orchestra entitled *Wedding Fantasy.* I may say that in composing
this piece I was guided solely by an inner music sense, without
thinking at all of what goes on at weddings, of how our orthodox
people walk, or how a drunk, arriving late, might knock insistently at a door. Nevertheless, F. M. Tolstoi (Rostislav) himself told
me how, at a rehearsal of the *Kamarinskaya*[12] (as this piece was
later called at Prince Odoevsky's suggestion), he explained my
*Kamarinskaya* to Her Majesty the Empress (now the Empress
Dowager) Aleksandra Fedorovna. In the last part of this piece,
that is, where the trumpets first hold the pedal on B Sharp and
then the horns hold on C, he told Her Majesty that this repre-
sented a drunk knocking at the door of a peasant hut.

This is the sort of friendly help I have suffered more than once
in my life.[13]

Friends and acquaintances came in the evenings—along with
tea, we offered our guests punch to warm the stomach (I confined
myself to warm red wine with a lemon rind and sugar), and for
the same purpose (that is, to warm the stomach) we had dances.
Angélique danced divinely, and if we needed others, two fairly

[12] P. P. Dubrovsky had this to say of the writing of the *Kamarinskaya*: "Some
parts of it he would rough out on paper and try them with the Prince's [Paske-
vich] orchestra, which would sometimes come to his house for the purpose. I
was present several times at these tryouts and was a witness to the preliminary
work on this outstanding creation. After this, M. I. delayed quite a while before
applying the finishing touches, but he constantly kept it in mind. During this
time, though, he scarcely touched the piano. One morning I arrived at his house
(this was in the summer) and found him in his room, with about fifteen birds of
the swallow family flying about behind a little screen. . . . He was sitting at a
little table in the center of the room, in front of his birds, writing something or
other on a large sheet of paper. . . . This was the *Kamarinskaya.* He had it all set
in his mind now and was writing it down boldly, with quick strokes, and all the
while talking and joking with me. Two or three other friends soon dropped in,
but he went right on amid the hubbub and conversation—not bothered in the
least—transferring to paper one of his most remarkable works."

[13] Opposite this sentence in the margin of the copy, a cat has been drawn.—
Note to Russian edition.

young Polish girls, the cook and the maid, would also join in. In addition to the birds flying about in the next room behind their netting, two tame rabbits ran around the sitting room and sometimes banged against the guests' legs.

This happy life went on to the end of October, when Angélique began to put on airs and we had a few quarrels. Well, so that I wouldn't be bored at home, Novoselsky provided me with a few agreeable acquaintances. I might mention the family of Dr. Grünberg: his daughters were most charming and talented, the elder, Julia, played the piano very well and had studied with Henselt[14] at the expense of Her Majesty Princess Elena Pavlovna. The younger daughter, Izabella, sang with feeling and understanding. I spent some pleasant evenings with them, as I also did at some friends of theirs, the Aleksandrovs.

In November the weather took a turn for the better and since I had heard that my mother was in Petersburg, I decided to go there to see her. With his customary kindness Novoselsky secured a carriage for me. Despite the fact that the Dvina was already covered with shifting ice and that there was snow for 150 miles west of Petersburg, Don Pedro and I reached our destination safe and sound in the middle of November (Old Style).[15]

After I had rested for a few days, I went to see my friends and visited at the estate of Ekaterina M. Koniar, whose family and Kastrioto were then in Petersburg. At the end of November I became ill and settled down during that time in order to be near

[14] Adolph Lvovich Henselt (1814–1889), pianist, composer, and teacher. Born in Bavaria, he lived in St. Petersburg from 1838. Grove has this to say of him: "Henselt's success in 1838 at St. Petersburg was unprecedented. He was at once made Court pianist and teacher to the Imperial children, and soon after Inspector of 'the Imperial Russian female seminaries,' in which latter capacity his firmness and disinterested zeal [bore] good fruit."

[15] The "Old," or Julian, Calendar was retained in Russia until 1918, when the "New" Style, or reformed Gregorian Calendar, was adopted—about 170 years after it had been adopted in Great Britain, for example. In the nineteenth century the difference between the two systems was twelve days.

my mother and brother-in-law, V. I. Fleri, who lived near the Krasny Bridge at the School for Deaf-Mutes. My sister Olga was there with her husband, and so was Maria and the children. We were rather crowded, but I found it pleasant despite my illness.

In the winter of 1848–49, Frezzolini[16] wanted to take my opera *A Life for the Tsar* for his benefit performance. He himself made the first visit and brought me a ticket to his benefit. My opera was not given by the Italians because the public was unhappy over the unsuccessful attempts of Russian composers and greatly irritated after the tremendous fiasco of F. M. Tolstoi's opera *Il Birichino di Parigi.* An order came from the highest authority banning the productions of Russian composers in the Italian theater. *Gloire à M. Tolstoi!*

During my convalescence, in the early part of 1849, I went to a party given by Prince P. A. Vyazemsky[17] to celebrate V. A. Zhukovsky's fifty years of literary activity. Bludov read verses written by Prince Vyazemsky for the occasion, and we also sang a chorus composed by Count Mikhail Yurevich Vielegorsky. His Majesty the Emperor Aleksander Nikolaevich (then Tsarevich) also attended this affair, and I was happy to be remembered and honored by the friendly inquiries he made about me.

Prince Odoevsky invited me and many mutual acquaintances to one party where, on the advice of the Prince, I renamed my

[16] Erminia Frezzolini (b. 1818), Italian opera singer appearing in Petersburg in 1848, whence the climate is said to have driven her back to Italy after two years. Grove lists this quotation from Chorley: "She was an elegant, tall woman, born with a lovely voice, and bred into great vocal skill (of a certain order); but she was the first who arrived [in London] of the 'young Italians'—of those who fancy that driving the voice to its extremities can stand in the stead of passion. But she was, nevertheless, a real singer; and her art stood her in stead for some years after nature broke down. When she had left her scarce a note of her rich and real soprano voice to scream with, Madame Frezzolini was still charming."

[17] Peter Andreevich Vyazemsky (1792–1878), lyric poet and critic. From 1810 to 1820 he sided with the Decembrists but later became a "reactionary," serving in the Ministry of Finance and with the censorship office. As a youthful army officer he fought at Borodino in 1812. He was a friend of Pushkin.

jota the *Spanish Overture* and the *Wedding Fantasy*—combined village wedding and traditional dance pieces—the *Kamarinskaya*.[18]

In the spring I got to know Vladimir V. Stasov, an exceptionally well-grounded musician, a lover of the fine arts, and in general a highly cultivated person. With him one day I tried to write some music to Obodovsky's *Palermo* (written to commemorate the visit of the Empress Aleksandra Fedorovna to Palermo), but I couldn't do it, and took the words on with me to Warsaw.

Heidenreich did a fine job of getting me back on my feet, and in very early spring I started going out, usually with Novoselsky, who had returned from Warsaw that winter. He introduced me to young people and writers of another[19] generation—unhappily, some of these got into trouble that same year of 1849.

I resolved to go to Warsaw again that spring, all the more so since I had received letters that promised a pleasant stay there. Leaving Petersburg on May 9 (Old Style) we traveled by post carriage in the most enjoyable manner; the weather was wonderful, there was the fresh green of spring, the birds were singing, and in fact, just about everything disposed one's soul to happiness, and when we crossed the Nieman at Kovno the whole aspect of nature fairly sparkled with an air of holiday and festival.

[18] V. A. Sollogub writes in his *Reminiscences*: "I happened to meet Glinka there at Odoevsky's. He sat at the great organ and extemporized thoughtfully, smoothly, magnificently. Two or three persons listened enraptured to this very personal improvisation, which even Beethoven would have envied."

[19] On the copy "another" has been amended in Glinka's hand to read "new." —Note to the Russian edition.

# 14

## Second Stay in Warsaw. St. Petersburg

IN Warsaw I soon saw that I had erred in my optimistic think-ing. After moving into an apartment on Netsala Street which belonged to an absent colonel, I began to feel an attack of de-spondency coming on. On one side the little windows of our apartment looked out onto the Sakonsky Garden. The thick, leafy poplars (not the pyramidal ones) shut off the light on dark days and the rubbing of the branches against the house in windy weather brought melancholy into my soul. In the suite of His Imperial Majesty, then in Warsaw, were several intimate ac-quaintances of mine and some old schoolmates. I would go ca-rousing with them from time to time and with other friends, too. We had some great reunions at my place and at my schoolmate's, General A. N. Astafiev. Once in a while I also saw Prince Mikhail D. Volkonsky.

Although I did manage to pass the time enjoyably on occasion, I did not really like this dissipated life, nor did it provide me with any musical inspiration. In the summer of 1849, however, I man-aged to derive deep musical satisfaction from the playing of Freier, organist at the Church of the Evangel. He was marvelous playing Bach, working the pedals with precision, and his organ was so finely tuned that in certain pieces, for example in the Bach *Toc-cata and Fugue in F Major*

he moved me to tears.

Toward the end of the summer my dejection finally threw me into a state of the most profound apathy and I would stay home most of the day lying on the couch. At this time the Hussar Regiment of His Majesty Grand Duke Mikhail Pavlovich was lying just outside Warsaw. A colonel in this regiment, my countryman and namesake Mikhail Ivanovich Kubarovsky, whom I sometimes saw at parties, dropped by and prevailed upon me to visit him. I don't know how he did it, what with my apathy. Anyhow, we first went to see some of our mutual friends, and then, after that, at one o'clock in the morning, we knocked on the doors of Ohm's establishment (anyone who's ever been in Warsaw knows the place very well), and since they wouldn't open up, we climbed over the fence and, after drinking some champagne there, went back to Kubarovsky's. He and the rest of the regiment were quartered in cottages, with little gardens, about a quarter of a mile away from Ohm's.

Kubarovsky took me to his lodgings—a small room—and the next day, after having tea and after getting dressed, we went on foot to Ohm's, along with some of Kubarovsky's fellow soldiers. The weather was superb (no question about it—August and September are the best time of the year in Warsaw and Paris). Ohm's establishment had quite a large and well-arranged garden, a fine public room with a fairly decent piano (and the acoustics were good); a clean kitchen and a good cellar further provided everything one could wish for a pleasant passing of the time. In addition to all this, the proprietor had two daughters. The elder, Rosamunda (Rusya for short) pleased us all by her pretty little face, and some of us—by her stoutness. Most of the customers tried to make love to her. The second daughter (the youngest was away at school), Emilia (or Mitsya for short), was small, with a nice little figure, lively and impish—a frolicsome girl. My singing created something of a furor with the Hussars and with the family of the host as well. While I was staying with Kubarovsky I went to Ohm's quite regularly, and I sometimes ate there. Looking upon the lively, pretty Emilia I couldn't help arranging to get better acquainted with her. In the course of my visit Kubarovsky suggested Mickewicz' romance, *Rozmowa*,[1] to me, which Mitsya, very amusingly, taught me how to read and pronounce, while I taught her something about the piano and singing. I returned to Warsaw, staying only a short while and then went back to resume my visit with Kubarovsky. Mitsya and I gradually became friends, and when my Hussar regiment, and Kubarovsky, left Warsaw, I visited Ohm's practically every day. In these little adventures of mine I had the company of Rosenberg, brother of Madame Grünberg, whom we called simply Daniel, as my aide-de-camp; Mitsya and I shared good conversation and music, and I also helped her pick apples, pears, and other fruit.

In October we moved to Dlugu Street across from the arsenal. Daniel and I continued to visit Ohm's every day. When the fruit had been gathered, we turned to the vegetables, and during the fall and the first part of winter we processed corn, peas, poppies, and so on. This eclogue lasted right into winter—and my poetical feeling for the dear Mitsya stirred me to some musical activity: that autumn I wrote music for Mickiewicz' romance *Rozmowa* and dedicated it to Emilia Ohm. I also wrote music to Pushkin's *Adèle* and *Mary*, dedicating the first one to Olga Izmailov and the second to Maria Stepanovna. At Ohm's that autumn I often met Kurpinsky,[2] the Polish composer, well known in his time, an old man then. He was a well-informed person and I had a good time talking with him about art.

The winter of 1849–50 was an extremely harsh one; I had to

---

[1] Mickiewicz' *Rosmowa*—literally, "conversation," "discourse," "talk."
[2] Carol Kurpinsky (1785–1857), Polish opera composer and conductor.

give up my visits to Ohm's because of illness. In the spring I hired Tekla, a girl still young and of quite pleasing exterior, as my nurse. She was good, kind, and attentive to duty, but these fine qualities were marred by one big flaw, unfortunately quite a common one in Warsaw: periodically, she would drink too much brandy, and by the end of summer I had to part with her.

In the summertime I often saw Dubrovsky,[3] Korsak, Daniel, Sobolevsky (passing through Warsaw at that time), and A. P. Grigorovsky, a high government official. In early fall Her Majesty the Empress (now Empress Dowager) visited Warsaw. The day after Her Majesty arrived I composed music for Obodovsky's romance *Palermo*, dedicated to Her Majesty and later published as *The Gulf of Finland*.

In October, 1850, I was invited to a reception by Her Majesty the Empress because of the following circumstances: Olga Niko-laevna, also in Warsaw, declared to Prince Paskevich that she would not leave Warsaw without hearing and seeing Glinka.

Invited along with me were the Grünbergs, mother and two daughters. The Empress greeted me most cordially, in approximately these words, in Russian: "Good evening, Glinka! What are you doing here?" To my reply, that I was in Warsaw because of the climate, which was not as harsh as that of Petersburg, Her Majesty was good enough to say: "There's not so much differ-ence, but I'm glad to see you, anyway, very glad."

I had been obliged to shave off my mustache and beard, so that when I entered the room where the guests were gathered, Prince Paskevich, who had seen me before with mustache and beard, bowed to me in a mocking manner; I returned a proper enough bow, but mocking in a different way, after which the Prince bowed to me correctly, as did I to him. I never saw the Prince again after that.

They soon had me seated at a grand piano with the Grünberg

[3] Ivan Petrovich Dubrovsky (1812–1882), Polish language professor at the Main Pedagogical Institute; he wrote reminiscences of Glinka.

girls around me. If I remember correctly, Olga Nikolaevna and Barteneva were sitting right on the piano.

Here my chronological order is disrupted. Back in the spring of 1849 while I was staying in Petersburg, I. K. Cavos[4] had asked me to write a graduation chorus for the girls of the Smolny Monastery. I agreed to this request with some hesitation because I did not wish to compete with Duke Peter Oldenburg, Lvov, and Count M. Yu. Vielegorsky, who had written—unsuccessfully—graduation choruses for the girls of the Smolny Monastery.

Toward the end of the summer of 1850, Cavos sent me some verses by Timaev, inspector at the Smolny Monastery. The content was good, but the verses were too long. There was not time enough to send them back to Peter[sburg] for revision, so I could only do the best I could to condense them. Moreover, Cavos had asked me to write the orchestra as softly as I could, suggesting that I use piano, harp, and a few wind instruments.

Knowing from experience that one could not expect a decent performance from the boobies (as Kukolnik, with good reason, called them), along with the piano and harp I used a full orchestra, after instrumenting the piece as clearly and softly as I could[5] in order thereby to bring out the voices of the girls as much as possible. When the work was finished, I sent it to Cavos, with detailed

[4] Ivan Katerinovich Cavos (1805–1861), outstanding conductor of Russian opera, teacher of voice at the Smolny and Ekaterinsky Institutes. Son of Cattarino Albertovich Cavos, who wrote his *Ivan Susanin* (one of his three operas) in 1815. "In this work Cavos combined, without great distinction, though with a certain charm, several of the idioms of Western Europe and occasional touches of Russian folk song." C. A. Cavos, a Venetian, came to Russia in 1788, where he had great success, conducting and composing for the St. Petersburg Opera and Theaters from 1803 to 1840. Although Glinka's *Ivan Susanin* (or *A Life for the Tsar*) drove Cavos' own work from the stage, he recognized Glinka's superiority and, in fact, conducted the *première* performance in 1836.

[5] This chorus was *distorted because of the laziness of Cavos*; those who wish may find the *true copy* at D. V. Stasov's.—Written on the copy in Glinka's hand.

Below this, taken from the original of the *Memoirs*, a donkey's head is reproduced, along with the words "Bravo! Bravissimo!" Glinka had made the donkey's ears bigger—Note to the Russian edition.

instructions on how to arrange the orchestra and the girls. There is no doubt that Cavos, in his natural flightiness, disregarded my instructions. The chorus did not have the hoped-for effect and as a consequence, I got a funny letter from Cavos. In this letter, among other things, he said: "Sa majesté l'empereur a trouvé que l'instrumentation du choeur est faible et moi, *je partage parfaitement* l'opinion de sa majesté." *Cavos partage l'opinion de s. m.!!*[6]

The first part of October, 1850, we moved to Notanson's house in Nalevki, where we occupied a very nice, roomy apartment. The sitting room, or parlor, was quite large and during the winter of 1850–51, I often had young *grisettes* in for dancing and merriment. By the end of the winter my health had begun to deteriorate considerably, partly from smoking cigarettes (a number of ladies I knew had told me this before) and partly from Hungarian wine, which had a very bad effect on my nerves. I later gave up both these things completely.

In the spring, too, I felt a sort of general indisposition. In June, 1851, one time after dinner I was playing the piano while near by sat A. A. Nevakhovich (in Warsaw at that time), who had brought with him a Roman Catholic priest and the Italian *maestro* Ricci.[7] Don Pedro interrupted my playing to bring me *two letters* from the village. I asked my guests' permission to read them, adding that *two letters at once* usually means bad news. The letter did, in fact, tell me of the death of my mother. She, like the righteous, had died of old age.

This news was a blow to me, but I did not weep. The next day, after dinner, in the thumb and index finger of my right hand, by which I had taken the fatal letters from Pedro and at the very same time that Pedro had brought them to me the evening before,

---

[6] "His Majesty the Emperor finds the instrumentation of the chorus lacking in strength and I, well I *entirely share* His Majesty's opinion." *Cavos shares His Majesty's opinion!*—Glinka's note.

Here, on the original notes, Glinka had drawn the head of an ass and [had written] the word "Bravo."—Note to the Russian edition.

[7] Federico Ricci (1809–1877), Italian composer and teacher of voice.

I felt a weakness, and also a strange sensation, as if flies were crawling over them. In a few minutes my right hand had become so enfeebled that I could scarcely move it. My doctor, Moritz Wolff, assured me, however, that this was only a passing nervous disturbance—and it turned out that he was right.

I wasn't able to write without assistance at first and even had the greatest difficulty in signing my name. At my request, Don Pedro informed my sister Ludmila of the misfortune that had overtaken me. At that juncture I gave her and her husband full powers to administer my property.

Ludmila came to Warsaw in July and, with her sisterly love, comforted me beyond words. My spirits revived a little; but we set about putting our affairs in the best order we could. When my sister left in August, I revised the potpourri of Spanish melodies, *Recuerdos de Castilla,* developed the piece, and called it *Spanish Overture No. 2.* During this period I found it easier to write music than to sign my name.

I was also seeing to my passport for travel abroad and in this connection sent a physician's certificate to St. Petersburg along with my application.

Not getting any decision on the passport and learning from Ludmila's letters that the papers we had signed to cover the ordering of our affairs would have to be revised, I decided to go to Petersburg myself. With a rented post carriage (two seats), I, Don Pedro, Daniel, and my cook left Warsaw in early September. The weather was very good and we arrived safe and sound. Soon after we got to Petersburg, though, the weather worsened and with it so did my health. Heidenreich treated me with a purgative, which only made my trouble worse, so I decided to go to Doctor Jal,[8] a homeopathic physician. I felt some improvement in my hand from the very beginning of his treatment.

---

[8] Here Glinka makes a pun in the margin, to wit: *Jal*, the doctor's name, is *zhal* in Russian, and can mean "too bad." Glinka's note was thus: "Zhal that I went to Zhal."

Soon after arriving in Petersburg I moved into Melikhov's house. V. P. Engelhardt often stopped in there and once introduced me to the younger brother of Vl. Stasov, Dmitri Vasilevich Stasov, a very well-educated young man and a fine musician. I had a good piano in my apartment; Engelhardt did the honors in providing the music, and we were soon *playing four hands*. In October my sister Ludmila came to Petersburg; after consulting with our very helpful relative A. V. Kozodaev, the papers we had drawn up in Warsaw proved not to be needed after all.[9]

Ludmila stayed at V. I. Fleri's when she came to Petersburg. On November 17, her birthday, she had a party at which she told me she was going to stay with me all winter and that she had already rented an apartment for us. This display of sisterly concern touched me deeply.

On December 1 my sister and I moved into Zhukov's house on Nevsky Prospekt and Vladimirsky Street. The place was quite comfortable, and the sitting room a large one. Before long we rented two grand pianos from Meltsel, and later Engelhardt sent his piano over to us. We began to play, first eight, and then even twelve hands. As far as I can remember, on one Friday night the following were present:

| | |
|---|---|
| Dmitri Stasov | |
| A. N. Serov[10] | } piano 1 |
| | |
| V. P. Engelhardt | |
| K. P. Vilboa[11] | } piano 2 |

[9] On October 27, 1851, Glinka made his will, leaving all his property to his sister Ludmila I. Shestakova, "as a sign of [my] true brotherly feeling toward her."

[10] Aleksander Nikolaevich Serov (1820–1871), music critic, composer. He did much to promote the success of Glinka's work, wrote reminiscences of him.

[11] Konstantin Petrovich Vilboa (1817–1882), composer, wrote many romances that were popular in his time. In the 1850's he became a friend of Glinka (also of Dargomyzhky and Ostrovsky) and transposed his two operas for piano and for voice and piano. On a well-noted trip along the Volga, Vilboa wrote down many folk tunes.

Moreover, Dubrovsky, transferred to Petersburg even before my arrival as professor of Polish at the Pedagogical Institute, introduced me to a first-class pianist, and a very nice person besides, by the name of De Santis.

Engelhardt provided the musicians required for our playing and himself diligently transposed for twelve hands, mostly from my operas.

On the whole, we lived quite nicely and happily, but my health got progressively worse. I had no appetite at all and ate practically nothing all through December. I imagine the reason for this serious disturbance of my stomach lay in the fact that, having started homeopathic treatment, I got the idea (I don't know why) of drinking water, eating cold food, and so on. This ailing state continued up to January 21, 1852, and then, during the night, I had the most severe and painful stomach-ache (*colique*): vomiting and extreme (nearly bloody) diarrhea tore me to pieces for a day and two nights. Heidenreich, whom Jal (I had quit him)[12] had called upon for help, brought me out of the threatened danger within a week.

When I felt a little better, at Lvov's request I started readying the singers (in the major parts) who were to perform his *Prayer and Cross* (*Stabat Mater*). That year (1852) witnessed the fiftieth anniversary of the Philharmonic Society; the Germans wanted to present one of my compositions, but Count Mikhail Yu. Vielegorsky and Lvov forced me out—there were no hard feelings on my part—and, as I have already said, I had at any rate taught the singers and even acted as a sort of nursemaid to them.

On February 28 we had a big musical party featuring Gluck's arias with oboes and bassoon; a piano replaced the orchestra. Gluck's music made more of an impression on me at that time— you see, I did not have such a clear understanding of his music when I had heard it in Warsaw.

[12] Since that time I have had absolutely no confidence in French doctors.— Glinka's note.

In March, when I was beginning to feel still better, I went with Engelhardt and Heidenreich to the imperial orangeries on Aptekarsky Island. I thought they were better planned and richer in *great palms* and other tropical plants than the Paris orangeries (*serres*) in the Jardin des Plantes.

In April my sister (and it was my sister, not I) arranged a second concert for the Philharmonic Society.[13] Shilovskaya took part and sang several of my pieces. The orchestra played the *Spanish Overture No. 2* (A Major) and the *Kamarinskaya*, which I then heard for the first time. F. M Tolstoi (Rostislav) was at the rehearsal and there was some talk about how he had explained to Her Majesty the Empress (now the Dowager Empress) the meaning of the pedals on F Sharp and C in the conclusion (*péroraison*). Our *eminent* (!)[14] critic, with his *profound* (!) formative mind could find nothing better or cleverer to say than that *some drunk or other* was knocking at the door![15]

Around Easter time, at my sister's request, I wrote the *First Polka* (that's what it was called when published).[16] I had played this polka four hands on the piano since the 1840's but wrote it down only in April, 1852.

At the party that Prince Odoevsky arranged for me that same April, and to which many of my friends came, Count M. Yu. Vielegorsky started to make fun of me, but I managed to break off from him in a very accomplished fashion.

At the end of April there was also another party (*a mon intention*)[17] at Novoselsky's (he was already married). Here some

---

[13] The second Jubilee Concert of the Philharmonic Society, conducted by K. Shubert, was on April 2, 1852. Among Glinka's works performed then were the *Kamarinskaya*, *A Night in Madrid*, two romances, and an aria from *Ruslan and Ludmila*.

[14] Before the exclamation point, in parentheses, there is a profile of a person with a long nose and a mustache.—Note to the Russian edition.

[15] A cat with long whiskers and tail has been drawn in parentheses. On the copy [of the *Memoirs*] a cat sitting down was drawn.—Note to the Russian edition.

[16] A very bad and untrue edition!—Glinka's note.

of the pieces performed at our February 28 party were repeated, with bassoon and oboe.

In May there was a party (in my honor) at Prince Mikh. Volkonsky's. Quartets were played and Shubert, Sherinz, and Beling were there.

Shubert visited us twice in the spring and we played some quartets.

About the middle of May (May 20) my sister and I went to the Exchange with D. A. Shestakov and A. N. Serov. The ale (which my sister provided for us, as we demanded) had very diverse effects: I (contrary to my custom) retained my equilibrium, D. A. Shestakov became terribly jolly and talkative, but the ordinarily garrulous A. N. Serov could not seem to find his tongue.

On May 21 (my name day) I set free (in the summer garden) two haybirds (pewits) and a lark, which had amused me all spring. After breakfasting at Donon's, my sister and I spent the day at Tsarskoe Selo, and that evening we had some friends in for supper—our own group, that is.

17 Given in my honor.—Glinka's note.

# 15

---

## Third Trip Abroad and Return to Russia

O N May 23 my sister and a group of friends saw Don Pedro and me off on our trip abroad. We were traveling by coach to Warsaw. On the second day we took quite a pretty woman into our carriage. Her society provided me with some distraction during the journey, and I composed a little mazurka for her in the style of Chopin—this mazurka was well received in Warsaw and Paris.

From Warsaw, where we stopped for only a short while, we went via Chenetokhov and Breslau to Berlin.

The morning we checked into the Römischen Hotel, Meyerbeer came to see me and, among other things, said: "Comment se fait-il, M. Glinka, que nous vous connaissons tout de réputation, mais nous ne connaissons pas vos oeuvres?"[1]

"Cela est très naturel," I told him. "Je n'ai pas *l'habitude de colporter* mes productions."[2]

Incidentally, Meyerbeer was extremely affable and easy to get along with.

S. Dehn showed me all the sights and I also spent many hours

[1] "How is it, M. Glinka, that we know you only by reputation and not through your works?"

[2] "Oh, that is quite natural. You see, I am not in the habit of *peddling* my compositions."

in the museum and at the zoological gardens. Dehn provided further diversion for me in the form of quartets and Moselle wine.

On one trip we took from Berlin we spent the first night in Hannover and went on the next day to Cologne. We were there a whole day and saw the cathedral. It's a shame the way they are restoring and rebuilding it—the same, but yet not the same. From Cologne we went up the Rhine to Strasbourg—a nice trip.

We spent several days in Strasbourg, visited the cathedral, and looked at the world-renowned clocks. The railroad between Paris and Strasbourg had not been completed, so we had to suffer part of the way in a coach.[3] After having spent several hours in Nancy (quite a nice, clean city) we reached Paris early the next day by railroad.

I entered Paris not without some feeling of anticipation for I could recall many enjoyable times out of the past. I installed myself in the Hôtel de la Marine, where I had stayed before and where I found familiar faces.

I looked up some acquaintances immediately: Henry Mérimée, for example (whose article about *A Life for the Tsar* is cited at the end of Part III of these Notes), whom I had already met back in the winter of 1845 through Melgunov, and apropos of that article. We had become good friends at that time; when he was in Paris the summer of 1852, we visited together the Hôtel de Cluny, the museum, and the old streets of Paris.

D. A. Shestakov arrived in Paris for a brief stay and for two days we were inseparable, abandoning ourselves with childlike joy and without a care in the world to the varied pleasures of Paris.

Since I was bound for Andalusia, and specifically Seville, in July we went to Châlon-sur-Saône by railroad. We had left in the

---

[3] Coaches in France are really instruments of torture. They are loaded unmercifully beyond capacity, the passengers packed in tightly, while the drivers are ill-mannered slobs.—Glinka's note.

evening; that night, during the journey, I suffered for several hours from a nervous sinking or fainting sensation with feelings of terror such as I had experienced in 1847 in Novospasskoe and in Smolensk.

Toward morning I felt a little better, and we proceeded on our way by Saône steamer to Lyons, where we spent the night. Despite the beauties of Lyons and its lovely location, I felt vaguely uncomfortable and benumbed after the agony of the night before. We went from Lyons by steamer again (on the Rhone) to Avignon, where we docked at about five in the afternoon. The banks of the Rhone are not so interesting as those of the Rhine—and besides all means of travel in France were at that time incomparably worse than in Germany.

In Avignon we inspected the former papal palace, now used as a barracks. In the cliffs close by the palace a very fine promenade has been made, with evergreen trees planted alongside it among the bare rocks. This walk leads to a terrace from which a magnificent panorama may be had: beneath one's feet (*à vol d'oiseau*) lies a great part of the city and the Rhone, split up into several branches, while on one side the Alps can just barely be discerned, and on the other—the Pyrenees. We stood and admired this panorama for a long time. The next morning in Avignon, where we had spent the night, my nervous irritation returned with frightening impact. I took homeopathic ignatia and, since that soothed me some, after breakfast we took the train to Beaucaire to see the fair. I wasn't quite up to that, though, nor Vaucluse either, and instead we hurried on to Montpellier and Toulouse in order to get to Spain sooner. Things worked out otherwise, though.

Montpellier, which has been so highly extoled, did not please me at all, nor did the promenade called Peyrou. We got to Toulouse in twenty-four hours by coach from Montpellier. Here we spent the night at the Hôtel Casset, *tenu par* Schaubart,[4] and which we knew well from an earlier trip. We stayed there for

4 "Run by Schaubart."

about two weeks, during which I felt pain every day. In Toulouse I met Émile Delille, with whom I had often visited in Paris. He was well educated, very obliging, but a gascon.

The continuous suffering made me change my mind about going to Spain,[5] and I decided to return to Paris. In order to travel more restfully I had hired an enclosed coach, and, by stages, we reached Poitiers in a little less than two days. Thence by railroad to Tours, the next day Blois, third day Orléans, and the fourth, Paris. Because of the bad weather and my low spirits I did not see the chateaus of Chambord or Chenonceaux. To me, the banks of the Loire were less picturesque than those of the Seine—but I'm not really sure this opinion is a well-founded one.

We had returned to Paris on August 15, St. Napoleon's Day, and all the hotels were full. There were no rooms at the Hôtel de la Marine, either, where we spent the night in the dining room sleeping on sofas or tables.

Very soon, though, we found comfortable quarters in the rue Rossini, near the Académie de Musique. Our rooms were sunny, and consequently cheerful and gay. In the same building we were able to find a young woman, Mme. Jean, who cleaned our rooms and cooked for us. There was also an old woman living there, Mme. Beaucé, of a very lively and jolly nature, and a pretty good music teacher. Her daughter, Mme. Ugolde, was prima donna at the Opéra Comique. Soon after we moved to the rue Rossini we had become acquainted with Mme. Beaucé and one evening she collected some of her pupils in our sitting room where we enjoyed a little music together. Afterward, during the fall and winter, they would come to see me every other day or so to discuss music and to sing Italian songs, for the most part.

September was a wonderful month, and I recovered my health to such an extent that I got to work again. I ordered some large-

[5] Glinka wrote his sister Ludmila: "Carefree Spain is not for me right now—here in Paris I can find new, untried intellectual pleasures." And in another letter: "I turn away from Spain—I'm too old for that happy land."

size manuscript paper and began to write my *Ukrainian (Taras Bulba) Symphony* for orchestra.[6] I wrote the first part of the first allegro (C minor) and the beginning of the second part, but since I didn't have the energy or the desire at the time to work my way out of the German rut in the development, I dropped the whole thing, and what I had done, Don Pedro later destroyed.[7]

At the end of October the weather began to get bad and, to fight off boredom, with Don Pedro's assistance I found a pretty young nurse by the name of Léonie (Ninie for short).

Ninie was nineteen years old, born in the Department of the Jura (a few hours from Geneva), but she was more like a Swiss girl and distinguished by the special freshness of her face. She was quiet, but a little bit bad in some ways. As for the rest, I had a pretty good winter in 1852–53—staying at home quietly and passing the time very agreeably. Mornings we would have a fire in the sitting room, and before breakfast we looked like a library reading room, each one sitting there with his own book. After breakfast one of Mme. Beaucé's young lady pupils usually dropped in. At five o'clock we had dinner, sometimes with a mixed group of friends, nor did we pass lonely evenings.

That winter, at the urging of Henry Mérimée, I read Homer's *Iliad* and the *Odyssey* (Mme. Dacier's prose translation) and nearly all of Ovid. Émile Delille (whom we got to know in Toulouse) had settled down in Paris and provided me with books from his own library. He gave me a superb edition of Ovid, with beautiful engravings, and Ariosto's *Orlando Furioso*, which I liked very much.

There was nothing especially noteworthy in the way of music.

[6] In letters to a number of friends Glinka revealed a new project: "I began work on a symphony this morning, with this very pen" (letter to A. N. Serov, August 20, 1852). "I have started on *Taras [Bulba]* and it is already going well enough . . . a cold has interfered with my work—but I hope to get back to it soon" (letter to Ludmila, September 7, 1852). "The symphony has been suspended—it's not yet ripe, but God willing, we'll live to see the thing finished" (also to Ludmila, October 2, 1852).

[7] What a nice one he was!—Written in the margin in Glinka's hand.

Soon after we arrived in Paris Henry Mérimée introduced us to the family of M. Duport, where lovers of music sometimes gathered of an evening and very competently sang various *morceaux d'ensemble*. I rarely went to the theater because the Parisians use perfume so unsparingly that the air becomes unbearable. However, I did hear Méhul's *Joseph* two times at the Opéra Comique. It was very well done, that is, without any kind of affectation, and so coherently and intelligently that despite the fact that Joseph and Simon were rather bad, the effect of the whole moved me to tears. Bussine was excellent as Jacob.

Volkov provided Ninie and me with a box at the Opéra Comique for the *première* performance of Auber's *Marco Spada*. The first part of the overture was very nice indeed and promised a lot, but the allegro of the overture and the music of the opera in general proved to be highly disappointing.

Volkov had a season ticket for the concerts at the Conservatoire. He knew of my unfavorable opinion of the pretentious manner in which these concerts were performed, especially Beethoven's music, so he sacrificed one of his concerts to me solely that I might confirm my prior impression. One of the numbers played at this concert was Beethoven's *Fifth Symphony* (C minor). I found the execution just exactly as before, that is, very affected, the *pianissimo* descended to the stupid nonsensical depths of a Rubini, and where the wind instruments were supposed to come in just a little, they were overplayed most deplorably—in a word, there was no Beethoven symphony (*elle a été complètement escamotée*).[8] Other pieces, however, such as the dervishes' chorus from Beethoven's *The Ruins of Athens* and a Mozart symphony were performed very accurately and very satisfactorily.

In the winter of 1852–53, Steiner, married to Mme. Beaucé's elder daughter, often visited me, and from time to time her son Henry Beaucé also came. The latter was a good musician and could sing pretty well in a high tenor voice—a little too much

8 It vanished into thin air.

through his nose, though. Steiner amused us with various funny stunts and tricks.

In early spring Ninie went off to see some relatives, and I, in turn, made ready for my return trip. My health was deteriorating little by little again, and I had begun to be weary of Paris. The Eastern Question came up, and this further increased my desire to return home and there is no doubt that I would have left Paris if my friend Don Pedro had co-operated with me, but he was deeply infatuated with Paris and had already given evidence of his reluctance to leave. On the other hand, the railroad frightened me and I was trying to find some other way of traveling. I commissioned the husband of our cook, Mme. Jean, a man with some knowledge of coaches and coachmen, to see if we couldn't get hold of a second-hand double-seat carriage and to find out also if there were still post horses to serve people traveling in their own vehicles. He found that we could get a carriage, but there were no more post horses in any area through which the railroad ran. This put me in an unhappy position—with my upset stomach and shattered nerves I didn't know what to do. Meanwhile, I had somehow happened to meet a lively, quite pretty young *grisette* from Bordeaux. At the end of April we moved from rue Rossini to No. 43 rue Richer into a very nicely arranged, newly furnished apartment. Next to our apartment we found a small one for Amalia, the girl from Bordeaux.

At our request Mme. Coupé (wife *d'un tapissier*,[9] and the one who had rented us the apartment), a woman of agreeable qualities, had recommended an Indian woman, Zòe, from Pondichery as maid servant and cook. Zòe was almost forty, a small woman, swarthy, very nearly brown or cinnamon in color, and possessed of an utterly childlike voice. She was exceedingly neat and tidy and a good cook—she could roast things to perfection on the spit. Although the Eastern Question was becoming more of an issue every day, and even then I could see it would lead to war, and my

[9] Wife of an upholsterer.

stomach and my nerves frequently bothered me,[10] well, regardless of all this, and also regardless of the fact that these miseries and sad reflections made me long for home (*nostalgie*), there were still many happy and exciting moments to be enjoyed.

In early spring Prince Aleksei D. Saltykov arrived in Paris from Egypt. I had known him for a long time and had seen him often in 1853. We would go riding in the Bois de Boulogne so early in the season that there was scarcely anything green about, and later, in the summer, we dined and otherwise passed the time together. He was an artist at heart and a diplomat (monstrously polite) in appearance.

The Jardin des Tuilleries is glorious in the spring—the sharp green of the chestnut trees, the lilacs in full bloom, and particularly the swarm of pretty, nicely dressed children—especially the girls—in short, the spectacle charms and delights one.

Amalia sometimes amused me but more often I found her excessive animation annoying. Around the first of June she went to Bordeaux. Just by chance, before she left we had come across a Spanish girl we had met on the return trip from Seville to Madrid in 1847. Antonia was a very attractive, frisky and merry Andalusian; unfortunately, she soon returned to Spain.

Adeline H., a milliner, sometimes called Amalia, had often visited me at my invitation, and that summer she moved in as my nurse. She was close to thirty, a pleasant, quite well brought-up and very literate lady.

Once, at the start of summer, when I returned from my morning stroll, I found Meyerbeer in our parlor with Don Pedro. Meyerbeer was talking of this and that with his usual amiability. When he asked about the publication of my operas, I showed him some printed copies of *A Life for the Tsar* and *Ruslan* which I happened to have with me. The talk then turned to Gluck, and to my question "Would his music be effective on the stage?" Meyer-

---

[10] Despite this, I didn't see a doctor—actually, I was afraid of quacks, French and other.—Glinka's note.

beer replied that it was precisely on the stage and nowhere else that Gluck would become magnificent. He assured me that when I left he would pass the word to Berlin in good time and see what he could do about having one of Gluck's operas performed for me. At that time four of Gluck's operas were being produced: the two *Iphigénie*'s, *Armide*, and *Alcestis*. From Gluck we passed to a discussion of other classical composers, whereupon I expressed my views on art.

"Mais vous êtes très difficile,"[11] said Meyerbeer to me.

"J'en ai complètement le droit," I replied. "Je commence par mes propres oeuvres, dont je suis rarement content."[12]

I never saw Meyerbeer again after this meeting. In the winter, or perhaps it was early spring, he had the opera *Star of the North* put on at the Opéra Comique. I did not hear it, but I was indignant that in it he had treated Peter I very disrespectfully.

At the end of 1853 an Egyptian pasha sent the French emperor a young hippopotamus (*hippopotame*), but the crowds at the Jardin des Plantes were so great that it was a long time before Pedro and I could see this curious beast. There was also a newly arrived chimpanzee (*chimpanze*)—a small one, to be sure, but perfectly genuine. During the summer months he would sit in a large cage and frolic in the most surprising way with a few monkeys that had been left there.

In addition to visiting the Jardin des Plantes and taking walks in the neighborhood, I sometimes liked to entertain my countrymen at dinner. At my insistent request every newly arrived friend had to come to me for dinner. Zòe and I used to go out shopping for fruit, and we did very well at it, too.

In late autumn a stove was placed in my bedroom, certainly a good idea because it made things so comfortable that in winter, when it was freezing outside, I was warm even though there were

11 "Ah, how difficult you are!"
12 "I have a perfect right to be because I start with my own works, with which I am not often satisfied."

no double windows. Some of my friends even felt like taking off their coats and ties when in my bedroom. Nonetheless, I felt bad all winter long, probably partly because I was smoking cigarettes, despite repeated warnings from Adeline, who quite rightly noticed that smoking was not good for me. I stayed at home that winter, feeling depressed. Adeline would read to me, clearly and with verve, and we got through most of Paul de Kock's *"A Thousand and One Nights"* (too bad I hadn't read these tales before I wrote my opera *Ruslan!*), and Boccaccio's *Décaméron.* I didn't feel like serious reading or doing anything else of a serious nature.

Shortly after the declaration of war between Russia and France, Pedro and I left Paris, but not before visiting the Jardin des Plantes, one of my favorite spots. How warm and pleasant it was in this wonderful garden! The fruit trees and the magnolias were in bloom. . . .

The night before our departure I had a severe stomach-ache, but despite that we left the next morning on the Northern Railroad. This was at the beginning of April, 1854 (New Style). Adeline went with me to the station. At ten that night we arrived safely in Brussels, where we checked into the Hôtel de Suède.

They gave us something for supper, but so soon after my stomach upset I really couldn't eat a thing, and anyway the hotel food didn't look very good to me. The next day a brother of Henry Beaucé's invited Pedro and me to dinner. I didn't eat anything then either, but did not pass up the very excellent wines he brought out. In the evening we went to the theater and got a lot of laughs out of the play—it was about the current political situation. On the third day after our arrival in Brussels I visited the Feigen family. One of the ladies was the bride of Damke,[13] whom I met at this time. We visited the studio of a very talented but exceedingly mad artist whose name I don't remember. His pictures made a very unfavorable impression on me. That same eve-

---

[13] Berthold Damke (1812–1875), German music critic, composer, and conductor. In 1845, he moved to St. Petersburg, where he spent ten years.

ning we went with the Feigen family to the home of a Belgian amateur musician. The violinist Leonard[14] and his wife, as well as Serve[15] were there. At my request they played Beethoven's D Major *Trio*. The host himself played the piano very well, that is, simply (not affectedly), Leonard played his violin, but I don't know who played the cello, except that it wasn't Serve, who did not play anything; he merely put on airs and, incidentally, invited me to his estate for hunting.

When, at the end of the *Trio*, I started to thank my host, he, indicating Serve and the other virtuosi there, said to me: "Ce sont tous mes amis, mais je ne les aime pas!"[16]

We went to Berlin by railroad via Cologne and Hannover. We traveled *avec la grande vitesse* and I was shaken up and tossed about a great deal.

It was a pleasure to see Dehn again, and to be treated to quartets, Haydn in particular, nor did he forget the Moselle wine. My health was in some disorder and the days were becoming very raw and harsh. But I forced myself to a certain extent because I remembered they were doing Gluck at the theater, and I determined to hear one of his operas, never mind my complaints. On Dehn's advice I went to see the publisher Schlesinger.[17] He, with Israelitic obligingness, presented me to the Director of Theaters, who received me kindly and assured me of his co-operation. There was a German composer in Berlin then (I can't remember his name) who also wanted to hear one of Gluck's operas. At *Schlesinger*'s advice, this time I went to see the prima donna, Mme. Koester.[18] Finally, with the King's permission, they gave *Armide*.

[14] Hubert Leonard (1819–1890), Belgian violin virtuoso and teacher.
[15] Adrien-François Serve (1807–1877), Belgian cello virtuoso and composer.
[16] "They're all friends of mine, but I don't like them!"
[17] Heinrich Schlesinger (1807–1879), proprietor of a music publishing firm (in Berlin) founded in 1795 by his father, Martin Adolph Schlesinger. Heinrich himself founded the periodical *Echo* in 1851 and held control of it until 1865. Until 1846, his brother, Mortiz Adolph, had a Paris music publishing house which, according to Grove, was "nearly as famous as Paris itself."
[18] Luisa Koester (nee Schlegel), German soprano, was born in 1823.

The effect of this music on the stage exceeded my expectations. For example, the scene in the enchanted forest with the mutes, D Major, was beautiful. The scene in the third act with *hatred* (the *big scene*, as the Germans call it) was extraordinarily impressive. In my opinion, Mme. Koester was good—she sang truly, and acted intelligently, and besides all that her fine figure fitted the role to perfection. I must say I also thought the orchestra was incomparably better than the one at the Conservatoire in Paris— they played without any affectation, pretentiousness, or mannerisms—in other words, they played with precision and clarity. The composition of this orchestra was more than satisfactory: twelve first violins, twelve second violins, eight violas, seven cellos and just as many basses, plus two each of the wind instruments. The production was good (*zweckmässig*)—the gardens—Claude Lorrain landscapes—the ballet, and all the rest. This was the seventy-fourth performance of *Armide* and the theater was full.

I also went to a *Singverein*, where, on Good Friday, they gave Graun's *Tod Jesu.* Here the singing was pretty good, but the orchestra was poor and the music worse.

I got to Warsaw satisfactorily and stayed there an extra week for the simple reason that I had a swelling on my right leg—a tumor, or something of the sort (no doubt because of my tight Paris shoes). Korsak, the poet Volsky,[19] and N. Volkov, who had been made director of the Fine Arts Theater, often visited me, and the latter let me have his *pianino* for the time being.

Wolff quieted my fears about my leg; thanks to Prince A. M. Golitsyn (Director of Posts in Warsaw), on May 11 we set out for St. Petersburg in a government post carriage and arrived safely early on the morning of May 16, 1854. I was a little drowsy, but Pedro, who knew my sister's address at Tsarskoe Selo, took me there, half-awake as I was. There I found my sister Ludmila Ivanovna and my little godchild, my niece Olenka, in perfect health.

[19] Vlodzimezh Volsky (1824–1882), Polish poet and writer. He wrote the libretto for Moniuszko's opera *Halka,* performed in Warsaw in 1858.

*Appendices*

# I

## *Chronology*

1804    May 20. Glinka born at Novospasskoe, near Smolensk.[1]

1812    War with Napoleon. Glinka family leaves Novospasskoe for a time.

1814–15 Piano and violin lessons.

1818    February. Enters Blagorodny School in St. Petersburg. Also studies music with John Field and Charles Mayer.

1822    Graduates from Blagorodny School.

1823    January. Journeys to the Caucasus to take the waters.

1824    Assumes post in Ministry of Transport. Writes *My Harp*.

1825    Writes several romances. On December 14, witnesses part of Decembrist Conspiracy in St. Petersburg.

1828    Publishes short poem *Alsand*.

1829    With N. Pavlishchev, publishes *Lyrical Album*.

1830    October. First trip abroad—to Italy.

1832    First expresses desire to write a "Russian" opera. Composes several instrumental compositions.

1833    July. Leaves Italy. From October, 1833, to April, 1834, studies in Berlin with Dehn.

1834    Death of father. Returns to Russia (spring). Writes instrumental compositions, romances. Meets Maria Petrovna Ivanova.

---

[1] The reader may well find "authoritative" evidence disputing some of the dates given here. For example, leaving aside the twelve-day difference between Old Style and New Style dates, *three* different dates are given, in three different national encyclopedias, for Glinka's birth.

1835    Marries Maria Petrovna.

1836    November 27. First performance of *A Life for the Tsar* at Bolshoi Theater in St. Petersburg.

1837    January. Appointed Kapellmeister of the Imperial Chapel Choir. Begins work on *Ruslan*. Pushkin dies on January 27. Works sporadically on *Ruslan* until 1842. Also writes instrumental and vocal compositions.

1838    April–August. Goes to the Ukraine to engage singers. Stays at Kachanovka. Writes songs to words by Ukrainian poet Zabella.

1839    Spring. Beginning of affair with Ekaterina Kern. In December, resigns as Kapellmeister because of friction with A. F. Lvov.

1840    Writes music for Kukolnik's *Prince Kholmsky*, many romances to Pushkin poems. Also *Midnight Review* to Zhukovsky's words and *Farewell to Petersburg* to Kukolnik's words.

1841    Sues Maria Petrovna for divorce.

1842    April. Score for *Ruslan* completed; first performance on November 27.

1844    June. In Paris. Performances of *Ruslan* discontinued when Russian opera moves to Moscow.

1845    March. Concert in Salle Herz. In May, goes to Spain for two years.

1846    Marriage legally dissolved. Romance with Ekaterina Kern also ended.

1847    Returns to Russia.

1848    Spring. In Warsaw. Composes *A Night in Madrid*, *Kamarinskaya*, and *Jota Aragonesa*.

1850    March. *Kamarinskaya* performed for first time.

1851    Revises *A Night in Madrid*.

1852    Director of Imperial Chapel Choir and Imperial Opera. Begins work on symphonic composition *Taras Bulba*. Sets out for Spain but stays in France. Visits Berlin.

1854    Returns to St. Petersburg. In summer, edits score of *Ruslan*. That fall, scores Weber's *Invitation to the Dance*. Remainder of year devoted to revision and editing of his own romances. This year and the next, in Tsarskoe Selo and St. Petersburg, writes his *Memoirs, Notes on Instrumenta-*

*tion*, and dictates a brief autobiography to A. N. Serov for a Belgian biographical dictionary.

1855    Becomes acquainted with Balakirev.

1856    May. In Berlin. Visits Dehn. Begins study of Russian church music.

1857    February 3. Dies in Berlin at age fifty-three. In May, his remains are moved to the Aleksander Nevsky Monastery in St. Petersburg. In October, V. V. Stasov publishes a monograph on him.

1858–59  *Ruslan* revival at St. Petersburg.

1864    *Ruslan* performed at Marinsky Theater in St. Petersburg.

1866–67 Balakirev attempts to produce *Ruslan* and *A Life for the Tsar* in Prague.

1870    *Memoirs* first published in entirety in journal *The Russian Past*.

1871    *Memoirs* first published in book form.

1872    *Ruslan* successfully performed at Marinsky Theater, St. Petersburg.

1879    December sees 285th performance of *A Life for the Tsar*.

1885    Monument to Glinka erected in Smolensk.

1886    Fiftieth anniversary of *A Life for the Tsar*. Performances throughout Russia.

1887    "Third" edition of *Memoirs*, edited by V. V. Stasov.

1892    Jubilee, 500th performance of *A Life for the Tsar*.

1906    Death of sister, Ludmila Ivanovna Shestakova. Monument erected on Glinka's grave in St. Petersburg.

1930    Fourth edition of *Memoirs*, edited by A. N. Rimsky-Korsakov.

1937    V. Ya. Shebalin finishes Glinka's *Unfinished Symphonic Overture*.

1939    Revival of *A Life for the Tsar* in Leningrad. Title changed to *Ivan Susanin*, libretto altered to stress devotion to country and people rather than to the Tsar.

1945    *Ivan Susanin* performed at the Bolshoi Theater in Moscow, text by S. Gorodesky, edited by People's Artist of the USSR A. M. Pasovsky and Merited Artist L. V. Baratov. (The Tsar is replaced by a "folk hero," Kozma Minin, and the Russian fighting forces become the "People's Army.")

# 2

## Glinka's Family and
## Relatives Mentioned in His Memoirs

Fleri, Viktor Ivanovich (d. 1856), brother-in-law. Married Glinka's sister Elisaveta Ivanovna.

Gedeonov, Fyodor Dmitrievich (b. 1797). Brother of N. D. Gedeonov.

Gedeonov, Nikolai Dmitrievich, brother-in-law. Married Glinka's sister Natalya Ivanovna.

Glinka, Afanasy Andreevich (1772–1828), uncle (mother's brother).

Glinka, Andrei Ivanovich (1823–1839), brother.

Glinka, Elisaveta Ivanovna (1810–1850), sister. Married V. I. Fleri.

Glinka, Evgeniya Andreevna, nee Glinka (1784–1851), mother. Married I. N. Glinka, her second cousin.

Glinka, Evgeniya Ivanovna, first cousin. Daughter of I. A. Glinka.

Glinka, Evgeny Ivanovich (1815–1834), brother.

Glinka, Fekla Aleksandrovna, nee Sokolovskaya (d. 1810), grandmother (father's mother).

Glinka, Grigori Andreevich, "a relative."

Glinka, Ivan Andreevich (1777–1852), uncle (mother's brother).

Glinka, Ivan Nikolaevich (1777–1834), father.

Glinka, Ludmila Ivanovna (1816–1906), sister. Married I. V. Shestakov.

Glinka, Maria Ivanovna (1813–188?), sister. Married D. S. Stuneev.

Glinka, Natalya Ivanovna (b. 1809), sister. Married N. D. Gedeonov.

Glinka, Olga Ivanovna (1825–1859), sister. Married N. A. Izmailov.

Glinka, Pelageya Ivanovna (1805–1828), sister. Married Ya. M. Sobolevsky.

Glinka, Sofiya Ivanovna, first cousin. Daughter of I. A. Glinka.

Ivanov, Aleksei Petrovich, brother-in-law (wife's brother).

Ivanova, Luisa Karlevna, mother-in-law.

Ivanova, Maria Petrovna, wife. Later married Nikolai Nikolaevich Vasilchikov.

Ivanova, Sofiya Petrovna, sister-in-law (wife's sister). Married A. S. Stuneev.

Izmailov, Nikolai Aleksandrovich, brother-in-law. Married Glinka's sister Olga Ivanovna.

Kazadaev, Aleksander Vasilevich, "a distant relative."

Kiprianov, Aleksander Ivanovich (1780–1872). Husband of Glinka's cousin Aleksandra Vasilevna Potresova.

Potresova, Aleksandra Vasilevna (1801–1830), cousin (ward of Glinka's father). Married A. I. Kiprianov.

Shestakov, Dmitri Alekseevich (1821–1853). First cousin of I. V. Shestakov.

Shestakov, Illarion Vasilevich (d. 1857), brother-in-law. Married Glinka's sister Ludmila Ivanovna.

Shestakova, Olga (1853–1863), niece. Daughter of Ludmila Ivanovna and I. V. Shestakov.

Sobolevsky, Nikolai Yakovlevich, nephew. Son of Pelageya Ivanovna and Ya. M. Sobolevsky.

Sobolevsky, Yakov Mikhailovich (d. 1844), brother-in-law. Married Glinka's sister Pelageya Ivanovna.

Stuneev, Aleksei Stepanovich. Married Glinka's sister-in-law (wife's sister) Sofiya Petrovna Ivanova. Brother of D. S. Stuneev.

Stuneev, Dmitri Stepanovich, brother-in-law. Married Glinka's sister Maria Ivanovna. Brother of A. S. Stuneev.

Ushakov, Aleksei Andreevich, "a relative."

Ushakova, Elisaveta Alekseevna, "a relative." Daughter of A. A. Ushakov.

Zelepugina, Maria Nikolaevna, nee Glinka, aunt (father's sister).

# 3

---

## A Life for the Tsar

RUSSIA is in peril in 1613, torn by civil dissension and under attack by King Sigismund's Polish armies. Michael Fedorovich Romanov has just been chosen Tsar by the boyars, first of his dynasty, but he is hiding in a monastery. In the course of events a roving Polish unit, disguised as ambassadors, comes upon the village of Domnino. Here they seek to force the peasant Ivan Susanin to lead them to the Tsar. Susanin seemingly agrees, but first he sends his adopted son, Vanya, to warn the Tsar. Then he leads the Poles deeper and deeper into the snowy forests and the wild morasses, to be killed when his deception finally becomes clear. The simple story ends with the magnificent, triumphal entry of the Tsar into Moscow, before the Kremlin, with Ivan Susanin's dead body lying in a place of honor.

There is a romantic interest between Susanin's daughter Antonida and the Russian soldier Bogdan Sobinin.

# 4

---

## Ruslan and Ludmila

THE story is a fairy tale of the very complicated and involved type, based on Pushkin's poem written in 1820.

Ludmila, daughter of Prince Svietozar of Kiev, is being courted by Ruslan (a brave knight), Farlaf (a Varangian coward and braggart), and Ratmir (a wandering poet—and prince—from the East). She loves Ruslan, but just before they can be married (during the chorus to Lel, god of matrimony), the dwarf Chernomor, a wicked sorcerer, carries her off. Her father the Prince now offers her hand to whichever of the three suitors rescues her.

In *his* efforts, Ruslan repairs to the cave of the *kindly* sorcerer Finn, who suggests he take a magic sword to attack the Giant's Head, which happens to be the brother of Chernomor, bewitched by the wicked enchantress Naina. (Incidentally, Glinka had placed a small male chorus inside this really huge stage Head; the breathing of the thing caused fierce storms, accompanied by thunder and lightning.) Ruslan does overcome the Head as a step toward rescuing Ludmila, but he is then entrapped by the sorceress Naina and delayed for a while, partly because of the lovely Gorislava, whom he had jilted for Ludmila. Finn arrives in time to save him from succumbing completely to Gorislava and a bevy of dancing girls. Farlaf, meanwhile, has been advised by the evil Naina to allow Ruslan to do all the work of finding Ludmila, simply so that he can carry her off again. Ruslan finally defeats Chernomor and finds Ludmila hidden away in his castle, but is unable to awaken her from the magic spell which has been cast upon her. Farlaf now carries her off all over again, according to plan, and claims her in marriage, although he cannot wake her either. Finn and Ratmir now collaborate to help Ruslan, giving him a magic ring with which he breaks Chernomor's spell and brings Ludmila back to consciousness. Farlaf flees in abject terror, and Ruslan and Ludmila will live happily ever after.

# Index

Aachen, Germany: 25, 55f.
Abbondio, Signora Giuseppa: 59, 72, 80
Adèle: *see* Rossignole, Adèle
Adeline: 190–91, 194f.
Adeline H.: *see* Amalia
Afanasiya (cook): 23
Akhtyrka, Ukraine: 126
Albrecht, Karl Frantsevich: 166
*Alcestis*: *see* Gluck, C. W.
Aleksander I: 35
Aleksandrinsky Theater: 18n., 106
"Aleksei": *see* Ulyanovich, Aleksei
Alisa: *see* Goronovich, Alisa
*Allgemeine musikalische Zeitung*: 87n.
Alyabiev, A. A.: 29n., 88
Amalia (girl from Bordeaux): 236f.
Andreev, Ivan Nikolaevich (tenor): 93, 118
Andreeva, Princess: 138
Andreyanova II (dancer): 162
Angélique: 214
Anichkov Palace: 132
*Anne Boleyn*: *see* Donizetti, Gaetano
*Ansald* (poem by Glinka): 40n.
Ansano, Italy: 66
Antonia: 237
Apukhtin, General: 35
*Armide*: *see* Gluck, C. W.
Arseniev (professor of geography): 12
Artemovsky: *see* Gulak-Artemovsky, Simon S.
*Art Journal*: 119
*Askold's Tomb*: 141n.
Astaviev, General A. N.: 99

Auber, Daniel François Esprit: *Marco Spada*, 235
Avignon, France: 232

Bach, Johann Sebastian: 27, 50, 116; *Clavecin bien tempéré*, 44, 163; *Toccata and Fugue in F Major*, 219–20
Baden, Germany: 83f.
Bakhmetiev, Nikolai Ivanovich: 138
Bakhturin, Aleksander Nikolaevich: 30
Bakhturin, Konstantin Aleksandrovich: 32, 33f., 93, 136
Balakirev, M. A.: 118n., 178n.
Baratynsky: 33
*Barber of Seville, The*: *see* Rossini, Gioacchino A.
"Baron Brambeus" (pseudonym): *see* Senkovsky, Osip Ivanovich
Barteneva, Praskovya Arsenyevna: 90, 99–100, 133, 136
Basadonna (tenor): 70
Basel, Switzerland: 57
Bashutsky, Aleksander Nikolaevich: 46
Basili, Domenico Andrea: 60
Battaglia, Dr.: 59, 62
Batyushkov: 44
*Beatrice di Tenda*: *see* Bellini, Vincenzo
Beaucé, Mme: 233
Beethoven, Ludwig van: 27ff., 32, 95, 123, 164; *Fidelio*, 27, 56; E Flat Major Quintet, 30; *Seventh Symphony*, 95; *Clärchens Tod*, 128; *Egmont*, 128; F

Major *Sonata*, 159; E Flat Major *Concerto*, 163; *Sixth Symphony*, 192; *Fifth Symphony*, 235; *The Ruins of Athens*, 235; D Major *Trio*, 240

Begnis, Ronzi di: 70

Beine, Karl Andreevich: 198

Belgiojoso, Prince Emilio: 62

Belgiojoso, Count Pompeo: 62, 78

Belikova (soprano): 99

Belinsky, V. G.: 67n.

Bellini, Vincenzo: 61, 70, 74, 77, 79; *La Sonnambula*, 61, 72; *I Capuleti ed i Montecchi*, 64; *Norma*, 75, 120, 204; *Beatrice di Tenda*, 78f.; *Il Pirata*, 95

Belloli (voice teacher): 31, 42, 93

Bender (clarinetist): 104

Benediktov, Vladimir Grigorevich: 148

Bergamo, Italy: 66

Berger (pianist): 88

Berlin: 69, 86

Berlioz, Hector: 114n., 191–93; article on Glinka in *Journal des Débats*, 194

Bernet (pseudonym): *see* Zhukovsky, A. K.

Bers, Dr.: 56

Besana (friend in Italy): 66

Bessonov (drawing teacher): 20

Bezzabotie (*Sans Souci*): 187

Bianchi, Eliodoro: 59, 65, 67

Bilibina, Aleksandra Yakovlevna: 138

Bitton (professor at Blagorodny School): 12–13

Black River: 46

*Black Shawl, The* (Henisht): 90

Blagorodny School: 11, 12n., 40n.

Bludov, Count Dmitri Nikolaevich: 182

Bogaev, V. I. ("Chevalier Bobo"): 140, 142–43, 165

Böhm, Franz: 22, 28n., 32, 95, 103

Boieldieu, François A.: *My Aunt Aurora*, 10; *The Little Red Cap*, 18; *Dame Blanche*, 46

Bolgakov, A. Ya.: 107n.

Bologna, Italy: 72

Bolshoi Theater ("Grand Theater"), St. Petersburg: 18n., 106, 132

Borgovico, Italy (Lake Como): 78

*Boris Godunov*: 36n., 105n.

Borromean Islands (Italy): 57

Bortniansky, D. S.: 113n.

Brailov, Dr.: 37

Branca (lawyer, brother of Dr. Branca): 72

Branca, Dr.: 73–74, 81, 83

Bravura (amateur musician): 89

Brescia, Italy: 66

Brest-Litovsk: 55

Brianza, Italy: 65–66

Brod (oboist): 104

*Bronze Steed, The*: 119

Brotherhood, The: 116, 118n., 120, 140–43, 151, 154; farewell dinner for Glinka, 152n.; dissolution, 164; parties, 165

Brullov, Karl P.: 70, 116, 121, 133, 159, 165

Brussels: 239

Bryansk, Russia: 3, 51

Bulgakov, Konstantin Aleksandrovich ("Kostya"): 115n., 162

Bulgarin, Faddei Venediktovich: 109, 169, 173

Bull, Ole: 123, 206

Bykovsky, Dr. Lazar Petrovich: 24, 26

Cambiaggio, Isidoro: 74, 80–81

*Cantatrici Villane, Le*: 59

Cantú (bassoonist): 78

Capri: 68

*Carneval*: *see* Schumann, Robert

Cassera, Contessina: 76

Catherine II: 6

Caucasus: 22, 24, 56

Cavos, Catterino Albertovich: 103, 120f.

Cavos, Ivan: 107, 223

Cefirina: 203

*Cenerentola*: *see* Rossini, Gioacchino A.

*Chao-Kang* (ballet): 63

Charlottenburg, Germany: 88

Charpantier (Leonov): 104, 170

Chernigov, Russia: 124

Cherubini, Maria Luigi: 17ff., 29; *The Water Carrier*, 18, 30; *Faniska*, 27; *Les deux journées*, 27; *Hôtellerie portugaise*, 27; *Lodoiska*, 27; *Medea*, 27, 56–57

"Chevalier Bobo": *see* Bogaev, V. I.

Chirkov (schoolmate): 43, 86, 88

Chopin, Frédéric François: 16n., 73, 164

Circassians: 25–26

Civitavecchia, Italy: 67

*Clärchens Tod*: *see* Beethoven, Ludwig van
*Clavecin bien tempéré*: *see* Bach, Johann Sebastian
Clementi, Muzio: *Gradus ad Parnassum*: 210
*Clemenza di Tito*: *see* Mozart, Wolfgang Amadeus
Colico, Italy: 83
Colombi (dancer): 62
Como, Lake: 65f., 73, 75ff.
*Complete School of Singing, The*: 177n.
*Comte d'Ory, Le*: *see* Rossini, Gioacchino A.
*Conqueror, The* (Zhukovsky): 73
Cramer, Johann Baptist: 50
*Crociato*: *see* Meyerbeer, Giacomo
Crusell, Bernhard Henrik: 7

*Da brava Catina* (Venetian barcarole): 46
*Dame Blanche*: *see* Boieldieu, François A.
Damke, Berthold: 239
Danchenko (Koko): 141
"Daniel": *see* Rosenberg
Dargomyzhsky, Aleksander Sergeevich: 94, 118n.
Dashkov: *see* Vorontsov-Dashkov, Count
*Dawn*: 160n.
De Filippi, Dr.: 62, 66, 72–73, 77f.
Dehn, Siegfried: 86–88, 98, 239f.
Delille, Émile: 233
Delvig, Baron: 47ff., 49n., 88
Demidov, D. P.: 32, 44, 93, 95
Demidova, Elena Dmitrievna: 32
Desna River (Russia): 3
Dessauer, Joseph: 66
*Deux aveugles, Les*: *see* Méhul, Étienne N.
*Deux journées, Les*: *see* Cherubini, Maria Luigi
Dever, Count: 38
De Vitte, Nikolai Petrovich: 179
Didina (Milanese girl): 60, 72, 80
Diefenbach, Dr. (surgeon): 85–86, 88
Doctors in Glinka's life (partial listing): Battaglia, Bers, Branca, Bykovsky, De Filippi, Diefenbach, Frank, Gaevsky, Gasovsky, Hauke, Hermann, Hindenberg, Kreisig, Lichtenstet, Malfatti, Marn-Zeller, Pizzati, Sadovsky, Salomon, Schuster, Shering, Shpindler, Stuhler, Volsky, Whering, Wolff
Domodossala Valley (Italy): 57
Donizetti, Gaetano: 70; *Gianni di Calais*, 61; *Anne Boleyn*, 61, 63, 71 f., 74; *Faust*, 77; *L'Elisir d'Amore*, 78
*Don Juan*: *see* Mozart, Wolfgang Amadeus
Don Pedro: *see* Fernandez, Don Pedro
Don River (Russia): 24
Don Santiago: 192
Donzelli (singer): 75
Dresden, Germany: 55
Dubelt, General Leonti Vasilevich: 135, 172
Dubrovsky, Ivan Petrovich: 222
Dubrovsky, P. P.: 214
Dupré (singer): 59
Dzhiafar: 20

*Egmont*: *see* Beethoven, Ludwig van
Eichberger (tenor): 56
"E. K.": *see* Kern, Ekaterina Ermolaevna
Ekaterinsky Institute: 23
Ellena (professor at Blagorodny School): 13
Elnya, Russia: 3
Ems, Germany: 55f.
Engelhardt, Pavel Vasilevich: 85
Engelhardt, Vasily Pavlovich: 18, 19n., 28, 50, 84n., 88, 98f., 226ff.
Engelhardt, General Vasily Vasilevich: 18, 19n.
*Eralash*: 143n.
*Ernani*: *see* Verdi, Giuseppe

*Fair at Sorochintsk, The*: 105n.
*Faniska*: *see* Cherubini, Maria Luigi
*Faust*: *see* Donizetti, Gaetano, *and* Spohr, Louis
Fernandez, Don Pedro: 202ff., 230ff., 236
*Fidelio*: *see* Beethoven, Ludwig van
Field, John: 16, 69, 163; *First Concerto*, 16; *Second Divertissement* (E Major), 16
Filimonov, Vladimir Sergeevich: 148
Findeizen, N. F.: 37n.
Fioravanti, Valentino: 59n.
Fischer, Mme (soprano): 56

Five, The: 39n.
Fleri, Viktor Ivanovich: 180
*Flowers of the North*: 49n.
Fodor-Mainvielle, Josephine: 69–70, 82
Frank, Dr. (University of Vilna): 78, 81
Frankfurt am Main, Germany: 55, 57
Free School of Music: 134n.
*Freischütz, Der*: see Weber, Carl Maria von
Frezzolini, Erminia: 217
Fuchs (piano teacher): 22

Gaevsky, Dr.: 92
Gagarin, Princess: 79–80
Gaidukov: 165
Gaivazovsky: 122
Galli (singer): 61
García: see Viardot-García, Michelle Ferdinande Pauline
García, Dolores (Lola): 201
Garegnani, Mme: see Mayer, Henriette
Gasovsky, Dr.: 43, 48
Gauman (violinist): 193
Gedeon, Bishop of Poltava: 125–26
Gedeonov, A. M.: 81n., 100, 103, 107, 119, 123
Gedeonov, Fyodor Dmitrievich: 85
Gedeonov, Nikolai Dmitrievich ("Théodore"): 81
Gedeonov, Stepan Aleksandrovich: 121
Gedeonov, Théodore: see Gedeonov, Nikolai Dmitrievich
Geitsinger (tenor): 56
Geneva, Switzerland: 57
Genoa, Italy: 67
*Gianni di Calais*: see Donizetti, Gaetano
Gillies, John: 40
Giulini (husband of Pini's sister): 75–78
Giulini, Carlotta: 75
Giulini, Luiggia: 75, 78
Glinka, Afanasy Andreevich (uncle): 3n., 17ff.
Glinka, Ãndrei Ivanovich (brother): 144
Glinka, Elisaveta Ivanovna (sister): 91
Glinka, Evgeniya Andreevna (mother): 3, 3n., 4n., 50, 209f.; death, 224

Glinka, Evgeniya Ivanovna (first cousin): 23
Glinka, Evgeny Ivanovich (brother): 91
Glinka, Fekla Aleksandrovna (grandmother): 3, 5n.
Glinka, Grigori Andreevich: 34
Glinka, Ivan Andreevich (uncle): 3n., 18n., 19, 22–23
Glinka, Ivan Nikolaevich (father): 3, 3n., 4n., 36f., 39, 41, 51f.
Glinka, Ludmila Ivanovna (sister): 4n., 5n., 51, 86n., 225f., 241
Glinka, Maria Ivanovna (sister): 91, 135
Glinka, Maria Petrovna (wife): 92–98, 114, 116–18, 122, 131, 139–40, 145–47, 158, 177, 207
Glinka, Mikhail Ivanovich: health, 3f., 26, 36–39, 41, 43, 48ff., 52, 56, 72, 77–79, 92, 105–106, 137f., 153–55, 157, 181, 189, 209, 224, 227, 231–32f., 236; interest in drawing, 4, 6, 20; interest in birds, 20f., 36, 180–81, 206, 212, 229; in civil service, 21, 29–30, 42–43; mineral baths, 22n., 25–26, 36, 55–56, 66, 83; witnesses Decembrist uprising, 33; studies with S. Dehn, 86–88; domestic troubles, 98–99, 117, 122, 131, 139, 145–46, 147, 158, 158n.; life at Kachanovka, 124f., 127, 128–30; comments on wife's appearance, 140; life in Paris, 187ff.; studies Spanish, 189f., 196; concerts in Paris, 192–94; musical compositions: *Adagio* (B Major), 28n., 41; *Ah, se tu fossi meco (Il Desiderio)*, 73; *Always and Everywhere Thou Art My Dear Unseen Companion*, 124; *Andante cantabile* (unfinished), 28n.; *Ask Not the Songstress for a Song*, 144; *Le Baiser*, 37; *La Barcarolle*, 210; *Beatrice di Tenda* cavatina, 78; *The Beggar Singer*, 36; *Call Her Not Heavenly*, 89; *Can It Be I Hear Thy Voice?* (Lermontov), 214; *Capriccio brillante (Spanish Overture)*, 196; *Cherubim Song* (C Major), 119; *A Collection of Musical Pieces*, 131; *Come di gloria al nome* (quartet in F Major), 44, 50; *The Conqueror*, 73; *Could I But Know You*, 94; *Darling*, 210; *Doubt*, 123; *Farewell*

to Petersburg, 102n., 150; *First Polka,* 228; *Flame of Desire,* 124; *Goblets Wand'ring o'er the Table,* 141, 142; *Grandfather, Once Maidens Told Me,* 47; *Greeting to the Fatherland,* 210; *Gude viter,* 129; *The Gulf of Finland,* 222; *Heart's Remembrance,* 44; *Howl, Wind, Howl!* 128; *How Sweet to Be With You,* 155; *If I Should Meet You* (Koltsov), 143; *I Love You, Lovely Rose,* 177; *Impromptu en galop,* 78; *Inezilia,* 94; *I Recall That Wondrous Moment* (Pushkin), 48n., 149; *Jewish Song* (*Prince Kholmsky*), 86; *Jota,* 197; *Kamarinskaya,* 215, 218, 228; *L'amo, l'amo, e a me più cara* (variations on a theme from Bellini's *I Capuleti ed i Montecchi*), 76; *Lila in the Black Mantilla,* 46; *Marguerite* (from Goethe's *Faust*), 214; *Melancholy Waltz,* see *Waltz Fantasy* (B minor); *Midnight Review* (Zhukovsky), 116; *Moonbeams on the Graveyard,* 36; *My Harp,* 32n.; *A Night in Madrid,* 228n.; *A Night in Venice,* 73; *The Nightingale* (Alyabiev) variations for piano, 88; *Not the Heavy Autumn Shower* (Delvig), 49; *O Beautiful Maid of Mine,* 150; *O Gentle Autumn Night,* 49; *Oh, Night! Oh, Gentle Night!* 47; *O mia dolce, mia carina,* 44; *Pavlovsk Waltz,* see *Waltz Fantasy* (B minor); *Pour un moment,* 44; *Prayer* (F Major), 38, 210; "Prologue" on the death of Aleksander I, 35; *Quartet* (D Major), 32; *Quartet* (F Major, for strings), 50; *Rakhili's Dream,* 154; *Recuerdos de Castilla,* see *Second Spanish Overture; Le Regret,* 143; *Rustle of the Forest,* 88; *Say Not That Love Shall Fade,* 88; *Second Spanish Overture,* 197, 225; *La Séparation* (F minor), 143; *Septet* (unfinished), 28n.; *Sestetto originale,* 73; *Sing Not, Little Nightingale,* 129; *Sogna chi crede esser felice* (quartet in G minor), 44; *Sonata* (D minor), 32, 41–42; *Souvenir d'une Mazurka,* 210; *Spanish Overture,* 218; *Tarantella,* 155; *Tell Me Why,* 44; *Tempt Me Not Without Need!* 33; *The*

*Toasting Cup* (Pushkin), 214; *To Her,* 177; variations for harp and piano (E Flat Major), 20; *Voice from the Other World,* 50; *Waltz* (B Major), 149; *Waltz* (F Major), 20; *Waltz* (G Major), 139; *Waltz Fantasy* (B minor), 151; *Wedding Fantasy,* 215; *Will I Forget You?* 48; *The Wind Is at the Gate,* 154; *Woe Is Me!* 38

Glinka, Natalya Ivanovna (sister): 50–51, 81, 91 f.
Glinka, Olga Ivanovna (sister): 3n.
Glinka, Pelageya Ivanovna (sister): 35
Glinka, Sofiya Ivanovna (first cousin): 19, 23
Glinkina, Elena Aleksandrovna: 133
Gluck, C. W.: 27, 213, 227, 237–38, 240; *Les fureures d'Oreste,* 213; *Iphigénie en Tauride,* 213, 238; *Iphigénie en Aulide,* 238; *Alcestis,* 238; *Armide,* 238, 240–41
Godefroy, Romulus: 34n.
Gogol, Nikolai: 94, 109n.; *The Marriage,* 94
Goldsmith, Oliver: 40
Golenishchev-Kutuzov, Count Arkady Pavlovich: 70, 175
Golitsyn, Prince A. M.: 241
Golitsyn, Prince Sergei Grigorevich: 37, 44ff.
Golitsyn, Prince Vasily Petrovich: 45, 191
Gorgol, General Ivan Savvich: 42
Gorgol, Polixena: 42
Goronovich, Alisa: 177
*Gradus ad Parnassum:* see Clementi, Muzio
Granada, Spain: 200
Granovsky: 109n.
Graun, Karl H.: *Tod Jesu,* 241
Griboedov, A. S.: 12n., 29n., 47, 118n.
Grigorich, Boris: 34
Grigorich, Dmitri: 34
Grigorovka (Skoropadsky's estate): 130
Grisi, Giuditta: 60
Grisi, Giulietta: 61, 75
Grünberg, Dr.: 216
Guelbenzu, Don Juan: 207
Guerrero, Biesma: 189
*Guido et Ginevra* (Halévy): 138
Gui-Stefani (dancer): 198

Gulak-Artemovsky, Simon S.: 126, 128, 133
Gurskalin, Peter Ivanovich: 133, 150
*Gypsies, The*: *see* Vielegorsky, Count Mikhail Yurevich
Gyrowetz (Czech composer): 10
Gzhatsk, Russia: 41

Halévy, J. F.: 138
Handel, George Frederick: 26, 87
Hauke, Dr. (German royal obstetrician): 85
Havemann (fencing instructor): 20
Haydn, Franz Joseph: 28, 32, 116, 240
Hebel, Francis Xavier: 90
Heidenreich, Dr.: 105, 142, 209; Brotherhood poem describing him, 142
Hempel, Karl Fedorovich: 17, 35, 98, 149
Henisht (composer): 90, 128
Henselt, Adolph Lvovich: 216
Hermann, Dr.: 92
Herz, Henri: 85, 189
Herzen, A. I.: 67n.
Hindenberg, Dr. Wilhelm Danilovich: 51
Hippius (bass): 30
*History of Little Russia* (Markovich): 28n.
Höck (professor at Blagorodny School): 13
Holtz (dancing teacher): 31
Horn-music: 49
*Hôtellerie portugaise*: *see* Cherubini, Maria Luigi
Hugo, Victor: 65n.
Hummel, Johann N.: 19, 29; *Concerto* (A minor), 17, 19, 24; *Septet*, 50, 163

*Idylls* (Panaev): 113
"I. E.": *see* Kolmakov, Ivan Ekimovich
*Illustrated Album*: 143n.
Ilya (valet): 23, 28
Imatru, Finland: 49
Imperial Chapel Choir: 52, 113–15, 138n.
Imperial Music Society: 134n.
Innsbruck, Austria: 83
Iogannis (conductor): 100
*Iphigénie en Aulide*: *see* Gluck, C. W.
*Iphigénie en Tauride*: *see* Gluck, C. W.

*I Recall That Wondrous Moment* (Pushkin): 48n.
*Iskra (The Spark)*: 143n.
Isouard, Nicolo: 18
Itri, Italy: 68
Ivanov: 46f., 51–52, 55ff., 67, 69–70, 71–72
Ivanov, Aleksei Petrovich: 145
Ivanov, Nikolai Petrovich: 102
Ivanova, Maria Petrovna: *see* Glinka, Maria Petrovna (wife)
Ivanova, Sofiya Petrovna: 92–93, 116n.
Ivanovna, Rosa: 6
*Ivan Susanin* (Cavos): 103
Izmailov, N. A.: 3n.

Jal, Dr.: 227
*Jessonda*: *see* Spohr, Louis
*Joconda* (Isouard): 18
*Joseph*: *see* Méhul, Étienne N.
*Journal de St. Petersbourg*: 22

Kachanovka (Tarnovsky's estate): 125ff., 135
Kaisarov: 70
Kalinich, Mikhail: 125, 129, 130
Kamensky, Pavel Pavlovich: 162
Karatygin, Peter Andreevich: 141
Kashtalinsky, Fyodor Stepanovich: 99
Kastrioto-Skanderbek, Vladimir Georgievich: 212
Katenka: 37
Kauer: 23
Kazadaev, Aleksander Vasilevich: 145
Kern, Anna Petrovna: 48, 49
Kern, Ekaterina Ermolaevna ("E. K."): 48n., 137, 139, 144, 178
Kharkov, Ukraine: 24, 26, 45n., 126
Khmelnitsky, N. I.: 117
Khovanskaya, Princess: 32, 35
Khovansky, Prince: 99
Khovansky, Yuri Sergeevich: 32
Khozrevamirz: 50
Kiev, Russia: 42, 126
Kiprianov, Aleksander Ivanovich: 30f.
Kireeva (amateur musician): 89
Kislovodsk, Russia: 26
Klammer, Varvara Fedorovna: 9, 11
Klimovsky (tenor): 18
Knecht (cellist): 123
Koblenz, Germany: 56
Kochubei, Count: 46
"Koko": *see* Danchenko

Kolmakov, Ivan Ekimovich ("I. E."): 13–15, 16, 40, 49, 82, 180
Kolomna, Russia: 3n.
Konarskaya, P.: 213
Kopiev: 94
Korsak: *see* Rimsky-Korsak, Aleksander Yakovlevich
Kozlov, I. I.: 73, 122n.
Kozodaev, Aleksander Vasilevich: 97
Krasovsky, General: 130
Kreisig, Dr.: 55
Kreutzer, Rodolphe: *Lodoiska*, 10
Kryudner (bass): 30
Kryukovskaya, Mme (soprano): 30
Kubarovsky, Mikhail Ivanovich: 220–21 ff.
Kuchelbecker, Ustina Karlovna: 34
Kuchelbecker, Wilhelm Karolovich: 12, 34, 118n.
Kukolnik, Nestor: 86, 94n., 102f., 105, 108, 116, 118ff., 122ff., 133, 140, 164
Kukolnik, Pavel Vasilevich: 156
Kukolnik, Plato: 122, 133, 140
Kulikov, N. I.: 107n.
Kunitsyn (professor of law at Blagorodny School): 12
Kurpinsky, Carol: 221
Kutuzov: *see* Golenishchev-Kutuzov, Count Arkady Pavlovich

Labitsky, Josef: 139
Lafin (glove manufacturer): 199
La Harpe, M.: 7n.
Lanner, Josef: 83, 85
Lansky: 118
Lausanne, Switzerland: 57
Laveno, Italy: 57
Lebedev, M. S.: 168
Lecco, Italy: 65f.
Lehren (oculist): 38
Leipzig, Germany: 55
*L'Elisir d'Amore*: *see* Donizetti, Gaetano
Leonard (violinist): 240
Léonie (Ninie): 234
Leonov (stage name): *see* Charpentier
Lermontov, M. Y.: 134n.
Lichtenstet, Dr.: 92
*Life for the Tsar, A*: 46, 89, 103n., 120, 122; subject suggested, 37n., 94; cracovienne, 85; *When They Killed Mother* (orphan's song), 88; writing

of, 95f., 96n., 97, 99–100, 101–102; *Bridal Chorus*, 97; *Pine Not, My Dearest*, 97–98; dances, 103; rehearsals, 104; *My Children! Let There Be Peace and Love Amongst You!* 106; change of title, 107; first performance, 107; critical reaction to, 108–109, 183; *At An Open Field I Gaze*, 192
Liglya (Viennese girl): 32
Lindquist, A. A.: 11, 22
Linz, Austria: 83
Lipinsky, Karl Joseph: 123
Lisette (assistant to Dr. Heidenrich): 181
Liszt, Franz: 16, 64, 175–76, 188; visits St. Petersburg in 1842, 162–64; reaction to *Ruslan and Ludmila*, 175
*Literary Gazette*: 49n.
*Little Red Cap, The*: *see* Boieldieu, François A.
Livorno (Leghorn), Italy: 67
Lobanova, Princess: 118, 138
Lodi, Andrei Petrovich ("Nestor"): 118ff., 142
*Lodoiska*: *see* Cherubini, Maria Luigi, *and* Kreutzer, Rodolphe
Logachevo (I. V. Shestakov's estate): 149
Lomakin, Gavril Ekimovich: 99, 134
Luinate, Italy: 72f.
Luisa: 89, 91
Lukyanovich (schoolmate): 40
Lumberg (professor at Blagorodny School): 13
Lvov, Aleksei Fedorovich: 18, 114–16, 131f., 227
Lvov, Fyodor Petrovich: 52, 113f.
*Lyrical Album*: 48

Madrid: 197
Maggiore, Lake: 57f., 73
Main Pedagogical Institute: 11, 12
Mainvielle: *see* Fodor-Mainvielle, Josephine
Mainz, Germany: 56
Malfatti, Dr.: 83
Malibran, María Felicia: 76
Malov, Aleksei Ivanovich: 97, 147
Marche d'Ancona, Italy: 72
Maria (Taeschner's pupil): 86ff., 91
Maria Fedorovna, Empress Dowager: 34

Maria Kristina (Spanish pianist): 207
Maria Nikolaevna, Grand Duchess: 93, 139, 143
Maria Petrovna: see Glinka, Maria Petrovna (wife)
Marino (Count Stroganov's village): 47
Markovich, N. A.: 128–29
Marn-Zeller, Dr.: 84
Maroketti (Italian-language teacher): 43
Marras (tenor): 194
*Marriage, The*: see Gogol, Nikolai
*Masquerade* (ballet): 78
Maurer (composer): 27
Maurer (violinist): 95
Mauri (voice teacher): 76
Mayer, Charles: 17, 22, 28–31, 35, 46, 101 f., 109, 163
Mayer, Henriette: 29
*Medea*: see Cherubini, Maria Luigi
Méhul, Étienne N.: 17, 19; *Les deux aveugles*, 10; *Joseph*, 18, 27, 235; *Le Trésor supposé*, 27; *L'irato*, 27; *Une Folie*, 88
Meingart: 170
Melgunov, Nikolai Aleksandrovich: 36n., 41, 63n., 67, 89, 109n.
Memel, Andrei Bogdanovich: 104, 167
Mendelssohn-Bartholdy, Jakob Ludwig Felix: 66
Mérimée, Henry: 182, 231, 234; article on Glinka, 183
Merti (Belgian singer): 169
Mes (violinist): 166
Meshchersky, Prince Elim: 65, 188
Meshkova, Irina Fedorovna: 6
Meyerbeer, Giacomo: 230, 237f.; *Crociato*, 63; *Star of the North*, 238
Mickewicz, Adam: 48; *Rozmowa*, 221
Mikhailov: 70, 133
"Mikhailova": see Ostroumova
Milan: 57ff., 63, 64–66, 72ff., 80ff., 86; Duomo, 58; Conservatory, 60; Carcano Theater, 60–62; La Scala, 60, 74–75, 77–78
Miller, Johann Heinrich: 29
Monuments to Glinka: 4n.
Moscheles, Ignaz: 50
Moscow: 41, 89, 100
*Moscow Observer*: 109n.
*Moskvityanin*: 67n.
Mozart, Wolfgang Amadeus: 19f., 27

ff., 32, 116, 126n., 178f.; *Clemenza di Tito*, 27; *Nozze di Figaro*, 27; *Zauberflöte*, 27; *Don Juan*, 27, 46, 179–80; biography by Ulybyshev, 178n.
Müller, Iwan: 76
Muraviev, Sergei Nikolaevich ("Timei"): 148
Muravsky: see Petrovsky-Muravsky
Murcia, Spain: 203ff.
Murciano (guitarist): 199
Mussorgsky, Modeste: 105n.
Myatlev, Ivan Petrovich: 155
*My Aunt Aurora*: see Boieldieu, François A.

Naples: 67–68, 70ff., 82; Bay of Baiae, 68; Sybil's Grotto, 68; Fondo Theater, 70; Conservatory, 70; Teatro Nuovo, 70; Teatro San Carlino, 70; Teatro San Carlo, 70f.
Naryshkin, Dmitri Lvovich: 49, 99
"Nestor" (stage name): see Lodi, Andrei Petrovich
Netoev, Yakov: 28, 91, 124f.
Nevakhovich, A. L.: 103
Neva River (Russia): 49
Neverov, Ya. M.: 107n., 109n.
Nicholas I: 33–34, 106, 108, 114, 118, 131–32, 156
*Night in Venice, A* (Koslov): 73
Nolde, Sofiya Ivanovna: 149
Norov, Nikolai Nikolaevich: 44
*Northern Bee*: 46, 109, 170, 211
Novgorod, Russia: 97
Novospasskoe, Russia: 3, 97f.
Nozzari, Andrea: 69, 70n., 82
*Nozze di Figaro*: see Mozart, Wolfgang Amadeus

Obodovsky, P. G.: 156
Odoevsky, Prince Vladimir Fedorovich: 29n., 94, 96n., 101, 107, 109n., 110, 118, 228
Oginsky, Aleksei Grigorevich: 40, 49, 180
*Oh, My Darling* (Cavos): 14
Ohm, Emilia (Mitsya): 221
Ohm, Rosamunda (Rusya): 220
Ohm's (establishment in Warsaw): 220ff.
Oka River (Russia): 23
Oksaya, Russia: 24
Oldenburg, Duke Peter: 223

Oman (piano teacher): 16
*On, On, O Faithful Sail* (elegy by
  Henisht): 90
Opekunsky Council: 158–59
Orel, Russia: 7, 23, 26
Orlandi (singer): 61
Ostroumova (protégée of Prince M.
  D. Volkonsky): 122
*Otello*: *see* Rossini, Gioacchino A.
Ovid's *Metamorphoses*: 16

Paër, Fernando: 19
Paganini, Nicolò: 123n.
Palagin, Dmitri Nikitich: 119, 124ff.,
  132
*Palermo* (Obodovsky): 218, 222
Palibina, Countess: 163
Panaev: 113
Paris: 75f., 181; July Days, 188; Chan-
  tereine Theater, 189f.; Montmartre
  Theater, 191; Théâtre de Variété,
  191; Conservatoire, 192, 241; Salle
  Hertz, 193; Opéra Comique, 235,
  238; Bois de Boulogne, 237; Jardin
  des Tuilleries, 237; Jardin des
  Plantes, 238f.
Parma, Italy: 72
Pashkov, Andrei: 118
Paskevich, Prince: 212, 222
Pasta (Italian singer): 61, 75, 79, 81f.,
  157
Paul I: 69
Pavlishchev, Nikolai Ivanovich: 48
Pavlov, Nikolai Filippovich: 89
Pavlovich, Grand Duke Mikhail: 220
Pavlovsk, Russia: 45, 151
Pelikan: 105
Pello (dancing girl): 201
Pereyaslavl, Russia: 125–26
Peter I: 21n., 238
Petrov, Osip Afanasievich: 100n., 105,
  108, 120
Petrova, Anfisa (understudy): 171
Petrova, Anna Yakovlevna: 100, 105,
  107–108, 170
Petrovna, Maria: *see* Glinka, Maria
  Petrovna (wife)
Petrovsky-Muravsky (government
  official): 24
Pini (friend in Italy): 66, 75ff.
*Pirata, Il*: *see* Bellini, Vincenzo
Pizzati, Dr.: 70
Plain of Erba (Italy): 66

Planeta (singer): 206
Pletnev: 94
Pogodin, M. P.: 39, 67n.
Pollini: 64, 66, 72, 74
Poltava, Ukraine: 125f.
Potemkin-Tavrichesky, Prince: 18
Prévost, M.: 7n.
*Prince Kholmsky*: 86, 154
Protasov, Count: 46
Puritani Quartet: 179n.
Pushkin, Aleksander Sergeevich: 12n.,
  36n., 40n., 47, 48n., 65n., 94, 110, 116,
  121, 124, 129, 136, 139, 160, 221
Pushkin, Olga Sergeevna: 48n.
Pyatigorsk, Russia: 24ff.

Quattrini (orchestra conductor): 60

Raimondi, Pietro: 70
Ral, Fyodor Aleksandrovich: 167
Rastopchina, Countess: 163
Raupach (professor of German): 12
Ravinsky (Korsak's brother-in-law):
  40–41
Remer (schoolmate): 70, 72
Rémi (violinist): 39
*Revolt in the Harem*: 123
Rhine River (Germany): 56
Ricci, Federico: 224
Ricordi, Giovanni: 79–80, 82
Ridiger, Count: 48
Righini (composer): 19
Rimsky-Korsak, Aleksander Yakov-
  levich: 33, 35, 37ff., 49, 124
Rimsky-Korsakov, N. A.: 118n.
*Robert le Diable*: 105n.
*Rokeby*: 33n.
Rolla, Alessandro: 74
Roller, A. A.: 104, 165
Romani (composer): 63n.
Romani, Felice: 73
Romberg, Bernhard: 27, 95
Rome: 67, 72, 79; St. Peter's, 67
*Romeo e Giulietta* (Zingarelli): 61
Rosen, Baron E. F.: 94n., 95ff., 96n., 99,
  102
Rosenberg ("Daniel"): 221
*Roses noires, Les*: 65n.
Rossignole, Adèle: 182
Rossini, Gioacchino A.: 17, 19, 28, 43n.,
  47, 59, 61, 63n., 64, 69n., 179n.; *Cene-
  rentola*, 17; *La Gazza Ladra*, 43n.; *Il
  Barbiere di Siviglia*, 47, 105n.; *Semi-*

ramide, 61; *Otello*, 64, 75; *Turco in Italia*, 70; *Le Comte d'Ory*, 76; *Guillaume Tell*, 175; *Semiramis Overture*, 193; *Variations on Russian Themes*, 193

Rostislav (pseudonym): *see* Tolstoi, Feofil Matveevich

Rousseau, J. J.: 5

*Rozmowa*: *see* Mickewicz, Adam

Rubini ("Ivan Ivanovich"): 59, 61, 71, 82, 95, 176

*Ruins of Athens, The*: *see* Beethoven, Ludwig van

*Rusalka* (Kauer): 23

*Ruslan and Ludmila*: 38, 121; *The Deep of Night Falls o'er the Field*, 128, 168; Finn's ballad, 49, 128, 135; writing and casting of, 119–20, 121, 131n., 135, 137, 143, 153, 154; first idea of, 121, 136; *Lezghinka*, 121, 162, 166; *Black Sea March*, 128, 135; Persian chorus, 128; *Resplendent Star of Love* (Gorislav's cavatina), 135, 137; *Sad Am I, Dear Father* (Ludmila's cavatina), 136; *Burning Heat and Scorching Sun*, 160, 172; *Thanks Be to Thee, My Wondrous Protector*, 160; *Warriors! Trait'rous Naina!* 160; critical reaction to, 160n., 161, 171 ff.; sets, 165–66, 168; *There Is a Desert Land*, 167; rehearsals, 167; *Why Love, Why Suffer?* 168; first performance, 171; number of performances, 183–84; performed in Paris, 192

*Ruslan and Ludmila* (Pushkin's poem): 36n., 121

*Russian Musical Gazette*: 115n.

Russian National Anthem: 115n.

Rybakov (Kolomna merchant): 3n.

Ryndin, P. P.: 85

Sadorozhnaya, Maria Stepanovna: 127

Sadovsky, Dr.: 148, 157

St. Petersburg Consistory: 158

St. Petersburg flood of November 7, 1824: 31

St. Petersburg Theaters Administration: 81n.

Salomon, Dr. (surgeon): 48, 181

Saltykov, Prince Aleksei D.: 237

Saltiykova, Countess Ekaterina Mikhailovna: 133

Samoilov (tenor): 18

Sandunova: 18

Saranchin, G.: 124, 126

*Save O Lord Thy People*: 132

*Scharivari*: 193

Schiller, Johann: 84

Schlesinger, Heinrich: 240

Schumann, Robert: *Carneval*, 123n.

Schuster, Dr.: 189

Scott, Sir Walter: 33n.

Semenov (vice-governor of Orel): 130

*Semiramide*: *see* Rossini, Gioacchino A.

Senkovsky, Osip Ivanovich: 169

Serov, A. N.: 39n., 164, 229

Serve, Adrien-François: 240

Severbrik (fencing instructor): 20

Shakhovsky, Prince A. A.: 121

Shcherbatova, Princess Maria Alekseevna: 134

Sheinov, Nafanail Nikiforovich: 124

Shemaev: 100

Shering, Dr.: 154

Shestakova, Ludmila Ivanovna: *see* Glinka, Ludmila Ivanovna (sister)

Shevchenko, T. G.: 127n.

Shevyrev, Stepan Petrovich: 67, 89, 107n.

Shimanovskaya, Elena: 48

Shimanovskaya, Tselina: 47–48

Shimanovsky (pianist): 47, 49

Shirkov, Vasily Fedorovich: 137, 151

Shmakovo (A. A. Glinka's estate): 3n.

Shpindler, Dr.: 51

Shterich, Evgeni Petrovich: 45, 50, 56ff., 65, 67

Shtericha, Serafima Ivanovna: 63, 65

Shternberg, Vasily Ivanovich: 127, 129f.

Shubert, Karl Bogdanovich: 167

Simplon Pass: 57

*Singing in Russia* (Lvov): 114n.

Sivers, Count: 30

Sivers, Countess: 30

Skochdopol (Czech conductor): 198

Skoropadsky, Peter: 128f.

Smoilev, V. V.: 130n.

Smolensk, Russia: 3, 4n., 35–36, 55, 62

Smolny Monastery: 9, 135

Snegirev: 108f.

Sobolevsky, Sergei Aleksandrovich: 14, 65f.

Sobolevsky, Yakov Mikhailovich: 35, 55, 145
Sofiya Petrovna: *see* Ivanova, Sofiya Petrovna
Soliva (professor of music at the Dramatic School): 95, 119f.
Sollogub, V. A.: 94n.
Solntsev, Fyodor Grigorevich: 159
Solothurn, Switzerland: 57
Solovieva: 120–21, 193
Somov, Orestes: 48f.
*Songs of Stenka Razin* (Pushkin): 36n.
*Sonnambula, La*: *see* Bellini, Vincenzo
Souza: 188
Spohr, Louis: 98; *Faust*, 56; *Jessonda*, 98
Spontini, Gasparo: 19, 63n., 86
Stankevich: 109n.
*Star of the North*: *see* Meyerbeer, Giacomo
Stasov, Dmitri Vasilevich: 226
Stasov, V. V.: 37n., 96n., 109n., 218
Steibelt: 10
Stepanov, Nikolai Aleksandrovich: 28, 143
Stepanov, Peter Aleksandrovich: 97, 99, 122; tells of Glinka's parties, 133n.
Stepanova: 119, 121
*Stone Guest, The*: 105n.
*Storm, The* (Steibelt): 10
Strauss, Johann: 83, 85
Stroganov, Count: 47, 210f.
Strugovshchikov, A. N.: 63n.
Stuhler, Dr. (Berlin homeopathic physician): 86
Stuneev, Aleksei Stepanovich: 43f., 91–93, 98, 116, 118
Stuneev, Dmitri Stepanovich: 91, 135
Stuneeva, Maria Ivanova: *see* Glinka, Maria Ivanovna (sister)
Stuneeva, Sofiya Petrovna: *see* Ivanova Sofiya Petrovna
Sukhanov (drawing teacher): 20
Sumarokov, Senator: 147
*Swiss Family, The* (Weigl): 20

Taeschner, Gustav: 86, 88
Tamburini, Antonio: 70, 179
*Taras Bulba* (Serov): 164n.
Tarnovskaya, Anna Dmitrievna: 127
Tarnovsky, Grigori Stepanovich: 124–25, 127–28, 130
Tassistro (clarinetist): 78

Tavrichesky: *see* Potemkin-Tavrichesky, Prince
Teatro della Cruz (Madrid): 198
Thalberg, Sigismund: 163
"Théodore": *see* Gedeonov, Nikolai Dmitrievich
Tikhmenev (flutist): 99
Tilicheev, Igor: 148
Tischner (piano maker): 12
Tityus, A.: 63n., 103; creates dances for *Ruslan and Ludmila*: 165–66
*Toccata and Fugue in F Major*: *see* Bach, Johann Sebastian
Todi (voice teacher): 17
Toledo, Spain: 197
Tolmachev, Yakov Vasilevich: 15
Tolstoi, Feofil Matveevich ("Rostislav"): 39, 43, 44ff., 228
Tozi (singer): 77
Transport Council: 29f., 42
*Travels and Wanderings*: 6
Trescorre, Italy: 66–67
*Trésor supposé, Le*: *see* Méhul, Étienne N.
Trevani (pianist): 76
Trippe (professor at Blagorodny School): 13
Tsarskoe Selo, Russia: 32, 46, 97n., 241
Tschaikovsky, P. I.: 118n.
*Turco in Italia*: *see* Rossini, Gioacchino A.
Turgenev, A. I.: 107n.
Turin, Italy: 58f., 65ff.
*Two Blind Men of Toledo, The* (*Les deux aveugles*): *see* Méhul, Étienne N.

Ukrainian folk music: 129n.
Ulyanovich, Aleksei: 28
Ulybyshev, Aleksander Dmitrievich: 178
"Uncle" Saranchin: *see* Saranchin, G.
*Une Folie*: *see* Méhul, Étienne N.
Unger (singer): 59
Ushakov, Aleksei Andreevich: 35

Valladolid, Spain: 26, 196
Varenna, Italy: 65, 83
Varentsov, Colonel: 34
Varese, Italy: 72ff.
Varlamov, A. E.: 38, 177
Vela, Sofia: 207
Venice, Italy: 79, 81, 102

*Ventaglio, Il* (Raimondi): 70
Verdi, Giuseppe: 60n.; *Ernani*, 198
Verstovsky, A. N.: 29n.
Vesuvius, Mt.: 71
Viardot-García, Michelle Ferdinande Pauline: 179
Vielegorsky, Count Matvei Yurevich: 94f., 110, 114
Vielegorsky, Mikhail Yurevich: 29n., 45, 100ff., 171, 176, 188; *The Gypsies*, 176
Vienna: 83ff.
Vieuxtemps (violinist): 123
*Viliva* (Shimanovsky): 49
Vilna, University of: 78
Visconti, Marquis: 62, 64
Vitkovsky, General Ivan Matveevich: 24
Vladislavlev, Vladimir Andreevich: 160
Volkonskaya, Princess Zinaida Aleksandrovna: 67, 70
Volkonsky, Prince Grigori Petrovich: 69, 113
Volkonsky, Prince Mikhail Dmitrievich: 122
Volkonsky, Prince Peter Mikhailovich: 69
Volkov, Matvei Stepanovich: 93
Volkov, Nikolai Stepanovich: 93
Volsky, Dr. S. F.: 92, 116
Volsky, Vlodzimezh: 241
Vorobiev, Yakov Stepanovich: 121
Vorobieva: *see* Petrova, Anna Yakovlevna
Vorontsov-Dashkov, Count: 61 ff.
Vyazemsky, Prince: 94, 110
Vyborg, Russia: 49

Wagner, Wilhelm Richard: 164n.
Warsaw: 55
*Water Carrier, The: see* Cherubini, Maria Luigi

Weber, Carl Maria von: 176; *Der Freischütz*, 56, 105n., 176
Weigl, Josef: 20
*Where Art Thou, O Youth's First Longing?* (Golitsyn): 48
Whering, Dr.: 138
*Woe from Wit*: 47, 118n., 141
Wolff, Dr. Moritz: 212, 241
Wurtemberg, Count: 34

"Yakov": *see* Netoev, Yakov
Yakovlev, Mikhail Lukyanovich: 47
Yakukevich (professor at Blagorodny School): 13
Yannenko, Yakov Fedoseevich: 122–23, 141
Yurevich, Count Matvei: 113
Yurevich, Count Mikhail: 46, 113
Yushkov, Peter Ivanovich: 19, 28
Yusupov, Prince: 99

Zabalburu: 207
Zabella, Victor: 129
Zamboni (Italian *buffo*): 43
*Zauberflöte: see* Mozart, Wolfgang Amadeus
Zelepugina, Maria Nikolaevna (aunt): 122
Zeller: *see* Marn-Zeller, Dr.
Zembnitsky, Yalim Grigorevich: 21
Zeuner, Karl: 16f.
Zherebtsov (wealthy landowner): 23
Zhukovsky, A. K. (Bernet): 148n.
Zhukovsky, Vasily Andreevich: 36, 45, 50, 73, 88, 94, 96, 102, 104–105, 110, 115n., 116f., 148
Zingarelli, Nicola A.: 61
Zlov (bass): 18
Zôe (maid and cook): 236
Zusman (flutist): 104
Zyablovsky, Professor: 21

The type used in *Mikhail Ivanovich Glinka's Memoirs* is Janson, a seventeenth-century European design adapted to modern machine-set book uses. The musical examples in the text are reproduced from the original Russian edition, in which Glinka's handwritten notations appeared.

UNIVERSITY OF OKLAHOMA PRESS
*Norman*